ABHANDLUNGEN FÜR DIE KUNDE DES MORGENLANDES

Im Auftrag der Deutschen Morgenländischen Gesellschaft herausgegeben von Florian C. Reiter

Band 97

2015
Harrassowitz Verlag · Wiesbaden

Stephen L. Field

The Duke of Zhou Changes

A Study and Annotated Translation of the Zhouyi 周易

2015

Harrassowitz Verlag · Wiesbaden

Bibliografische Information der Deutschen Nationalbibliothek
Die Deutsche Nationalbibliothek verzeichnet diese Publikation in der Deutschen
Nationalbibliografie; detaillierte bibliografische Daten sind im Internet
über http://dnb.dnb.de abrufbar.

Bibliographic information published by the Deutsche Nationalbibliothek
The Deutsche Nationalbibliothek lists this publication in the Deutsche
Nationalbibliografie; detailed bibliographic data are available on the internet
at http://dnb.dnb.de.

For further information about our publishing program consult our
website http://www.harrassowitz-verlag.de

Printed on permanent/durable paper.
Printing and binding: KN Digital Printforce GmbH, Stuttgart
Printed in Germany
ISSN 0567-4980
ISBN 978-3-447-10406-7

Contents

Preface

The earliest English translation of the *Yijing* 易經 was by the Reverend Canon Thomas McClatchie (1814-85): *A Translation of the Confucian Yih King or the "Classic of Change" with Notes and Appendix* (Shanghai, 1876). The second was by James Legge (1815-97), first professor of Chinese at Oxford University, and a Presbyterian missionary in China for thirty years. It was Legge who established the use of the words "trigram" and "hexagram" in English for the three- and six-line graphic symbols that constitute the numerological foundation of the text. James Legge is one of the most prolific translators of Chinese texts ever to have lived.[1] He was so meticulous about his translation of the *Yijing* that he conducted it twice, first in 1855 and then in 1882. Unsatisfied with his first attempt, he set it aside until he felt he understood it sufficiently. It remains a good translation, despite its outdated English usage. Its only drawback is the one it shares with all 19th and early 20th century translations. It does not make use of the wealth of information uncovered in archaeological excavations.

The first German translation was by Richard Wilhelm (1873-1930), who became pastor for the German settlement in Qingdao, Shandong province, in 1899. The book was published in Jena in 1924. The English version of Wilhelm, called *The I Ching, or Book of Changes* (Princeton, 1950), was translated from the German by Cary F. Baynes (born 1883), a student of C. G. Jung. Baynes was responsible for popularizing Legge's terms, "trigram" and "hexagram," which had not been adopted by Wilhelm. This version of the *Yijing* attained cult status in the 60s in the United States, and remains the most popular translation in the English-speaking world. Wilhelm's work was conducted in close consultation with his teacher, Lao Naixuan 勞乃宣, a former official of the Qing dynasty, who trained him in the tradition of Song dynasty scholarship.

The most masterful rendition to date, a worthy successor to Wilhelm, remains that of Richard John Lynn, whose *Classic of Changes* (Columbia, 1994) translates the commentary of Wang Bi 王弼 (CE 226-249), an important scholar of the post-Han, Three Kingdoms, period and founder of the *yili* 義理

---

1   He rendered into English the *Book of Odes*, the *Book of Documents*, the *Spring and Autumn Annals* with the *Zuo Commentary*, the *Book of Rites*, and the *Analects* of Confucius, as well as the *Yijing*. Most of these translations were not superseded for a hundred years after they first appeared.

(principles and meanings) exegetical method.[2] Wang's *Zhouyi zhu* 周易注, sometimes called the first philosophical interpretation of the *Yijing*, became the standard commentary until the Song dynasty.

The only published complete translation of the *Yijing* into English that is not affected by "philosophical" interpretation is the work of Richard Rutt, formerly Bishop of Leicester. His *Book of Changes* (Curzon, 1996) takes into account all the pertinent research conducted in the 20th century, while attempting to capture the intent as well as the spirit of the "original diviner's manual," which he does by mimicking in English the rhyme patterns of the original Chinese text. In his preface, Rutt acknowledges his debt to Edward Shaughnessy and Richard Kunst, West Coast graduate students who produced influential Ph.D. dissertations on the *Yijing* in the last decades of the twentieth century.

Kunst's thesis, "The Original 'Yijing': a Text, Phonetic Transcription, Translation, and Indexes, with Sample Glosses" (Berkeley, 1985), still remains the most rigorous study of the "original" *Zhouyi* 周易 (minus the "Ten Wings"), although it was never published. In 1996, Shaughnessy published the first English translation of the newly discovered Mawangdui 馬王堆 manuscript of the *Yijing*—dating from 168 BCE—which is useful to scholars mainly for its presentation of many variant characters that differ from the received version of the text. Since Rutt's study was conducted, Shaughnessy produced another translation of recovered manuscripts—the so-called Shanghai Museum manuscript of the *Zhouyi*—dating to 316 BCE, and the Fuyang *Zhouyi*—dating to 165 BCE. As Shaughnessy admits in his preface, "Paradoxically, each new discovery both adds a little bit to what we know and also undermines a little bit of what we knew."[3]

Most recently, John Minford, well known co-translator of *The Story of the Stone*, has produced a dual rendering of the text, called *I Ching (Yijing): the Essential Translation of the Ancient Chinese Oracle and Book of Wisdom* (Viking, 2014). In this work, Minford conducts two separate translations of the *Yijing*, beginning with the philosophical version—based to some extent on a 19th century Daoist commentary, followed by the Bronze Age "oracular" version—based on Kunst and more recent scholarship. Minford's translation is meant for the general reader, especially those who, in his words, will "find Part II [the Bronze Age oracle] completely irrelevant to their purpose."[4]

---

2   As distinguished from the *xiangshu* 象數 (images and numbers) method prevalent in the latter Han dynasty.

3   *Unearthing the Changes: Recently Discovered Manuscripts of the Yijing (I Ching) and Related Texts*, p. xx.

4   See Minford, p. xxvi.

The Duke of Zhou Changes also relies heavily on the work of Richard Kunst. Unlike any translator preceding him in the history of *Yijing* studies, Kunst has posted on the World Wide Web his unpublished notes recording the detailed research that led to his dissertation. Scholars are thus able to readily access his readings of dozens of classical and modern Chinese commentaries throughout the centuries, including relevant Japanese and continental scholarship.[5]

In the preface to his book, Richard Rutt admits that his translation is only "a possible one" since "all translations of *Zhouyi* must be provisional." His admission is also true for this work since it is based on the traditional understanding that King Wen's fourth son, Ji Dan 姬旦, the Duke of Zhou, is the author of the line texts of the *Zhouyi*. Assumptions are therefore made in the commentaries regarding allusions and metaphors in the text that pertain specifically to the personal history of the Ji 姬 clan of Zhou, especially the life of King Wen, posthumous founder of the dynasty, and his son, Ji Fa 姬發, or King Wu. For this reason, some scholars will claim that the commentaries construct a "seven-story pagoda."[6] That may be the case, but the alternative to the fanciful pagoda is a rickety scaffolding that no one but specialists may climb. To quote a scholar of Late Bronze Age Mediterranean culture, "we must come to this with an open mind and employ 'the scientific use of the imagination,' as the immortal Sherlock Holmes once said, for 'we must balance probabilities and choose the most likely'."[7]

The envisioned audience for this translation is also the general public, yet it maintains a minimum of exegesis so that the specialist can understand the derivation of what may initially appear to be unorthodox renditions of various passages.[8] It is hoped that the general reader will appreciate a translation that captures the divinatory intent of its presumptive authors and, in so doing, maintains a narrative cohesion unseen in its forebears. Since it is the average

---

5   Kunst utilizes a novel numbering system in his "Notes," identifying hexagram, line, and sentence numbers. Thus, 64.4.2 refers to hexagram 64, line 4, sentence 2: "Zhen used this omen to attack the Land of Ghosts." His "Notes" utilizes this system for pagination, which I will use to cite his work, including, when applicable, scholars that he references, most of which have been checked for accuracy.

6   Li Xueqin—the leading scholar of the *Changes* in China—says that seeking the original meaning of the *Zhouyi* is too difficult, because of the danger of building such a fanciful structure. See Shaughnessy, *Unearthing*, p. xiv.

7   Eric H. Cline, *1177 B.C.: The Year Civilization Collapsed*, p. 139.

8   For those scholars who do make use of this translation, all citations to ancient Chinese texts conveniently cite the page numbers of library resources accessible on Donald Sturgeon's "Chinese Text Project" webpage (located at http://ctext.org), for which the author is indebted. Furthermore, the Chinese text of each hexagram of the *Zhouyi*, based on the *Zhouyi zhengyi* version, is appended after each commentary.

reader who will be consulting *The Duke of Zhou* Changes, it is also assumed that its main use will be for the purposes of divination. Therefore, the commentaries address the reader as if he or she were inquiring from an oracle.

There are many individuals to whom I am grateful for the publication of this book. First, I would like to acknowledge the work of three writers who have preceded me as interpreters and transmitters of the *Book of Changes*—the aforementioned translator Richard Kunst, also *Yijing* historian and longtime colleague Richard Smith, author of *The I Ching: A Biography* (Princeton, 2012), and finally Steve Marshall, author of *The Mandate of Heaven* (Curson, 2001), the book that first inspired me to conduct a translation from the point of view of the Duke of Zhou. I also would like to thank two friends who have supported my literary peregrinations over the years—anthropologist Richard A. Nisbett, my oldest and dearest friend, who first gave me the Legge translation upon my college graduation in 1974, and Steve Moore, editor of *The Oracle: The Journal of the I Ching Society*, who published my article on the *bagua* in 1999. I also owe a deep debt of gratitude to Humboldt University Professor Florian C. Reiter, convener of the fifth and sixth International Conference on Scientific Fengshui, who recommended my translation for publication. To all of these learned and generous men, I express great appreciation for their sharing of profound knowledge and friendship. Clearly, any mistakes that remain herein are my sole responsibility.

Since I have been a professor of Chinese for thirty years, I should like to acknowledge my students from the College of William and Mary and Trinity University for their insights through the years. I also gratefully acknowledge the J.K. Lee Family Foundation whose funding support over the past six years has allowed me to dedicate a good portion of my time to this project. Finally, for her unstinting moral support since the project's inception, and for her unfailing love since my senior year in high school, I thank my wife, Gail Reynolds.

While some may say that this 21st century confluence of three Richards and three Stephens is a coincidence, in the world of *Yijing* lore, such synchronicity is surely meaningful. It is thus with great reverence that I dedicate this book to Stephen James Moore, who graciously read an earlier version of this translation and, most unfortunately, died unexpectedly before the book could be published. May this publication preserve his memory for generations as yet unborn.

Stephen L. Field
March 21, 2015
Austin, Texas

Introduction

The *Yijing* 易經 is the oldest book of divination in continuous use in the history of the human race. The casting of yarrow stalks—the origin of the *Yijing*—has been an important way to seek guidance from the spirits at least since the end of the 2nd millennium BCE. Its written form, originally called the *Zhouyi*, or *Changes of Zhou*, dates at the latest from the beginning of the 1st millennium BCE. Thus, the authors of the *Zhouyi* were contemporaries with Ramses XI of Egypt and King Saul, first king of Israel. When a man or woman of the 21st century taps into the wisdom of the *Yijing*, he or she will be consulting with the spirit of a culture that has been called the most advanced in the history of the pre-modern world.

In its earliest written form, the *Zhouyi* consisted of 64 linear symbols called *gua* 卦 hexagrams, their names and omen statements, and their line texts. This is the manuscript that is translated in Part 2 of this book. After the *Zhouyi* was written, the ensuing centuries saw the development of cosmological theories on such subjects as *yin* 陰 and *yang* 陽, *qi* (ch'i) 氣, and *wuxing* 五行, or the five element/phases. These new concepts were then used to analyze the structure of the hexagram symbols. The result was a commentary tradition called the *Shiyi* 十翼 "Ten Wings" that attempted to explain the order in the universe. New theories based on sequences of the *gua* gained popularity in philosophical circles. The *Zhouyi* and its commentaries were then canonized in the Former Han dynasty (206 BCE-25 CE) as the *Yijing*, or *Classic of Changes*. It had now thoroughly transformed from a manual of divination into a book of philosophy. Much of the original religious importance of the texts was subsequently forgotten. Part 1 below describes the process of evolution from divination to philosophy, providing the reader with detailed explanations of the myth, legend, and history in the formative stages of the book's creation. Since the *Zhouyi* forms the core of the *Yijing*, the names will be used synonymously, especially since the latter is the more familiar title with the general public.[1]

---

[1] Some readers may be more familiar with the spelling, *I Ching*, which uses the Wade-Giles system of romanization, rather than the *pinyin* system that is now the universal standard for spelling Chinese sounds.

At the beginning of the 20th century, the vast oracle bone archives of the vanquished Shang 商 dynasty were discovered buried at Anyang 安陽, the site of the great Bronze Age city of Yin 殷. Heretofore unknown, these bones were a great repository of knowledge. As a result of their discovery, many of the previously forgotten traditions of divination were recovered, which allowed a complete reassessment of the language of the original *Zhouyi*. The translation in Part 2 makes use of much of the Chinese and Western research of the late 20th and early 21st centuries, which has attempted to reinterpret the book strictly from the point of view of divination. A consultation of the *Yijing* using this translation will be as close to the original intent of the ancient Zhou diviners as has ever been possible in the West. The metaphysical speculations of generations of Chinese commentators have given the *Zhouyi* an unprecedented richness. Yet, what reader of any sacred text from the ancient world would not yearn to hear the unmediated, original utterances of the gods or prophets? Such language has a freshness that no reader can miss.

Still, some clarification of the original language will be helpful to those unfamiliar with ancient Chinese culture. Each hexagram is therefore accompanied by a line-by-line commentary, the purpose of which is to provide detailed background for the situations presented in the texts, to interpret metaphorical language, and to explicate technical syntax. Occasionally, a context for the contemporary diviner is also provided, so that the archaic language may be appropriated for contemporary use.

Part 3 of the book gives detailed information on how to cast the oracle and how to interpret the resulting reading. It is followed by a glossary of technical terms utilized by the authors of the original *Zhouyi*, a bibliography of reference works consulted for the translation, as well as an index of terms and other important information appearing herein. Finally, the last printed page of the book is a Hexagram Location Chart, provided for those readers who utilize the translation for divination purposes. This chart juxtaposes upper trigrams over lower trigrams to derive the resulting hexagram number.

Chinese Periods and Dynasties

Legendary Period
    Three Emperors 三皇
        Fuxi 伏羲
        Shen Nong (Divine Husbandman) 神農
        Huang Di (Yellow Emperor) 黃帝
    Five Rulers 五帝
        Shao Hao 少昊
        Zhuan Xu 顓頊
        Di Ku 帝嚳
        Yao 堯
        Shun 舜
        (Yu, the Great 大禹, first emperor of the Xia 夏)

Prehistoric Period

Yangshao Culture 仰韶文化	ca. 5000 BCE
Longshan Culture 龍山文化	ca. 2500
Erlitou 二里頭	ca. 1850-1550
Xia dynasty 夏	ca. 2070-1600

Historical Period

Shang dynasty 商	ca.1600-1046 BCE
Zhou dynasty 周	1046-221
Western Zhou	1046-771
Eastern Zhou	770-256
Spring and Autumn Period	722-481
Warring States Period	403-221

Part 1. The Origin of the *Zhouyi*

1.1 A Short History of the Ancient Chinese

Before we can begin to contemplate the worldview of a people who walked the earth some three thousand years ago, we must know something about the land they inhabited, as well as the peoples that bordered them and the cultures that influenced them. There is some speculation that the Zhou Chinese shared roots with the nomadic proto-Tibetan peoples of Central Asia whose religion was shamanism, but they also shared agrarian roots with their Shang cousins to the east who believed in a cult of ancestors.[1] In this chapter we will follow the Zhou Chinese from their Neolithic origins around 5000 BCE to the foundation of the Zhou dynasty in 1046 BCE. We will visit the villages of a prehistoric millet farming community and the pleasure dome of a decadent Shang king. We will meet the ancestors of the House of Ji, founders of the Zhou dynasty, and follow them on their exodus and wandering, see their battles, and watch them construct their settlements. By the time the reader has digested this short history of the Zhou people, he or she will be ready to dig deeper into the line texts of the *Yijing*, which are quite literally "snapshots" of daily life in Zhou China at the end of the 2nd millennium BCE.

1.1.1 Prehistoric Chinese Culture

Consider a setting about seven to eight thousand years ago, inland west on the Central Plain 中原 near where the Wei 渭 tributary joins the great southern bend of the Yellow River. This basin is protected by the yellow silt

---

1 Some early scholars, such as the preeminent archaeologist K.C. Chang, theorized that shamanistic beliefs also defined the character of Shang religion. However, recent scholarship has rejected such views due to the lack of convincing proof in ancient texts that kings or their diviners made use of trance states—the prerequisite of Ural-Altaic shamanism (Shelach-Lavi, p. 219). For our purposes, the word "shaman" is the translation of the Chinese *wu* 巫, the ritual specialist charged by the king with mediation between the human and *shen* 神 spirit realms, including the practices of divination, prayer, and healing, but not necessarily spirit flight. Nevertheless, there remain isolated instances such as the omen texts of Hexagram 49 Molting, where it could be argued that something like spirit transformation is indeed being described, or the ritual of Hexagram 20 Observation, where the spirit descends to partake of the sacrifice.

highlands to the west, the Shaanxi 陝西 plateau to the north and the Qinling Mountains 秦嶺山 to the south, while the east opens out to the vast flood plain of the Yellow River. At least since the post-glacial climactic optimum that occurred around 6000 BCE, when increasing rainfall and warmer temperatures extended forest belts northwards across Asia, the geographical and climatic advantages of this terrain attracted hunters and fishers to exploit the herds of deer in the woods and fish shoals along the riverbanks.

However, these hunter-gatherers, as they became more "affluent," slowly became less mobile and more sedentary (Shelach-Lavi, p. 63). This sedentism likely stimulated experimentation by the tribe's herbalist with more efficient food procuring techniques (Chang, 1977: p. 81). Perhaps the discovery of seed germination resulted from underground storage of gathered plants; or maybe the first experiments were magical and religious, such as the sacrificial burial of foxtail grass (*Setaria viridis*) or some other important flora. The production of foxtail millet (*Setaria italica*; in Chinese, *ji* 稷) was the eventual result, stimulating a virtual revolution that raised the carrying capacity of the land. The proto-farmers, surrounded by mid-Holocene oak forests, out of necessity developed the technique of slash-and-burn cultivation, which cleared fields and fertilized the soil in one strenuous operation. As villages grew to capacity, daughter villages would bud off and carry on the new tradition elsewhere. This "swidden" form of agriculture, a transitional technology between seasonal and fully permanent settlement, opened up a vast new resource for the fueling and feeding of an expanding agrarian culture.

Agriculture, therefore, rather than the hunting of deer and gathering of acorns, cast the first mold of specifically Chinese culture. The transition from the gathering to the producing of foodstuffs took place in North China sometime around 5000 BCE and is known from more than a thousand sites of Yangshao Painted Pottery, named after the village of Yangshao 仰韶 in northwestern Henan 河南 province near where the first specimens were unearthed in 1920. It was the stability of year-round settlement that contributed to the surge of innovation that produced the red and black designs of Yangshao pottery (Chang, 1977: p. 111).

Although successful husbandry generated a need for storage facilities, which might suggest that people congregated for economical purposes, this was not the case (Wheatley, p. 225). Instead, the village centered around a ceremonial complex, usually a large, rectangular, aboveground, multi-hearth dwelling. This structure was quite imposing compared to the semi-subterranean hovels that surrounded it. It was occupied by a tribal lineage whose distinction was its religious leadership. The planned village layout plus the arrangement of burials in the village cemetery indicate a cult of ancestors (Chang, 1977: p. 108). On the other hand, the discovery of a tattooed face wearing a fish-shaped headdress painted on pottery bowls indicates the continued existence from Paleolithic times of the shaman (Wheatley, p. 25). Similarly, there is evidence that Yangshao farmers may have performed some kind of fertility rites for the sake of crop harvests and fishing and hunting gains. This is implied by the discovery of deer burials plus the frequent occurrence of fish patterns in ceramic decoration. Since one common method of recruiting shamans in Central and Northeast Asia was by hereditary transmission of the shamanic profession (Eliade, p. 13), it is possible that the clan leader of the Yangshao village was also a shaman.

The plan of the village of Banpo, near present-day Xi'an, was oriented along a north-south axis, with the ceremonial house at the center of the village plaza facing east toward the rising sun, while the dugouts faced south, evidence that the Yangshao Chinese already practiced a primitive type of *fengshui* 風水. This central area was enclosed by a ditch nearly twenty feet in depth and width which separated the residential and ceremonial center of the village from its cemetery and its communal kiln and pottery works. Every similar site on the Central Plain, of which there were thousands, was apparently a self-sufficient community, where the tenor of life seems to have been peaceful in the main, since evidence of both defensive measures and offensive weapons is scanty (Chang, 1976: p.28). The people were well provided with agricultural produce: two kinds of millet and soybeans, vegetables such as mustard and cabbage, not to mention pork and dog. Even chopsticks were already in use. Their homes may seem like hovels but they were probably quite comfortable. The semi-subterranean construction was ideal for passive air conditioning, and plastered floors and walls contributed to hygiene. Although the work was long and hard, conceivably everyone had more spare time now, because storage led to surplus. In Yangshao China, kinship and crop were the people's prime concerns.

The succeeding culture to the Yangshao stage is marked by an even finer grade of ceramic ware, the so-called Black Pottery, which was thin, hard, lustrous, and black. Its first discovery was in 1928 near the town of Longshan 龍山 in the province of Shandong 山東, thus its designation. Longshan culture was a southern extension of the Yangshao horizon that was innovative enough to import rice cultivation from the south and adapt it to a new environment. This innovation gave the farmers enough advantage to enable widespread settlement of the eastern and southeastern portions of China proper. Add to this the discovery of the well, which allowed a wider choice in the selection for settlement sites.

A transformation occurred between the early and late Longshan phases in which the earlier peaceful and largely egalitarian village life had been transformed into a warlike and ranked society (Chang, 1977: p. 144). The transformation may have been effected by revolutionary innovations in farming techniques. Perhaps fertilization with river silt and irrigation from rivers and wells made it possible to abandon the less productive swidden method (Stover, p. 24), or perhaps some system of crop rotation had replaced field rotation. This would set the stage for the first truly permanent settlement, since slash-and-burn techniques still required occasional long-term fallowing of depleted fields. This permanency may have been the factor that initiated intercommunity raiding. Now is where the first appearance of walls is noted, great barriers of pounded earth that signaled the end of the peaceful propagation of Neolithic China. Scapulimancy, or divination by animal bones, also appears, as does sericulture, an extremely labor-intensive industry. The accumulated culture of the prehistoric Chinese had propelled them to the threshold of civilization, where behind them now was the pristine age, and before them the unknown barriers of class-consciousness and the crushing arrival of the city.

The successor to Longshan culture and the culmination of urban civilization in the prehistoric past of China is known as Erlitou 二里頭 culture, named for the village in Henan province in the middle reaches of the Yellow River where it was discovered in 1959. The earliest bronze vessels made in China were cast here. Erlitou is the largest known city in China in the early 2nd millennium BCE, spanning some 750 acres and containing palaces, royal tombs, bronze foundries, jade and turquoise carving workshops, paved roads, and rammed earth foundations. The amount of manpower required to construct the massive architecture, and the equally impressive organization required to maintain bronze foundries and workshops, testify to the complexity of the governing structure of Erlitou. The city was also planned around a transportation grid, indicating that Erlitou was indeed a central hub of what is generally known as the first state in ancient China. In fact, most Chinese scholars claim that Erlitou is the seat of the Xia 夏, the legendary dynasty that preceded the first historical dynasty of Shang. Since Erlitou left no written records, this cannot be substantiated, yet it cannot be disproven.

Before leaving the discussion of prehistoric Chinese civilization, it will be helpful if the reader takes one last glimpse at the cosmological worldview available to the elite culture of the late Neolithic. A Taosi culture type excavated recently near the city of Taosi 陶寺 in southern Shanxi 山西 province has been called the oldest walled-city compound in China, dating to approximately 2100 BCE. More importantly, just outside the city wall, near the tombs of the city chiefs, was discovered a terraced, rammed-earth platform with a semi-circular outer foundation that would have permitted observation of the sunrise at specific dates along a mountain range on the eastern horizon.

Scholars speculate that the platform was roofed, allowing shafts of sunlight to shine through apertures in the walls into a darkened inner sanctum (Pankenier, 2008: p. 146). This "observatory" is the earliest of its kind in China and proves that the Neolithic Chinese were capable of determining the length of the solar year and constructing a calendar.

1.1.2 Shang Culture

It is no single factor alone that makes a civilization appear, such as bronze metallurgy or writing, prototypical forms of which even existed in Longshan times. But there is a point in the gradual intensification of all aspects of culture when economic, industrial, and military specializations extend beyond the village level. This phenomenon, the widespread eco-social interdependence among specialized communities, is one of the most decisive characteristics of Shang 商 urbanization. Its cities were composed of a plethora of small farming and handcrafting communities whose close ties were indicated by their clustering within eyesight distances and their sharing of a common administrative and ceremonial center (Chang, 1976: pp. 34-36). The ceremonial complex is familiar from previous ages, but has grown into a vast hub of temples and palaces housing the ruler. The authority that resided in this "forbidden city," whose great appetite required the combined urban effort to satisfy, was the theocratic court of the Zi 子 clan, which came to dominate the eastern plains around 1600 BCE.

The architecture of this urban complex was by no means monumental, compared to other centers of ancient civilization. Instead of impressing gods or immortalizing humans by erecting stone monuments, the ruling house of Shang lavished all luxury upon the ritual and ceremony that perpetuated the memory of its ancestral forebears. Though the buildings were made of wood and thatch, the bronzes that were cast now for largely ceremonial reasons are recognized as the world's finest. The reigning king of the House of Zi boasted a mythical progenitor and a complete lineage of ancestors. His role as king was pivotal—so that his people might live in well-being without the calamity of earthquake and drought, he sacrificed to the earth, rivers, mountains, and winds. For rainfall, harvest, and military victory, he prayed to the High God or Shang Di 上帝, who ruled the world from *Beiji* 北極, the celestial North Pole (Li Feng 李峰, 2013: 5.3). For personal well-being and for the good fortune of the state, he conducted five types of ancestral sacrifices, the grand ceremonies of which were public and were enacted both in the walled royal compound and the royal cemetery.

What perhaps had begun in Erlitou as a ruler's patriarchal control over his extended village family was now being applied by the Shang king as a patrimonial rule over the subjects of his city and state (Wheatley, p. 56). The bulk of the populace was the peasantry, reduced to the status of serfs by now, yet who may still have retained the small dignity of being the subjects of the divine Shang Di. It was to the king they brought their grain tributes every year, where they were treated to the spectacle of the beheading of human prisoners-of-war as part of the grand ancestral sacrifices. At the same time they might have been drawn into the pageantry associated with the labor of digging and filling the royal tombs (Stover, p. 39). Otherwise their whole life-needs were served by an underground pit-house a few meters in diameter located in a cluster in the midst of the fields on the outskirts of the Great Shang City.

The elite class consisted of the king, his family, and his high officials, on the one hand, who enjoyed the best quality life of the time, including lavish banquets and above-ground palaces. On the other hand there was a large retinue of lesser officials, including scribes, priests, and warriors who still lived within the walls of the ceremonial complex in houses built on platforms of rammed earth. It was this court that dictated the styles that became the art and cultural treasures of the era. Most of their ranks were filled by relations of the royal family. These upper and lower echelons of government were so superior to the productive class of commoners that the Shang period can be regarded as the beginning in this part of the world of organized large-scale exploitation of one group of people by another within the same society (Chang, 1976: p. 57). Such was the legacy of China's first historical dynasty. The Shang dynasty endured for seventeen generations, maintaining control over the whole of the North China plain until the close of the 2nd millennium BCE. But, finally the paternalism of the early ages degenerated into tyrannical oppression when Zhou Xin, son of Di Yi, became king in 1078 BCE.

Zhou Xin 紂辛, also known as Shou 受, was an intelligent and talented prince. According to legend, his strength was so great he could kill wild beasts with his bare hands. But when he ascended to the throne his interests turned to self-indulgence. When Shou began to eat his meals with ivory chopsticks, his uncle Jizi 箕子 recognized this as the first sign of his nephew's decadence and told him so. Like Hamlet, he escaped a grisly fate by pretending insanity. To satisfy his carnal desires Zhou Xin constructed a pleasure park stocked with wild animals and exotic birds. According to legend, it had trees hanging with delectable slices of meat and ponds filled with wine where the nude revelers swam. However, when the Lord of Gui 鬼侯 presented his daughter to Shou for his harem, she refused his advances, so the king killed her, had mincemeat made of her father, and distributed portions to his nobles. When the Lord of E 鄂侯 protested against this tyranny, he was chopped up, cooked into a stew, and offered to the royal ancestors. Shou is said to have been led astray by his vicious concubine Daji 妲己, whose appetites were insatiable. When she asked him if it was true that sages were sagely because their hearts had extra chambers, Shou had the heart of the wise minister, Bi Gan 比干, cut out in order to show her.

Lord Chang 昌, of the House of Ji 姬, and ruler of the western vassal of Zhou 周, heard of the murder of the Lords of Gui and E, and knew better than to respond—but he couldn't restrain himself from sighing deeply in sadness. Marquis Hu of Chong 崇侯虎 heard the sighs and reported them to his king. So Shou threw Chang into a dungeon where he remained for six years. According to legend, it was during this incarceration that Chang wrote the earliest layer of the *Zhouyi* 周易. Chang's ministers eventually ransomed him with beautiful women, horses, and other exotic objects, and Shou released him.

1.1.3 The House of Ji

The high ancestor of the Zhou people was Hou Ji 后稷, literally "Lord Millet," a culture hero celebrated as the giver of grain to the people and the founder of agricultural sacrifices. Although an officer of the legendary Xia kingdom east of the great southern bend of the Yellow River, when that dynasty began to decline his descendants returned to live among the nomadic Rong 戎 and Di 狄 tribes in the Ordos region to the west, subsisting on sheep herding. Hou Ji's great-grandson, Chief Liu 公劉, recovered his ancestor's patrimony at Bin 豳, and re-established agriculture for his clan. Liu's son Qing Jie 慶節 then led the tribe to the upper valley of the Jing River 涇水, where they remained for some nine generations and three hundred years (Wu, p. 414).

In the twelfth generation after Hou Ji (late 12th century BCE), in response to the increasing pressure of the Quan Rong 犬戎 tribes, and the encroaching armies of Shang King Wu Ding 武丁, descendant Danfu 亶父 moved his people to the Wei River 渭水 valley beneath Mount Qi 岐山 (see Hexagram 46). This region was the homeland of the Jiang 姜 peoples, who welcomed Danfu as an ally against the common enemy, the Quan, or Dog, Rong (Wu, p. 420), as well as the Shang. This was the final move of the Ji clan, and the place from whence the people took their name—the Plain of Zhou 周原.

On the southern slopes of Mount Qi, Danfu's people cleared the land of heavy woods and dug kiln-like huts and caves to live in while beginning large-scale construction of palaces and temples within a walled compound. They also raised a great moated earth-mound—the altar to the earth god, where excursions of war began. Danfu, Ancient Duke 古公, in fact is credited with beginning the aggression against the Shang realm to the east, and it was in his time that there began the rise of the Zhou as a people conscious of their own destiny. The posthumous title of Tai Wang 太王, Supreme King, was bestowed upon him by his descendants. Danfu had three sons by different wives and favored the youngest, born from his marriage to a Jiang woman after his tribe had migrated to Qi. This was Ji Li 季歷, otherwise known as Wang Ji 王季, or King Ji, who took a wife from the Shang court—the standard procedure for subduing a recalcitrant neighbor short of going to war with him. Ji Li is best known as the father of Chang 姬昌, who eventually became King Wen of Zhou 周文王.[2]

The fact that Ji Li married a Shang princess is proof that the Shang state was sufficiently worried about the rising power of its western neighbor. He was made Military Governor, ruling over a cluster of pastoral tribes in the western marches of the Shang realm, and led several military campaigns against northern tribes, such as Guifang 鬼方, or Ghost-land (see Hexagrams 8 and 64). The *gui* tribe probably belonged to the *xianyun* 獫允 people, ancestors of the *xiongnu* 匈奴 tribes of the Mongolian steppes. However, the relationship deteriorated between Ji Li and Di Yi 商帝乙, the next-to-last king of Shang. He was detained in the Shang court at Yin in 1099, and was ordered killed by King Wen Ding 文丁.

Ji Li was succeeded by his son, Chang, who was a just and wise ruler. In its rise to power, the ruling clan developed a new character of governance that emphasized *gong* 功, or devotion to the people (Wu, p. 428). His qualities of meekness and humility were so opposed to the cruelty and intimidation of the Shang kings that worthy people from all directions flocked to serve him.[3] Chang, like his father before him, was also married to a Shang

---

2   What we know about King Wen, and his illustrious ancestors, comes mainly from the *Book of Odes*, a collection of 305 songs dating between about 1000 and 600 BCE. Composed mainly of folksongs, the anthology also includes some forty sacrificial hymns that were sung in ancestral temples to praise the accomplishments of the venerated founders of the dynasty. Of these, there are nine odes that narrate the history of the Ji clan, beginning with Lord Millet and continuing down to King Wu, son of Wen, who completed the conquest of Shang. The central figure of this epic tale is King Wen.

3   King Wen's reign title "wen" captures his primary virtue of "cultural elegance" as distinguished from that of his son, King Wu, whose title emphasizes his "martial-heroic" qualities. King Wen is clearly more venerated in literature and history than his son, and the supremacy of his reign demonstrates how the Zhou emphasized cultural pursuits (especially agriculture) over military. One of the oldest books in the Chinese tradition, the *Book of Documents*, speaks of Wen as a leader who dressed in coarse clothing and farmed with his own hands. Such humility endeared him to his subjects, noble and commoner alike.

princess, Tai Si 太姒—daughter of King Di Yi—with whom he had at least ten sons (see Hexagrams 11 and 54). Eventually, Shang King Zhou Xin grew jealous of his western vassal, and on his next tributary visit to the capital, threw him into prison. After six long years, Chang was released, and, to insure his loyalty, the Shang king made him Xi Bo 西伯—Earl of the West, giving him control of all the western lands. Chang returned to his homeland, the Plain of Zhou under Mount Qi, and began to consolidate his power and rally support for rebellion. While Chang was a kind and compassionate leader, that does not mean he was not a capable military leader. He was, in fact, about to embark on one of the most important military campaigns in the long history of China.

In 1059 BCE, according to the *Bamboo Annals*: "there was a conjunction of the five planets in Fang; a red crow lighted on the altar to the spirits of the land in Zhou" 五星聚于房有赤鳥集于周社 (*Zhushu jinian* 竹書紀年, 卷上, "Di Xin" 帝辛, p. 70; tr., Legge, vol. 3, "Prolegomena," p. 140). This was proof to Chang that Heaven had chosen the Zhou to receive the Mandate of rule. Modern cosmologists have confirmed this conjunction of the five visible planets (Pankenier, 1981: p. 4). However, the conjunction did not take place in the *Fang* 房, or Chamber, constellation of the Azure Dragon, but appeared instead in the constellation of Beak 柳, the leading asterism of the great composite constellation of the Vermilion Bird. As the Vermilion Bird set in the northwest on the 28th of May, 1059 BCE, the planets hovered just ahead of the setting Beak in the shape of a scepter, the symbol of divine rule.

Chang declared the change of Mandate and initiated his rebellion with the help of the Jiang tribe, which shared the plain of Zhou with the Ji clan. Their leader was Lü Shang 呂尚, better known as Tai Gong, or Grand Duke Wang 太公望, who became a famous general. In five years time, Chang conquered five different states, beginning with the archenemy, Quan Rong, who had originally driven his ancestors out of their homeland (Wu, p. 432). Finally, he attacked the marquisate of Chong, whose lord had originally slandered him to King Zhou Xin. He toppled the high, thick walls of Chong with ladders and siege machines, then massacred its nobles, extinguishing its ancestral sacrifices for all time. From then on Chang was called King Wen, and throughout his kingdom none dared to oppose him. The following year, he moved his capital from Qi further east to Feng 豐, near present-day Xi'an 西安, in order to facilitate the rebellion (see Hexagram 55). Here he constructed the Lingtai 靈臺, his Numinous Tower, surrounded with a moat and a hunting park. On this earthen platform, King Wen could watch the sky for portents, since Heaven's commands were written there even more clearly than on an oracle bone. However, he died before he could complete his task.

King Wen died in 1050 BCE, in the ninth year of his undertaking. His son Fa 發, born in 1095, succeeded him as King Wu 武王. He continued in his father's steps, making covenants with other nobles against the Shang king, promising income of the second class and office of the first rank, then smearing the covenant with a victim's blood and burying it. After many delays, Heaven ordered King Wu to carry out the conquest, when the planet Jupiter once again returned to the constellation Beak early in the year 1046. On a winter day at dawn he held his court in the capital, sacrificed, and led his army of 45,000 troops east. He assembled with his allies at Mengjin 孟津, a ford on the Yellow River, sacrificed again, and crossed the river to confront the Shang army of 700,000 at Muye 牧野, the Wilds of Mu (see Hexagram 13). On March 20th the army entered and took the Shang capital at Yin. Shou was defeated when his own army turned against him. He ascended his ten-tiered Deer Tower 鹿臺, set the building on fire, and perished. King Wu entered and shot three arrows into the body and cut off its head off with a ritual sword. When he returned to his homeland in the spring, he offered sacrifices to Heaven, including the heads of many Shang grandees, and announced that the conquest was complete. At that point, King Wu moved the capital from Feng across the river to Hao 鎬, establishing it as the ancestral capital, Zong-zhou 宗周.

1.1.4 The Early Zhou Dynasty

Beyond the original Shang domain, in a hostile hinterland of scattered Neolithic villages, Zhou kinsmen, invested by the Duke of Zhou 周公 with new territories, set out with a party of soldiers, swidden agriculturists, and artisans to colonize the land. This might be the origin of the well-field system 井田 (see Hexagram 48), where each cadre of eight families cleared and farmed a nine-section field, the produce of the ninth section going to the maintenance of the non-cultivating elites in the fortress community (Wheatley, p. 176). Regardless of local factors of colonization, from a political worldview, this was the beginning of Zhou feudalism, more accurately termed *fengjian* 封建, or the founding of regional states (Li Feng, 2003: p. 143). In this work, the use of feudal terms will be with the understanding that the relationship between the king and his landed lineage was closer to king and subject than to king and vassal.[4]

---

4   "The regional rulers were not only local agents of the Western Zhou king, but were also members (or marriage partners in cases of non-Ji-surnamed states) of the king's lineage bound together by a common ancestral cult" (Li Feng, 2013: 7.5).

Zhou society at the very beginning of the era was divided into two classes: *junzi* 君子, or "sons of the rulers," and *xiaoren* 小人, the "lesser men," or commoners. The former term refers to the hereditary noblemen, consisting of the king and the five grades of landed aristocracy, plus two grades of ministers, sometimes also heritable. The five grades are related to the size of the state and were used to address the subjects at the royal court: *gong* 公, *hou* 侯, *bo* 伯, *zi* 子, *nan* 男, usually rendered into English as duke, marquis, earl, viscount, and baron. The second class mentioned above is *xiaoren*, or "common people." These were the serfs or peasantry, who possessed no family names, and therefore had no need of genealogies. They did not own the land they cultivated but were transferred with it whenever it changed hands. Also included in this class were the artisans and merchants, who, like the serfs, were not free traders but were attached to the cities as retainers of noble households.[5]

As regards worship, the essential religious forms of Shang were also inherited by the Zhou. That is, Zhou royalty and nobility still practiced an elaborate ancestor worship. However, Shang Di 上帝 became the guaradian of the Zhou people, while also "hosting" the deceased Zhou kings in his court in the celestial North Pole (see p. 9 above). These ancestors would then descend to their royal temples on the proper sacrifice day to receive honor from their descendents. The position of supreme ruler over the natural world was then usurped by Tian 天, or "Heaven," which from then on dominated the realm of profane men, dealing out fortune as well as calamity (Li Feng, 2013: 7.2). The Zhou king proclaimed himself *Tianzi* 天子, or "Son of Heaven," becoming in effect the sole link between Heaven and man. Heaven "mandated" that the charismatic Ji clan of Zhou succeed the degenerate Zi clan of Shang, and with the semi-divine status of Son of Heaven the four generations that sat as the first kings of Western Zhou created a resounding glory that reached to all corners of the land.[6]

---

5 *Junzi* and *xiaoren* gradually evolved in meaning, so that by the time of Confucius (551 BCE) the *junzi* was the "gentleman," a man willing to pursue a moral agenda. And the *xiaoren* was the "petty man" who pursued only his own selfish ends. In the line texts of the *Zhouyi* the words retain their original meaning.

6 According to Li Feng, "From this concept of Heaven's Mandate, it was further theorized, probably by the Duke of Zhou, that the Shang once themselves hosted Heaven's Mandate when their sage kings ruled the kingdom, as did the Xia dynasty before it was conquered by the Shang" (2013: 7.2).

1.1.5 The Duke of Zhou

Three years after the conquest, King Wu contracted an illness and was close to death. Some accounts record that King Wu ordered his brother Dan 旦, his chief advisor, to succeed him, but he refused. Instead, Dan, better known as the Duke of Zhou 周公, prayed to the three immediate ancestors of the ailing king, offering his own life for that of King Wu. Consequently, his elder brother's health improved. Upon the king's final demise in 1043, the Duke of Zhou assumed the throne as regent, since King Wu's son and successor, Ji Song 姬誦, was only thirteen years old.[7]

Since the dynasty was still quite young, the death of King Wu initiated an uncertain chapter in the history of the House of Ji. This was the thinking behind the duke's decision to rule in his young nephew's place—how could a boy withstand the intrigues of the court? Some of the duke's brothers did indeed slander him, claiming that the Duke of Zhou was merely biding his time before usurping the throne from the young king. Ji Song believed them at the time, but could do nothing about it. After the conquest, Dan's elder brother, Ji Xian 姬鮮, Lord of Guan 管, had been charged with overseeing the former Shang capital at Yin in the east, so he was very familiar with the remaining Shang nobles. Perhaps jealous that the regency did not go to him, Xian revolted, aiding and perhaps leading the rebellion of the prince of Shang, Wu Geng 武庚, and the armies of the eastern Yi 夷 tribes. The Duke of Zhou, with his elder half brother, Shi 奭, the Grand Protector 太保, and his younger brother, Feng 封, the Lord of Kang 康叔, led the six Zhou armies east to suppress the rebellion, which took a long three years.

The Duke of Zhou remained regent for four more years. It was probably at this time that he recorded the Zhou liturgies and the great political addresses that formed the core of what would eventually become the *Shi* 詩 and the *Shu* 書, the classics of the *Odes* and the *Documents*. He may also have recorded descriptions of the governmental offices of the kingdom, which eventually became the *Rites of Zhou* 周禮. To him is also attributed authorship of the *Erya* 爾雅, or *The Literary Expositor*, the earliest dictionary or thesaurus. Most importantly, he added the 384 line texts to the Zhou dynasty manual of divination called the *Yi*, or *Changes*.[8]

---

7   However, bronze inscriptions record that King Cheng as well as his uncles would eventually lead troops in the east to consolidate the realm, so his youth may have been exaggerated (Li Feng, 2013: 6.3).

8   In regard to the text of the *Zhouyi*, Li Feng acknowledges that "Some of these records were probably formed as early as the pre-dynastic Zhou time based on sources similar to the oracle bone inscriptions from Zhouyuan" (2013: 7.6).

In 1036 BCE, the Duke of Zhou established a secondary capital called Chengzhou 成周, near modern Luoyang 洛陽, and returned the throne to his nephew, whose reign title became Cheng 成, the Accomplished. He then retired (some say in exile) to the state of Lu 魯 in the east, near present-day Qufu 曲阜, the birthplace of Confucius, where his eldest son was enfeoffed. He died there in the 11th year of the reign of King Cheng, in 1032 BCE. It was at this time that the young king finally learned the Duke of Zhou had offered his own life in sacrifice to save the life of his father, King Wu. He then regretted his former distrust of his uncle and ordered his body returned to Chengzhou to be buried with the honors due a king.

For his exemplary service to his nephew Song as regent and minister, and for his skill as author of the literary foundations of Zhou culture, the Duke of Zhou was exalted by Confucius as a paragon of virtue and the ideal minister to the king. As someone who edited the *Odes*, wrote his own history of the early Zhou dynasty (*Spring and Autumn Annals* 春秋), and purportedly wrote the first commentary to the *Changes*, Confucius certainly understood the Duke of Zhou. He is recorded to have said, in lamenting the degeneration of his times, "It has been a long time now since I dreamed again of meeting with the Duke of Zhou" 久矣吾不復夢見周公 (*Lunyu jishuo* 論語集說, 卷 4, "Shu Er" 述而, p. 6; Ames and Rosemont, p. 112).[9]

---

9   Unless otherwise noted, as in the case with this translation by Roger Ames and Henry Rosemont, all translations of Chinese texts are the author's.

1.2 Ancient Chinese Divination

Divination is the art of divining or seeking unknown information directly from nature or by personally appealing to spirits or unseen powers. Often called "fortune telling," one of the most common reasons for divining is to tell the future. The art of divination is universal; every human culture has used it at some stage of their development.

Perhaps the reader has heard of a "divining rod"—the forked stick of the dowser or water witch. In rural America today there are still drilling companies that will dowse for water if their customers are unsure where to put their well. Dowsing for water, metallic ores or diamonds is called rhabdomancy, or divination by rod. Probably, the most common form of fortune telling in the West today is Tarot card reading, a form of sortilege—divination by the drawing of lots. But the Chinese practice of *fengshui* is becoming as well known as Tarot. *Fengshui* is the art of divining currents of *qi*, or life energy, in the earth. Since *geo* is Greek for "earth" and *-mancy* is Greek for "divination," the word "geomancy" was borrowed to translate *fengshui*.

1.2.1 Forms of Divination: Portents

In China divination appears in three main forms—portents, augury, and oracles—depending on how the diviner seeks the unknown knowledge. The information can appear spontaneously and sometimes traumatically in nature; such appearance is unexpected or abnormal and is of sufficient import to demand explanation by those who witness it. These are called portents, and in the Chinese tradition they indicated a disturbance of the normal patterns of the cosmos. Examples of such portents or signs of cosmic upset are eclipses, comets, and earthquakes, but also the appearance of strange creatures such as phoenixes and dragons. To this day, when an earthquake occurs in China, the rural people believe heaven and earth are responding to a particular human imbalance—those in power are abusing their positions. This is a remnant of the ancient belief in the *Tian Ming* 天命, or Mandate of Heaven. In the *Yijing* there are suggestions of this type of divination. See Hexagram 51, "Earthquake" and Hexagram 30, "The Lia-Bird."

Portents can also indicate good fortune. Chinese mythology is full of stories that tell of the birth of prodigies. The most conspicuous example, perhaps, is that of Hou Ji, or Lord Millet, the first ancestor of the Zhou people. It is said that his mother walked upon the footprint of a god and became pregnant. Thinking this was an evil omen she threw the child in the street when it was born. But oxen and horses avoided the baby. Then she placed it on the ice, but birds covered it with their wings. From these auspicious signs she realized the child was divine and therefore brought it up.

1.2.2 Forms of Divination: Augury

The unknown information is obtained from the observation of natural phenomena by those gifted with certain powers or trained in a particular form of observation. Reading signs or omens of impending danger or continued well-being in nature is called augury. In the Chinese tradition such omens generally could only be recognized and interpreted by diviners. Since the cycles of the cosmos were regular, any deviation from the norm was a potential message. Wind change, cloud patterns, and the flight of birds were all open to interpretation. Most of the common forms of divination in China fall into this category. Following are brief discussions of six forms of augury: astrology, chronomancy, physiognomy, geomancy, oneiromancy, and ornithomancy.

1.2.2.1 Astrology

Ancient Chinese astrologers, like their Western counterparts, made predictions based on the heavenly bodies. For example, the following prediction is recorded in the 100 BCE text, *Shiji* 史記 or *Records of the Grand Historian*: "If the Fire planet (Mars) forces its way into the Dragon's Horns, then there will be fighting. If it is in the Dragon's Heart this will be hateful to kings" 火犯守角則有戰房心王者惡之也 (*Shiji jijie* 史記集解, 卷 27, "Tian Guan Shu" 天官書, p. 111). In the *Yijing* there are also suggestions of this type of divination. See the commentary for Hexagram 1, "The Vigorous."

Chinese astral divination utilizes the observation of the movement, position, color, and brightness of heavenly bodies, as well as their relationship to each other, to determine the auspicious or inauspicious nature of human affairs. Divination by the Wood Star 木星, for example, determines fortune according to the movement of Jupiter (also known as the Year Star 歲星 in ancient China). If the color of Jupiter is bright with a yellow center, the world will be at peace. The direct movement of Jupiter represents human-heartedness. When Jupiter is out of sync, the people will encounter difficulties. When it moves in spring, there will be agricultural disasters. When it progresses and retrogresses, the region it shines upon cannot fall. It was Jupiter that signaled to King Wu that the time had arrived for his eastern march to capture the Great Shang city in 1046 BCE.

The color of the five moving stars (Venus, Jupiter, Mercury, Mars, and Saturn) is also portentous: white indicates mourning and drought; red indicates the military; green indicates grief and flood; black indicates illness and death; yellow means good fortune. The silk manuscripts excavated at

Mawangdui 馬王堆 in 1973 included a Five Star Divination manual (*Wuxing zhan* 五星占), which is a record of ancient Chinese astral divination dating to before the 2nd century BCE.

The earliest classical record of something like Western astrology is the following passage recorded in the 1st century: "Heaven sends forth its *qi*, and the stars send forth their essences, and the essences are in the midst of the *qi*. Men imbibe this *qi* and are born. As long as they cherish it they grow. If they obtain a sort which means honor, they will be men of rank, if not, they will be common people. Their position will be higher or lower, and their wealth greater or lesser, according to the position of the stars concerned" 天施氣而 眾星布精天所施氣眾星之氣在其中矣人稟氣而生舍氣而長得貴則貴得賤 則賤貴或秩有高下富或賞有多少皆星位尊卑小大之所授也 (*Lun Heng* 論 衡, 卷 2, "Ming Yi" 命義, p. 61).

Until recently, our understanding of ancient astrology was limited to the few references in classical texts such as these. However, in 1975, a Qin dynasty tomb was uncovered which contained two groups of bamboo strips that have been identified as *rishu* 日書, or "daybooks." This is the earliest known example of a type of book that is in common use in China today—virtually every household in China owns a copy of the *tongshu* 通書 or almanac.

1.2.2.2 Chronomancy

Chronomancy is the divination of lucky and unlucky days. In oracle bone records, which will be discussed in detail below, there are often questions about the fortune of particular days. Remnants of this practice can be found in lines of the *Yijing*. For example, in Hexagram 18 the hexagram statement says, "On the third day before and the third day after *jia* 甲, it is good to cross the great river." The first day of the ancient ten-day week was called *jia*. Three days after *jia* (day 4, named *ding* 丁), and three days before *jia* (day 8, named *xin* 辛), were considered lucky days. The recent discovery of the *rishu* 日書 "daybooks" proves that chronomancy was widely practiced.

In the Shang dynasty, days (or suns) were numbered according to a cycle of ten called the *tiangan* 天干 or Heaven Stems. The week was thus ten days long. Moons were enumerated with a cycle of twelve called *dizhi* 地支 or Earth Branches. When the 12 Branches and 10 Stems were paired (think of five 12-inch rulers laid alongside six 10-inch rulers) a cycle of 60 *ganzhi* 干 支 was formed. Six of these 60-day cycles formed a year of 360 days. Since this lunar year was a few days shorter than a solar year, a leap 13th month was added every few years.

1.2.2.3 Physiognomy, Geomancy, and Oneiromancy

Other forms of divination that fit this category are physiognomy—fortune telling according to facial features, geomancy, or *fengshui*, and oneiromancy—prognostication by dreams, which also has a long history in China. A famous record of oneiromancy was the basis of the overthrow of a dynasty. The last king of the Xia dynasty was Jie 桀, a tyrant whose wickedness is comparable to that of Shou, the last king of Shang. One night he dreamed that there were two suns in the sky, one in the east and one in the west. There was a struggle, and the western sun was victorious. This dream was told to spies by the neglected queen and eventually reported to Tang 湯, the Successful. The next day he led his troops around to the western border before beginning his attack. Jie fled before a blow had been struck, and Tang became the first king of the Shang dynasty.

1.2.2.4 Ornithomancy

Although there are other examples of augury in ancient China, this category will close with an illustration of ornithomancy, divination by the observation of birds. King Wu assembled his allies at Mengjin and began to ford the Yellow River. Halfway across a white fish jumped out of the river and landed in his boat. When he reached shore he observed fire shooting up to heaven and then falling back down to earth. When it reached where King Wu stopped to camp, it transformed into a flock of vermilion crows. Taking this as an auspicious omen, they confronted the Shang army at Muye.

1.2.3 Forms of Divination: Oracles

Differing from the previous two categories in one major aspect, the third type of divination is called the oracle. Unlike augury or the interpretation of portents, oracles are not based on natural signs. They are a deliberate search for the answers to particular questions by the artificial production of signs. In ancient Rome this type of divination is represented by such techniques as haruspicy, the reading of the entrails of the sacrificial victim. In China the oracle is represented by pyro-osteomancy, or divination by the burning of bones, and sortilege, or divination by the casting of lots.

1.2.3.1 Scapulimancy and Plastromancy

The oldest known form of divination in China, identified since Neolithic times, is scapulimancy or plastromancy, otherwise known as "oracle bones." Scapulimancy is divination using the scapula or shoulder blade of a mammal. Plastromancy is divination using the plastron or breastplate of a turtle. It was the Shang kings who perfected the practice of oracle bone divination. From the reign of Wu Ding 武丁 (1324-1264 BCE) we have literally tens of thousands of fragments of oracular texts, all of which were excavated from the ruins of the ancient capital of Yin, near present day Anyang 安陽. Because of their sacred value, the bones with their oracular texts were stored in archives by the Shang diviners. Historians of ancient China owe their profession to these archivists. The words on the oracle bones are the oldest Chinese characters in existence, and tell us most of what we know about the Shang dynasty.

Before the actual divination took place the bone of the ox or the shell of the turtle was specially prepared. The spine and socket of the shoulder blade were sawn off so that it was flat on both sides. The carapace or shell of the turtle was sawn apart from the plastron. All surfaces were scraped and planed to present the smoothest face possible. Then on the back were carved several rows of paired indentations, each pair consisting of a shallow, circular bored pit and, tangent to this, a vertical, oblong, deeply chiseled pit (see figure 1). When a red-hot brand was applied to the center of the chiseled pit two cracks would appear on the opposite side of the bone or shell—a vertical crack corresponding to the oblong pit and, perpendicular to this, a horizontal crack extending into the circular hollow. The crack would thus look something like this Chinese character: ⼘ , which sounded like *pok*, representing the noise of the bone cracking. The word is now pronounced *bu*, and means "crack-making" or, by extension, "to divine."

At least in the formative stages of Chinese pyro-osteomancy, the crack answered the questions of kings, as put to the spirits by the diviner. It was the gods or spirits who were speaking, and the kings and their diviner interpreted the divine language of the pyromantic cracks in bone or shell. Here is a fanciful description of how such a ritual might have proceeded.

> At sunrise the king offers steaming grains in bronze caldrons to invite the spirits into the temple. Libations of millet wine are poured over the turtle shells placed on the earthen altar, consecrating them. The Grand Invocator approaches, grasps a flaming brand of peach wood from his assistant, and cries out the charge, "Ghost-land will attack!" Then he applies the fire. As his assistant fans the flame, seconds pass while the smell of singed bone mingles with that of millet wine and dried blood. Suddenly the most silent of creatures, the turtle, speaks, "*Pok!*" Moving across the plastron to the adjacent row, the royal diviner cries out again, "Ghost-land will not attack!" and the brand is applied. Seconds later another "*Pok!*" He repeats this process several more times. Then the king and assembled diviners consult. "Auspicious!" remarks the king, pointing first to one crack and then another. The king issues an order. There is the sound of bleating, then silence. Blood stains the

altar as the king dismembers the sacrificial victim. The Grand Invocator proposes another charge: "We sacrifice a sheep to our father" (Keightley, 1978, 1-2).

After the crack-making ceremony was completed the charges and prognostications plus the date and the diviner's name were written on the oracle bones with brush and ink. Then they were carried to the archive behind the temple. When the ten-day week was over and the result of the prognostication was known, the archivist carved the written information into the bones, as well as the result of the prognostication. The entire record would look something like the following, which became the standard formula for the oracle bone text:

Crack-making on *jia wu* 甲午 (day 31), the Grand Invocator divined...

"Ghost-land will not attack!"

The king, reading the cracks, said "Auspicious."

On *bing shen* 丙申 (day 33) Ghost-land presented tribute of ten strings of turtle shells.

The pair of antithetical questions appearing in the hypothetical crack-making ceremony above was also standard practice. It indicates that the oracle was a yes or no answer.

Scapulimancy and plastromancy continued down to the Former Han dynasty (206 BCE-CE 25), although for the most part their use in the court was superceded by the following form of divination.

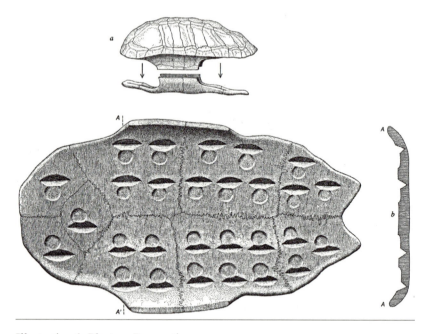

Illustration 1. Plastron Preparation
Source: Chou, p. 138

1.2.3.2 Milfoil Lots

Toward the end of the Shang dynasty another form of divination called *shi* 筮, or "divination by stalks," gained in popularity. The stalk of choice was the *Achillea* plant, or yarrow, sometimes called milfoil (thousand-leafed), because of the large number of stalks that grow from a single root. Scholars know much less about this system than scapulimancy because, unlike with bone and shell divination, there are no detailed records that survive from its formative period.

The earliest record of milfoil divination appears in the *Shangshu* 尚書, or *Book of Documents*. It is an address made by the Duke of Zhou to his brother, Prince Shi 君奭, the Duke of Zhao 召公, on the subject of the virtuous minister. He was serving as regent in the place of his young nephew, the future King Cheng, who ascended the throne upon the unexpected death of King Wu. There were those who did not trust the regent, thinking he was about to usurp the throne for himself. In reference to the great ministers of the Shang dynasty, this is what the Duke of Zhou had to say: "They set forth their virtue, and thus they directed their princes. Therefore, when the king sacrificed to the four quarters, and when he took turtle and milfoil oracles, there were none who did not have confidence in him" 惟茲惟德稱用乂厥辟故一人有事于四方若卜筮罔不是孚 (*Shangshu* 尚書, "Zhoushu" 周書, ch. 18, "Jun Shi" 君奭, p. 88; tr., Legge, vol. 3, p. 479). From this record we know the Zhou founders believed the Shang kings had always resorted to both plastromancy and milfoil divination. We have no need to doubt the words of the Duke of Zhou. Oracle bones from Shang king Wu Ding's reign contain inscribed figures that record the "cast" of a milfoil lot.

Humans have probably been using lots to make decisions since they were first able to count. Lots are objects such as stones or sticks placed in a container and drawn or cast out at random. The simplest technique requires stones of different color or sticks of different length ("drawing straws"). A more complex technique requires that the stones or sticks be inscribed with meaningful symbols such as numbers or words. The word lottery is derived from "lot" and means a system of distributing prizes based on the drawing of lots. The lots in this case are simply a sequence of numbers drawn from a series of digits (1 through 50, for example). In China, no less than two kinds of lots have been used at least since classical times. In 1993, near the town of Wangjiatai 王家台, Hubei province, the tomb of a Qin dynasty (221-206 BCE) diviner was uncovered. It contained two different types of dice, a bamboo box of counting sticks, and a divining board.

The Chinese divination technique known as *shi* is a type of lot casting. Unfortunately, we do not know the exact technique used by Shang and early Zhou dynasty kings to cast the stalks. We do know the stalks were manipulated and counted in such a fashion so that a number was derived. See, for example, the illustration of a late Shang oracle bone in figure 2. The symbols on the left represent the six numerals, 766718, followed by a short sentence. The number is the lot, and the sentence is the prognostication provided by the diviners based on the casting of the stalks.

The stalks of milfoil, like the shoulder blades of ox and deer, or the breastplates of turtles, were objects from nature. When these objects were ritually prepared, they could be encouraged to "speak," thus communicating to humans the intent of the spirits. In this sense, the *"pok"* of the turtle's crack and the cast of the milfoil stalks were no different from the streak of a comet in the night sky.

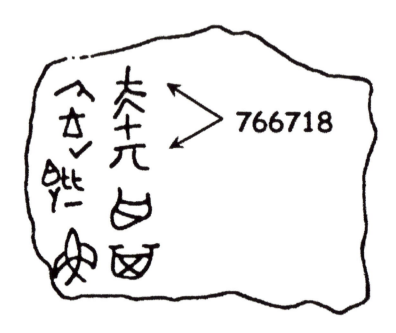

Illustration 2. Shang Dynasty Numerical Milfoil Lot
Source: Zhang Yachu, p. 156

1.2.3.3 The Numerology of Odd and Even

A curious fact surfaces when all the existing records of milfoil lot numbers are compared. The six-digit numbers consist only of the numerals 1, 5, 6, 7, and 8, while the numbers 2 through 4 do not occur in the record. Chinese sentences are written vertically, so the numerals appear to be stacked on top of one another as in figure 2. The Chinese numerals for 1 through 4 are sets of one to four horizontal lines. So scholars speculate that the numerals 2, 3, and 4 do not occur in the record because they were too difficult to distinguish if they appeared in succession in a vertical stack. What looked like a 4 (a stack of four horizontal lines) might actually be <1,3> or <2,2> or <3,1>. From a statistical analysis of the record, it was determined that the numerals 2 and 4 were transmuted into 6, and the numeral 3 was transmuted into 1.

As the record evolved, the numerals 5, 7, and 8 also disappeared, leaving six-term sequences of only the numerals 1 and 6. The example given above—766718—would now have been represented as 166116. In other words, the numeral 1 subsumed all odd digits, and the numeral 6 subsumed all even digits. This example would have appeared in an early Zhou dynasty bone or bronze record as in figure 3:

Illustration 3. Early Zhou Dynasty Numerical Milfoil Lot

The numeral one, then as now, was a simple horizontal stroke. The numeral six was a wedge or caret. This numerical symbol of lines and wedges is the origin of the *Yijing* hexagram. Hexagram is the word coined by early translators of the *Yijing* to represent the six-lined graphical symbol known as the *gua* 卦 in Chinese. The hexagram is composed of a combination of solid and broken lines that evolved from the horizontal ones and wedge-shaped sixes of the early Zhou dynasty numerical milfoil lot.

At this time in the evolution of Chinese divination the concept of *yin* 陰 and *yang* 陽 had yet to develop. But thanks to a characteristic of Chinese writing—the confusing similarity of the numbers one through four—we gain a rare insight into the mind of Shang dynasty diviners. By the 13th century BCE at the latest, the Chinese were aware of the even and odd values of numbers. This knowledge is important for the development of a complicated numerology, or number magic. The Chinese were the first to discover the magic square of three, for example, which utilizes the odd and even values of the digits 1 through 9.

1.2.3.4 Ancient Omen Texts

In the illustration of the Shang Dynasty Numerical Milfoil Lot (figure 2), following the number was a sentence of text. The illustration reads in full: "766718 says, 'It ... the king had already fished'" (七六六七一八曰：其...入王既魚). The instance of the word "says" indicates that the statement is "spoken" by the diviner or the divination text, and was not simply a factual recording made at the time of the divination (Field, 2000: p. 9). However, we do not know if this sentence is an omen that was traditionally attached to this milfoil lot, or if it is a prognostication determined spontaneously by the diviner who cast the lot. In other words, when the lot of 766718 was drawn, did the diviner search his memory or consult an archive for the image his forbears had traditionally associated with that lot? Or did he contemplate the charge or question that prompted the ceremony, and personally divine the prophecy? Since archaic Chinese had no tense markers, the statement could be past, present, or future.

What we can see from this milfoil text is the great similarity it shares with oracle bone texts. Certainly in the formative period of milfoil divination there was great influence from scapulimancy. Since we have more records from the bone and shell tradition, we can use those to speculate about the development of the milfoil tradition. An important question is this. How does the diviner interpret the crack, and thereby derive his forecast? And conversely, how is a particular omen statement or prognostication associated with a milfoil cast?

Firstly, the more horizontal the transverse crack—the branch perpendicular to the vertical crack—the more likely the prognostication is a good one. Actually, the chances of this T-shaped crack being exactly 90° are small. Similarly, the chances of rain in the semi-arid northern plain were small too, as were the chances the king's toothache would be cured by sacrificing a rooster. In other words, the chances the spirits would answer prayers were about the same as the chances of obtaining a 90° crack. But this does not help us understand how the diviner could derive more complex information from the crack.

1.2.3.5 The Origin of Yijing Line Texts

In 562 BCE, while the ruler of Wei 衛侯 was away on a military campaign, Huang'er of Zheng 鄭皇耳 attacked the state of Wei. Sun Wenzi 孫文子, a senior official of Wei, was considering whether to launch a counter-attack.

> Sun Wenzi cracked a turtle-shell regarding pursuit, and then presented the crack to Ding Jiang (mother of the Lord of Wei). Lady Jiang asked him for the omen. He said:
> A crack like a mountain overhanging.
> There was a chief who led a raid,
> Instead, 'twas he who lost his braves.

Still unclear as to what his course of action should be, the Lord of Wei consulted further with the old mother of his Marquis. She studied the omen, and replied:

> "The raider's loss of braves is what you will gain from opposing the bandits. You should plan accordingly." The people of Wei pursued

them, and Sun Kuai captured Huang Er of Zheng at Hound Hill. 孫文子卜追之. 獻兆於定姜, 姜氏問繇. 曰: 兆如山陵, 有夫出征, 而喪其雄.姜氏曰: 征者喪雄, 禦寇之利也. 大夫圖之, 衛人追之, 孫蒯獲鄭皇耳于犬丘 (*Chunqiu Zuozhuan zhengyi* 春秋左傳正義, 卷 31, "Xiang Gong 襄公," 10th year, p. 19).

This record from the middle of the Zhou dynasty is a wealth of information. Three things especially will help us to understand how the hexagram statements and line texts of the *Yijing* originated. First the crack is described: "A crack like a mountain overhanging." The word *ling* 陵, literally "hill" or "mound" (as in burial mound) can also mean "to usurp, to oppress."[1] So the diviner, by his choice of words, indicates that the mountain-shaped crack is oppressive, or symbolic of usurpation. Next, based on his reading of the crack, the diviner then supplies a rhymed couplet that specifically addresses the question or charge put to him by the inquirer: (As regards your question about military attack) "There was a chief who led a raid,/ Instead, 'twas he who lost his braves." The ominous image of the crack inspires an ominous association from the human world. Presumably, the omen about a raider who loses his warriors is directed at Huang'er, the usurper, but it could also refer to Sun Wenzi's counterattack. Since the omen text was still too cryptic to follow, secondary advice was requested from a wise woman of the realm. Her counsel—the third step in the divination process—is an interpretation of the omen according to the situation at hand.

If the old mother of Wei had added at the end of her counsel a prognostication such as this, "An attack will bring good fortune," the entire episode would be identical to the format of a hexagram text from the *Yijing* (see table 1):

Table 1

OMEN	COUNSEL	FORTUNE
There was a chief who led a raid; instead, 'twas he who lost his braves.	Now is time to resist the bandits.	(An attack will bring good fortune.)

This similarity between the language of the two different forms of divination is remarkable. But the differences are equally enlightening. The omen verse

---

1   The character occurs sixteen times in the *Zuozhuan*, three instances of which mean "usurpation" and seven meaning "to oppress."

quoted above was inspired by the ominous reading of a crack. Were this the omen text of a milfoil lot, we might ask what there is in the random sequence of numbers to inspire the sentence. To answer this question, we may examine a hexagram line text that is similar to this turtle shell divination—line 3 from hexagram 53, "Progression":

Table 2

OMEN	COUNSEL	FORTUNE
The wild goose pro-gresses to high land.	The husband goes to war and will not re-turn.... Now is the time to defend against ban-dits.	There will be misfor-tune.

In the turtle shell oracle the diviner was inspired by a burial mound-shaped crack, and thus extemporized the couplet about military matters. But as we can see by the hexagram line text, instead of a crack we have an image from nature, a lone goose migrating from the water to high land. The question is, with such an omen how would a diviner derive the original counsel text? In ancient China the lone goose was the symbol of the husband separated from his wife. Furthermore, military excursions usually occurred in the winter after the autumn harvests and before the spring rains. This was also when geese migrated south. So the counsel makes logical sense for this omen.

As to what the lone goose has to do with this particular hexagram, there are several possible answers. Perhaps a flock of wild geese flew over when the milfoil lots were being cast. Perhaps the hexagram symbol resembled geese flying in formation. Some hexagram symbols seem to have inspired the texts that accompanied them. There is, for example, Hexagram 50, "The Cauldron," whose line texts describe a sacrificial cauldron, but whose hexa-gram symbol also appears to be a representation of the cauldron's shape. The lower broken line mentions the cauldron's legs, the upper broken line men-tions the cauldron's "ears," and the top line mentions the cauldron's carrying pole. We may never know exactly how the ancient diviners linked particular omen verses to particular hexagram symbols, but thanks to the oracle bone records we can at least understand how the omen verses relate to the counsel texts.[2]

---

2   Edward Shaughnessy was the first to make this connection in his pioneering essay on the origin of the *Yijing* line text. See Shaughnessy, 1995, p. 231-235.

It is likely that by the end of the Shang dynasty the 64 six-digit numbers that would eventually evolve into the sixty-four hexagrams of the *Yijing*, had already received their associated omen statements. At this time there were at least three traditions of milfoil divination existing simultaneously—the *Lianshan* 連山, the *Guicang* 歸藏, and the *Zhouyi* 周易. These were probably oral traditions, known only to diviners and kings, and not written down until much later. The first of these is lost except for scattered fragments quoted in other texts. Parts of the second have been discovered recently in the Qin dynasty tomb at Wangjiatai. What still remains of the *Lianshan* and the *Guicang* are only hexagram statements, not line texts. It may be that these two divination traditions utilized only 64 hexagram statements. The *Zhouyi*, on the other hand, ancestor of the *Yijing*, is a collection of 64 hexagram statements plus 384 line texts. The *Zhouyi* most likely existed first as hexagram statements, and only later were the line texts added. This does accord with the legend that says King Wen wrote the hexagram statements while his son, the Duke of Zhou, added the line texts. However, since milfoil lot numbers have been found on Shang period oracle bones in Zhou temples, then the Zhou clan may have used the *Lianshan* or *Guicang* before they created their own *Zhouyi*. We cannot be sure how milfoil divination evolved, but as more archaeological discoveries are made, the picture will surely get clearer.

1.3 The Mythical Origins of the *Yijing*

Myth is the "history" of the prehistoric world, the oral record passed down through the ages before the discovery of writing. With writing, the record could be preserved unaltered. But with myth each generation changed the story according to its own understanding of what became more inscrutable as time passed. In this chapter some of the stories regarding the birth of China and her cultural symbols will be recounted so that the reader may derive a clearer picture of how and why the ancient Chinese created the *Yijing*.

1.3.1 The Sibling Gods, Fuxi and Nüwa

There are a considerable number of myths in China pertaining to culture heroes—those semi-divine beings who discovered fire and created the artifacts of culture, such as writing, weaving, and farming. Hou Ji, or Lord Millet, for example, was the first to grow the grain that became the staple of the ancient Chinese diet.

One of the most important culture heroes in the Chinese tradition is Fuxi 伏羲/犧, the first of the legendary rulers (traditionally reigned 2852-2737 BCE). He almost always appears in drawings with his sister, Nüwa 女媧. Some dynastic registers indicate that Nüwa ruled before Fuxi. The earliest representations of these creatures depict them as intertwined half-dragon, half-human forms. Fuxi usually is holding a carpenter's square, while Nüwa grasps a compass. As such, they are the creators or fabricators of the cosmos. There is no record of Nüwa's birth, but we do have some idea how Fuxi was born:

> In Thunder Marsh there lives a thunder god who has a dragon body but a human head. (It thunders when he) drums his belly. 雷澤中有雷神, 龍身而人頭, 鼓其腹 (*Shanhaijing* 山海經, "Regions Within the Seas: East, no. 13" 海內東經第十三, p. 117).

> Once, a giant footprint appeared by Thunder Marsh. (A girl named) Hua Xu stepped in it and later gave birth to Fuxi. 大跡出雷澤, 華胥履之, 生伏羲 (*Taiping Yulan* 太平御覽 135 卷, "Huang Qin, pt. 1" 皇親部一: "Baoxi mu" 庖犧母, p. 14).

This explains why Fuxi is pictured as half-dragon and half-human. He had a human mother and a dragon father. The second of the two fragments utilizes a particularly Chinese version of the motif of virgin birth. This was also how Hou Ji was born, although it was a different god.

A clue to the function of these culture heroes may reside in their names. The *fu* 伏 of Fuxi is a dog next to a man, and *xi* 犧 means "a sacrificial victim." Dogs, like oxen, swine and fowl, were important sacrifices in ancient China. Another name for Fuxi is Baoxi 庖犧. *Bao* means "to cook" or "kitchen." Fuxi is sometimes called the bringer of fire, so it makes sense that he would also be the inventor of cooking. He was the first hunter and wove baskets and nets for fishing. He also invented a stringed instrument like the zither.

The sister's name is the character for "woman" *nü* 女, plus a second character *wa* 媧, that combines "woman" with a phonetic element. The fact that the ideographs of her name are so predominantly female has prompted some scholars to speculate that remnants of her myth are evidence of an ancient matriarchal culture. Nüwa is credited with establishing the rites of marriage and inventing the reed pipe, but she is best known for creating human beings out of yellow clay.

At the risk of euhemerizing these myths, we might imagine that the mythical character of Fuxi embodied the memory of a particular clan leader with a dragon totem.[1] His inventions may have enabled his tribe to progress at a rate that propelled it culturally far ahead of surrounding tribes, thus assuring immortality in the memories of his descendants. Nüwa may precede Fuxi as the last matriarch; her institution of marriage would signal the beginning of patriarchy. A Later Han dynasty (25-221 CE) text describes the conditions of this primitive age.

> In the beginning, before there was either moral or social order, people knew their mothers only, not their fathers. . . . Then Fuxi looked up and studied the images in the heavens. He looked down and studied the patterns on the earth. He united man and woman, regulated the five phases, and established the laws of humanity. 古之時未有三綱六紀,民人但知其母,不知其父... 於是伏羲仰觀象於天,俯察法於地,因夫婦正五行,始定人道 (*Baihutong delun* 白虎通德論, vol. 1, 卷 1, "Hao" 號, p. 37).

Certainly the legend of Fuxi's miraculous birth (as well as Hou Ji's) would support this conclusion. Only his mother's name is known.

---

1   Euhemerus was a 4th century BCE Greek philosopher who believed that the pantheon of gods such as Zeus and Apollo arose from the deification of dead heroes. Our word euhemerize comes from his name. It means to explain a myth as originating in forgotten history.

1.3.2 The Invention of the *Bagua* 八卦

If Fuxi was indeed a historical figure, then the myths that describe him are a rare glimpse into the hunting and gathering society of pre-dynastic China. The following myth fragment shows Fuxi to be a contemplative ruler who attempted to fathom all aspects of his environment.

> In ancient times, Baoxi came to rule all under heaven. He looked up and studied the constellations in the heavens. He looked down and studied the patterns on the earth. He studied the markings of the birds and beasts and how they fit their habitats. Near at hand he learned much from his own body, and at a distance he learned much from external objects. Consequently, he drew the *bagua* in order to connect with the nature of the spiritual intelligences and to regulate the relations of all things. 古者包犧氏之王天下也, 仰則觀象於天, 俯則觀法於地, 觀鳥獸之文, 與地之宜, 近取諸身, 遠取諸物, 於是始作八卦, 以通神明之德, 以類萬物之情 (*Zhouyi zhengyi* 周易正義, "Xici xia" 繫辭下, 卷 8, p. 5).

Here, Fuxi has studied his world in an attempt to understand its regularities—the rising and setting of constellations, the ebb and flow of waters, the rise and fall of terrain. In the stripes of tigers and the tint of feathers he perceived the match between habitat and inhabitant. A gaze outward was balanced by a gaze inward—veins and arteries were obviously the streams and rivers of the body. With such keen perception he was able to mimic nature with ritual ceremonies and thereby maintain harmony between the known world and the unseen world of spirits. Undoubtedly, he began with sacrifices to these intelligences as a means of pleasing them. But eventually he improved the communication by creating a language that enabled the gods to speak back to him. Fuxi's language was a set of eight symbols called the *bagua*, which he could use to represent the relationships between all things.

1.3.3 The *Hetu* 河圖, or River Diagram

There are different versions of the origin of the *bagua*. We just learned from a passage in the *Yijing* that Fuxi intuited them from his environment. But myth fragments recorded in other texts depict a creature, either a dragon or a dragon-horse, emerging from a river with a series of markings on its body (see figure 4). These markings were then interpreted by Fuxi, who wrote them down in the form of the so-called *hetu* 河圖 or River Diagram. Mentioned briefly in one of China's oldest texts, the *Book of Documents* 尚書, the diagram is described in more detail in this Han dynasty commentary:

When Fuxi ruled the world, a dragon-horse emerged from the River. Fuxi imitated its stripes and drew the *bagua*. This is called the River Diagram. 伏羲氏王天下, 龍馬出河, 遂則其文以畫八卦, 謂之河圖 (Kong Anguo 孔安國, ed., *Shangshu* 尚書, "Zhoushu" 周書, ch. 24, "Guming" 顧命, p. 134).

Illustration 4. The Dragon-Horse
Source: Tang, p. 29

The dragon is a venerable figure in Chinese mythology. Dragon figurines have been uncovered in the oldest strata of Chinese civilization. Regardless of whether this creature is a Stone Age memory or an imaginary beast, its artistic representation since Han times is usually a composite of one or more of the five lucky animals: the head of a horse, the horns of a deer, the body of a serpent, the claws of a rooster, and the tail of a turtle.

A close look at the back of the dragon-horse reveals a configuration of white dots (or circles), which signify numbers based on their systematic organization into odd and even groups. The Chinese believed, generally speaking, that odd numbers were lucky and even numbers were unlucky. A person who could, by his contemplation of the world, extract the odd and even numbers, could thereby tell the future. Numbers, simply speaking, were the language of the gods.

1.3.4 The *Luoshu* 洛書, or Luo River Writing

The two versions of the origin of the *bagua* just discussed are not necessarily contradictory. When Fuxi looked up to study the constellations his eyes would have naturally followed the course of what we call the Milky Way, but which the Chinese call the Heavenly River 天漢. In the southern sky, just where the Milky Way splits into two tributaries, is a region called the Heavenly Ford 天津. On either side of this ford there are two important constellations. To the west, on the right bank of the river, is the Azure Dragon 蒼龍. To the east, on the left bank of the river, is the Heavenly Turtle 天黿. Both constellations appear to be emerging from the river. Only the dragon's tail (the constellation Scorpio) is still submerged, and the remainder of its body is stretched across the southern sky. One leg of the Heavenly Turtle (the constellation Corona Australis) is in the river, and the remainder is crawling out onto the eastern horizon. So Fuxi could have seen the dragon emerging from the *Heavenly* River as he studied the constellations, rather than an earthly river as he studied the topography of the land. The dots and circles in the illustration may have originally represented stars.

Some 500 years after the reign of Fuxi, the legendary period traditionally came to an end with the crowning of Yu, the Great 大禹 (2205-2197 BCE) as first king of the Xia dynasty. Yu, like Fuxi, was a culture hero. He is best known for quelling the floods and saving China from inundation. After his successful hydraulic engineering, when he had dammed the flooding Yellow River and drained the swamped domain, a sacred turtle is said to have emerged from the River Luo 洛水. On the turtle's back was another diagram, similar to that of the River Diagram (see figure 5). It is called the *luoshu*, or Luo Writing. Together with the River Diagram, the two figures were said to have been the cosmological models by which Yu rebuilt the devastated world.

Illustration 5. The Luo River Turtle
Source: Tang, p. 29

Scholars speculate that these models may represent ancient calendar re-
form (Porter, p. 36). In an agrarian society the most important knowledge that
a person can possess is the time when planting should begin. Ancient societies usually calculated planting times as so many days after the first day of
spring. Prehistoric farmers knew when this day had arrived by watching the
stars. When a particular star in a particular constellation rose above the horizon at dusk, that marked the first day of spring.

However, unknown to the ancients, the stars do not rise at the same time
every year. Due to a phenomenon called the precession of the equinoxes,
stars rise a little later every year. It would take three or four generations
before the change would be drastic enough to notice. But when a farmer is

counting on the appearance of a star to plant his crops, as the star rises later every year the planting is also later, and thus the growing season is progressively shorter. This will be disastrous unless the calendar is changed.

In prehistoric times, stars and constellations were spirits whose regulation of the seasons was unquestioned. A change of calendar was equivalent to a revolution in heaven. In the Yangshao period of prehistoric China the rise of the Heavenly Turtle would have marked the beginning of spring. During the reign of Fuxi, the Heart of the Dragon would have marked spring. Thus Fuxi's observation of the dragon-horse and his creation of the *bagua* may represent the victory of the dragon over the turtle and the creation of a new calendar. From now on the crops would be planted with the rise of the Dragon, not the Turtle.

1.3.5 The *Bagua*

As mentioned above, numbers were the language of the gods. The person who could extract the odd and even numbers from the environment could thereby know the future. Since Fuxi drew the *bagua* 八卦 from the River Diagram and both the Diagram and the Writing are numerical configurations, then it follows that the *bagua* must have a numerical basis. If the dots in the River Diagram and the Luo Writing are converted into numbers, we derive the patterns in figures 6 and 7.[2]

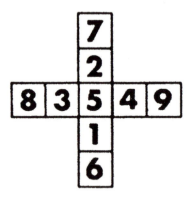

Illustration 6. The River Diagram

---

2   These figures (and all others not specifically attributed to other sources) were prepared by the author.

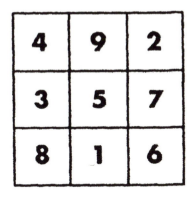

Illustration 7. The Luo Writing

The earliest we can prove the existence of the Luo Writing configuration of numbers is the Former Han dynasty (206 BCE-CE 25). As for the River Diagram numbers, they do not appear in the record until the late Song dynasty (960-1127), although they are implied in the Han dynasty text, *Guanzi*. No one doubts that the *luoshu* and *hetu* are ancient—their names are as old as the oldest Zhou dynasty texts, if not older. We just cannot be sure the numbers associated with the names are equally old, which is why scholars are compelled to find other reasons for the appearance of these strange creatures in prehistoric times.

There are two important organizational factors that are common to both of these figures—the centrality of the number 5, and the function of odd and even numbers. Both are keys to the derivation of fortune in Chinese divination systems. The number 5 is at the center for a reason. A look at both figures above will reveal that the numbers in adjacent cells differ by a factor of 5. On the River Diagram, for example, the difference between the two numbers on each arm is 5. On the Luo Writing each odd number on the cross differs by 5 from its counterclockwise neighbor on the corner. Because of the "magical" function of 5, the Luo Writing is called the Magic Square. Rows, columns, and diagonals all add up to 15, which is also the product of 3—the base value of the 3x3 square, times 5—the central number of the square. When this 5 is multiplied by 9, the largest number in the square, the product is 45, which is the total of all numbers in the square.

As mentioned above, the Chinese believed that odd numbers were lucky and even numbers unlucky. This may explain the value of the second organizational factor—the alternation of odd and even numbers. When we count sequentially from 1 to 10, odd and even numbers naturally alternate. Likewise, in both figures odd and even numbers alternate across adjacent cells, even though adjacent numbers in the figures are not sequential. For example, each arm of the River Diagram includes one odd and one even number. Also, in the Luo Writing the cross is occupied by the odd numbers, while the corners are filled with the even numbers.

These figures would later become the basis for a correlative theory of the cosmos. Each cell would be correlated with a related factor in other systems such as time (the four seasons), space (the eight directions), and more importantly, divination (the *bagua*). From configurations of odd and even numbers would be developed the theory of *wuxing* 五行, or the "five phases" (soil, metal, water, wood, fire) which, however, does not figure in the theoretical history of the *Yijing*. Knowing the current phase of a system, a person would be able to predict the next phase. So these figures were formulae for telling the future. For this reason they were carefully guarded secrets throughout the ages.

Since Fuxi drew the *bagua* from the River Diagram, and the Diagram was a configuration of numbers, we have speculated that the *bagua* has a numerical basis. That is certainly the case, and archaeological discoveries prove this to be so. In the last chapter we learned that the milfoil lot was a six-digit number that evolved into the six-line graph of the *Yijing* hexagram.

In one study of archaeological records of milfoil lots, Zhang Zhenglang 張政烺 discovered that 20% were three-digit numbers and 80% were six-digit numbers (p. 404). For example, one oracle bone record from the late Shang dynasty invokes the name of an early ancestor, Shang Jia Wei 上甲微, and then follows this invocation with the digits, 666 (Zhang and Liu, p. 160; see also Hexagram 23, whose lower trigram is 666, and whose line texts probably refer to Shang Jia Wei and his father, Wang Hai). A bronze vessel from the early Zhou dynasty bears an inscription that reads, "Father Zhongyou made this precious caldron, 758." There are even bone and horn arrowheads discovered in an early Zhou dwelling site that contain the isolated digits, 161 and 711. In this last example, the numbers must have been inscribed for good luck in the hunt.

If the six-digit milfoil lot corresponded to omen or prognostication texts, what about the three-digit numbers? Scholars cannot be certain because none of the three-digit records is accompanied by omen texts. However, there can be little doubt that these numbers correspond to the *bagua* (or "eight" *gua*). At this stage in the evolution of milfoil divination, the three-line graphs known as "trigrams" did not exist. The word *gua* 卦 is composed of the element *bu* 卜 on the right (meaning "to divine") plus a phonetic element on the left. Whereas *bu* specifically meant to divine by crack-making, *gua* meant to divine by milfoil stalks, and by extension, the figure derived from such divination.

There are precisely *eight* of these figures for this reason: as indicated above, odd digits of the six-place milfoil lot were eventually transposed into the number 1, while even digits were transposed into the number 6. By the middle of the Zhou dynasty the 1 and 6 had transformed into the familiar solid and broken lines. Eventually, these lines would lose their numerological meaning and derive metaphysical meanings. Thus, the "monogram," composed of a solid *yang* 陽 line, represented strength and movement, while the broken *yin* 陰 line represented pliancy and rest. These two lines when combined formed the "bigram" representing the four seasons. Two *yang* lines characterize summer, while two *yin* lines represent winter. Potential progress of lines within a figure is organically upward, so a *yang* line encroaching upon an *yin* line is spring, and an *yin* line encroaching upon a *yang* line is autumn.

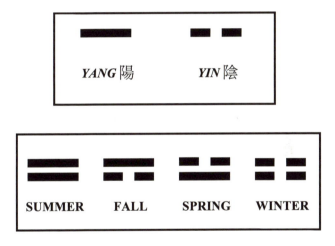

Illustration 8. Monograms and Bigrams

When an odd number—represented by a one (or a solid line)—and an even number—represented by a six (or a broken line)—are combined in threes, the result is the following eight combinations:

Qian 乾	Dui 兑	Li 離	Zhen 震
▬▬ ▬▬ ▬▬	▬▬ ▬▬ ▬ ▬	▬▬ ▬ ▬ ▬▬	▬ ▬ ▬ ▬ ▬▬
HEAVEN **1**	**LAKE** **2**	**FIRE** **3**	**THUNDER** **4**
Xun 巽	Kan 坎	Gen 艮	Kun 坤
▬▬ ▬▬ ▬ ▬	▬ ▬ ▬▬ ▬ ▬	▬▬ ▬ ▬ ▬ ▬	▬ ▬ ▬ ▬ ▬ ▬
WOOD **5**	**WATER** **6**	**MOUNTAIN** **7**	**EARTH** **8**

Illustration 9. The Eight *Gua* Trigrams

These eight combinations were given names at sometime in the tradition. While these interpretations are open to question, they were standardized in the *Shuogua zhuan* 說卦傳 "Explaining the *Gua*" commentary written in the Han dynasty.

1.3.6 *Bagua* Sequences

According to the *Records of the Grand Historian* (1st century BCE), when King Wen was imprisoned by the Shang king Zhou Xin, he combined the eight *gua* by pairs and created the 64 hexagrams. He then attached a statement called a *guaci* 卦辭 to each hexagram to explain its meaning. Since there are no Shang dynasty records of hexagram statements, we cannot refute the legend that Wen composed them. However, archaeological discoveries have proven that proto-hexagrams existed at least three centuries before the time of King Wen. Some scholars in fact think that hexagrams preceded trigrams, and the latter were derived from the former. Since it is not possible to prove either theory definitively, the traditional account will be accepted as the correct one. As to when the *bagua* were doubled to produce the 64 hexagrams, perhaps it was Fuxi. This is the understanding of Wang Bi 王弼 (CE 226-249), the first known commentator on the *Yijing*. Or perhaps it was Yu, the Great, the sage-king who discovered the Luo Writing.

1.3.6.1 The Post-Heaven Sequence of Bagua

In the "Explaining the *Gua*" commentary is recorded a saying of great antiquity.[3] It opens with a reference to Di (Shang Di, the High God of the Shang people). As such, it is probably religious in intent. It confirms the antiquity of the *bagua*, and verifies their original divinatory function. It reads as follows:

Di emerges in *Zhen*	帝出乎震
Is revered in *Xun*	齊乎巽
Reveals himself in *Li*	相見乎離
Is served in *Kun*	致役乎坤
Speaks words in *Dui*	說言乎兌
Is feared in *Qian*	戰乎乾
Rewards the suffering in *Kan*	勞乎坎
And fulfills his words in *Gen*	成言乎艮

(*Zhouyi zhengyi* 周易正義, "Shuogua" 說卦, 卷 9, p. 5).

If the trigram names are translated in the context of the passage, it reads as follows:

Di, manifest in earthquake,
Is revered by those who kneel,
Reveals himself as a bird of omen,
Is offered service by the compliant,
Speaks words to the mediator,[4]
Is feared by the vigorous,
Rewards those suffering in the pit,
And fulfills his words to those who obstruct.

The liturgy opens with a testimony to the power of Di whose might can shake the world. Each sentence then describes in narrative fashion the means by which the deity interacts with humans. He communicates his power indirectly through ominous signs, and directly to the mediator/shaman who interprets the omens and oracles. Those who tremble at the flight of the Dragon and kneel to Di are rewarded when they suffer the pitfalls of mortality. Those who obstruct him see his oracles fulfilled.

Immediately following this passage in the "Explaining the *Gua*" commentary is an interpretative annotation, as if the original passage were a quote from elsewhere which needed contemporary explanation. This alone attests to the antiquity of the original verse. The religious meaning had been lost or

---

3   This passage appears in a fragment of the *Lianshan*, the Xia dynasty book of divination.
4   In the *Shuogua* commentary, the trigram *dui* is characterized as the "shaman." See table 4 below.

was ignored by the time the commentary was written in the Han dynasty. For example, the "Di" is interpreted to mean *wanwu* 萬物, "the myriad things," that is, the phenomenal world. Religious intent is not what the commentators believed was in need of elucidation. Instead, the annotation locates each *gua* in one of the eight directions and identifies four *gua* with the four seasons. By securing the *bagua* in time and space, the passage allows us to draw a cosmological map.

The Chinese were masters at visualizing the cosmos and creating maps or models to represent heaven and earth. The River Diagram and Luo Writing are cosmological maps, as are the *bagua* sequences first described in the commentaries of the *Yijing*. But the cosmological map *par excellence* was the *shipan* 式盤, or cosmograph (a type of divining board; see figure 10), the ancient precursor to the *fengshui* compass. The cosmograph had a square base—representing earth, upon which revolved a round disc—representing heaven. Around the circumference of the heaven disc were inscribed the 28 constellations of the Chinese zodiac, including the seven segments of the Azure Dragon (Horn, Heart, Tail, etc.). At the eight directions of the earth plate were inscribed the *bagua* of the post-heaven sequence.

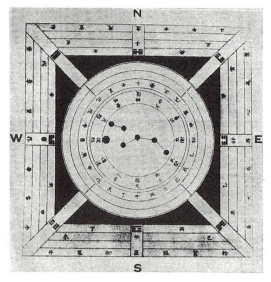

Illustration 10. The Cosmograph with *Houtian Bagua*
Source: Needham, vol. 3, p. 543

The "post-heaven," or *houtian* 後天, sequence of *bagua*, is represented in figure 11. It is also called the King Wen sequence, because Wen supposedly arranged the order of the 64 hexagrams in the *Yijing*. It has also long been associated with the Luo Writing in the cosmological history of the *Yijing* and thus corresponds to the number sequence of figure 7. The diagram in figure 11 is oriented with south at the top, which is the traditional Chinese placement, whereas the illustration in figure 10 is oriented in the Western fashion with north at the top. Because of the association of *bagua* sequence to the numerological sequence, each of the *bagua* has not only a directional correlation but also a numerical designation. The function of this diagram is crucial to the understanding of forms of divination derived from the *Yijing* in the post-classical period.[5]

Illustration 11. The *Houtian*, or Post-Heaven, Sequence of *Bagua*
Source: Zhang Qicheng, p. 73

1.3.6.2 The Pre-Heaven Sequence of Bagua

Another passage from "Explaining the *Gua*" commentary is not as descriptive as the one just quoted:

---

5 For more information on the function of the *houtian baqua* and the *luoshu* numbers, see Field, "The Numerology of Nine Star Fengshui: A *Hetu, Luoshu* Resolution of the Mystery of Directional Auspice."

Heaven and earth set the bearing.	天地定位
Mountain and lake communicate their *qi*.	山澤通氣
Thunder and wind arouse each other.	雷風相薄
Water and fire are not mutually hostile.	水火不相射
In such fashion do the *bagua* intersect.	八卦相錯

(*Zhouyi zhengyi* 周易正義, "Shuogua" 說卦, 卷 9, p. 4).

According to tradition this passage describes another cosmological map—the *xiantian* 先天, or "pre-heaven" configuration (see figure 12). Although this passage does not identify the sequence of *bagua* around the circumference of the square, it does capture the major characteristic of the map. Unlike the post-heaven sequence, opposites are arranged facing each other. Thus *Qian* "heaven" and *Kun* "earth" establish south and north, while *Li* "fire" and *Kan* "water" occupy east and west, etc. This configuration is traditionally coordinated with the River Diagram. For that reason it is also called the Fuxi sequence of *bagua*, since it was Fuxi who supposedly discovered the diagram on the back of the dragon-horse. A circular arrangement of the 64 hexagrams developed by the philosopher Shao Yong in the Song dynasty, is based on the pre-heaven sequence of trigrams and is called the Fuxi order.

Illustration 12. The *Xiantian*, or Pre-Heaven, Sequence of *Bagua*
Source: Zhang Qicheng, p. 77

1.4 The Historical Origin of the *Yijing*

1.4.1 The Author of the *Zhouyi*

According to the *Records of the Grand Historian* (1st century BCE), when King Wen was imprisoned by the Shang king Zhou Xin, he combined the eight *gua* by pairs and created the 64 hexagrams. He then attached a statement called a *guaci* 卦辭 to each hexagram to explain its meaning. However, archaeological discoveries have proven that hexagrams existed at least three centuries before the time of King Wen, and it may even be the case that hexagrams preceded trigrams, and the latter were derived from the former. So, while the origin of the hexagram figures may not be a fact, we do believe there existed a written record of divination early in the Zhou period. When King Wu contracted a serious illness and was about to die, his brother Dan, the Duke of Zhou, prayed to his ancestors using three turtles, all of which were favorable. Then, "He opened the bamboo tube and looked at the writings—they also indicated good fortune" 啟籥見書乃並是吉 (*Shangshu* 尚書, "Zhoushu" 周書, ch. 8, "Jinteng" 金縢, p. 18; Legge, vol. 3, pp. 355-56).[1] From this record we know there existed a written divination text just a few short years after the time of King Wen. This was either an early version of the *Zhouyi* or an earlier divination manual.

At this time there were also two other milfoil texts in existence—the *Lianshan* 連山 or "Linked Mountains" (reputed to date from the Xia dynasty) and the *Guicang* 歸藏 or "Return Within" (of the Shang dynasty). Although we know very little about them, their names are somewhat revealing. Lianshan is also a place name, the ancestral home of the second legendary sage-king, Shen Nong 神農. The *Lianshan* opened with the hexagram *Gen* 艮, composed of the doubled ("linked") trigram for "mountain" (see Hexagram 52). The *Guicang* opened with the hexagram for "earth." Thus the name *gui* 歸 ("return") *cang* 藏 ("hidden in") expresses the central concept of the text: "All things *return to lie within* the earth." The *Zhouyi* combines both of these naming schemes. Zhou is the name of the plain where the Zhou people originated, and *yi* means "to change," which is the central theme of the *Zhouyi*.

Only hexagram statements exist of the *Lianshan* and the *Guicang*, no line texts. The *Zhouyi*, on the other hand, is a collection of 64 *guaci* 卦辭 hexa-

---

1 In ancient China texts were written on bamboo or wooden strips, which were then tied together like stakes in a picket fence. This "book" could then be rolled up and stored inside a large bamboo tube.

gram statements plus 384 *yaoci* 爻辭, or line texts (six per hexagram). According to Ma Rong 馬融 (CE 79-166), a first century scholar, King Wen wrote the hexagram statements (*guaci*), while his son, the Duke of Zhou, added the line texts (*yaoci*). Several theories exist that explain the evolution of these lines. Some scholars speculate that the book was a hodgepodge, thrown together over the centuries from peasant omens and bone records. But these scholars apparently do not take into account the complexity of the structure of the text.

The King Wen sequence of hexagrams has baffled readers since the text was first subjected to intense study. In the Han dynasty and thereafter it was assumed the bigram and trigram basis of hexagram structure was most essential. In other words, the structure of individual hexagrams was considered more important than the relationships between different hexagrams. This bias made it impossible to determine the rationale for the sequence of hexagrams.

Only recently has anyone come close to deciphering the order of the traditional sequence of the hexagrams.[2] Such an elaborate construction could not have been an accident, and, in the absence of proof to the contrary, this book will accept the traditional account that King Wen and his son, the Duke of Zhou, were the original authors the *Zhouyi*.

1.4.2 The Naming of the *Zhouyi*

There is no structural difference between the *guaci* or hexagram statement and the *yaoci* or line text. Both are composed of omen, counsel, and prognostication or fortune texts. Apparently, the 64 hexagram statements alone did not give the diviner sufficient latitude for divining. So the original 64 texts were sextupled, which added 384 more possibilities. Back when the only means of divination was the oracle bone, the diviner was not limited to a finite number of omens. The crack could literally represent anything in the diviner's mind. With the 64-omen book, a divination ritual was limited to a relatively small set of readings. Sextupling the number of readings must have greatly enriched the divination experience and bolstered the survival of this new oracle.

The earliest testimonial evidence of the casting process contains an element that may be a clue to the name of the book. In these records the reading is expressed in the formula: "Hexagram A 之 [*zhi* "goes to"] Hexagram B." In most cases the two hexagram symbols differ only by one *yao* or line. In other words, if one *yao* line of Hexagram A changes into its opposite, then

---

2   See Scott Davis, *The Classic of Changes in Cultural Context: A Textual Archaeology of the Yi jing.*

Hexagram B results. And the text of the *changing* line in Hexagram A is the focus of the divination ritual. That is the line text that is utilized by the diviner to answer the inquirer's question. This may be the origin of the name of the book. It was called the *Yi*, or "the Changes," because the hexagram derived from the ititial casting of the yarrow stalks transitioned or changed into another hexagram. More importantly, the result of that change or transition was the prediction for the future.

1.4.2.1 Early Zhou Dynasty Book of Divination

Although scholars are not entirely sure how the milfoil was cast at this early stage, some two-dozen records of milfoil divination exist from mid-Zhou dynasty historical texts. Most of them are found in the *Zuozhuan* 左傳, or *Commentary of Zuo* on the *Spring and Autumn Annals* 春秋.[3] The earliest records of divination by milfoil occurred four centuries after the founding of the dynasty. As the Zhou dynasty progressed, the power of nobles slowly began to eclipse that of the king. The use of divination, originally a royal prerogative, spread from the capital to the regional states and permeated all of literate society. This cast of the milfoil dates from 645 BCE:

> Formerly, Duke Xian of the state of Jin cast the milfoil about his daughter's marriage to the ruler of Qin. He encountered *The Young Bride* (Hexagram 54) going to *A Sighting* (Hexagram 38). Interpreting, Diviner Su said, "It is unlucky. The line says, 'The young man stabs the lamb, and it does not bleed. The young girl offers a basket, but it has no fruit.' The neighbor to the west reproaches us and we cannot respond. *The Young Bride* going to *A Sighting* means it is a one-sided affair." 初晉獻公筮嫁伯姬於秦遇歸妹之睽史蘇占之曰不吉其繇曰士刲羊亦無衁也女承筐亦無貺也西鄰責言不可償也歸妹之睽猶無相也 (*Chunqiu Zuozhuan zhengyi* 春秋左傳 正義，卷 13, "Duke Xi 15th year" 僖公十五年, p. 19-23).

Line 6 of hexagram 54, a broken line, changes to a solid line to form hexagram 38. Thus the text of line 6 of The Young Bride is the basis for the

---

3 The *Spring and Autumn Annals* was a chronicle of the state of Lu from 722-481 BCE written by Confucius (551-479 BCE). As records of authentic events in the history of an important Zhou state, the *Annals* were prized by later generations. But they were difficult to understand because Confucius was very guarded in his narration—the bald facts about a duke's transgressions might result in a vendetta against the historian by the duke's descendants. Some 150 years after the last entry in the *Annals*—a time suitably distant from the actual occurrence of events—Zuo Qiuming wrote a very detailed commentary we call the *Zuozhuan*, or *Commentary of Zuo*.

consultation. According to this line, the sacrifice is a failure, and the basket is empty. Diviner Su interprets this to mean the proposed marriage will gain little for the state of Jin and much for the state of Qin.[4]

1.4.2.2 Spring and Autumn Period Book of Rhetoric

By the end of the Spring and Autumn period (770-476 BCE) even unlanded gentry were casting the milfoil. Uses ranged from medical prognosis to selection of auspicious days for travel. The text of the *Zhouyi* was so widely known by then speakers could allude to particular lines, and listeners would recognize them. This familiarity led to the ever-increasing use of the text to support one's argument. This is no different from contemporary uses of Biblical verses or quotations from the plays of Shakespeare, for example ("Something's rotten in the state of Denmark"). Eventually lines were being quoted out of context by those who needed revered texts on which to base their moral instruction. This moralizing slowly began to influence everyone's understanding of the *Zhouyi*, so that much of the original meaning was forgotten. The original divination text had become a book of rhetoric.[5] The following example will show how far the transformation had progressed. In 545 BCE, a treaty had been formed between various states so that the larger would protect the smaller. The smaller states were required to periodically send emissaries to the larger states to swear allegiance. The state of Zheng 鄭 sent an official named Youji 游吉 to the state of Chu, but he was turned back at the border. Chu claimed the treaty required a visit by the ruler of the state, not a mere servant. Youji made this report:

> The ruler of Chu will soon perish. Instead of cultivating a virtuous government, he is greedy and blind in his conduct toward the nobles. Will it be possible for him to continue long? The *Zhouyi*, under Return (Hexagram 24) going to Jawbones (Hexagram 27) says, "Losing the way back. Misfortune." Such is the case with the ruler of Chu. He seeks what he desires, but abandons what is essential, so there is no place to return to. This is what is meant by "losing the way back." How can he not meet with misfortune? 楚子將死矣不脩其政德而貪昧於諸侯以逞其願欲久得乎周易有之在復之頤曰迷復凶其楚子之

---

4   At this time Jin occupied the area east of the great bend of the Yellow River, while Qin occupied the frontier to the west. Qin would grow to be the most powerful of the warring kingdoms, eventually conquering all other states. Our name for China, in fact, is a Roman rendering of the Chinese "Qin" (pronounced like chin).

5   In ancient China a cultured man could sing verses from the *Odes* to embellish his stories, quote lines from the *Annals* to teach the lessons of history, and relate omens from the *Changes* to speculate about the future.

謂乎欲復其願而棄其本復歸無所是謂迷復能無凶乎. (*Chunqiu Zuozhuan zhengyi* 春秋左傳正義, 卷 37, "Duke Xiang 28th year" 襄公二十八年, p. 102).

Line 6 of Hexagram 24, a broken line, changes to a solid line to form hexagram 27. Thus the text of line 6 of Return is the basis for Youji's comment. However, no stalks were cast to derive this line, so is it a prognostication or simply a shrewd observation?

The *Spring and Autumn Annals* reports that the ruler of Chu died some months later. So Youji's comments were indeed a prediction, but one determined by mental power rather than divine power. Men from the growing "middle class" were using the words of the divination text without resorting to divination. And by now the ability of the *Zhouyi* to tell the future was invested in the text itself and not in the power of ancestral spirits. This backdrop prepared the way for philosophical interpretations of the *Zhouyi*.

1.4.2.3 Warring States Period "Ten Wings"

The Warring States period (403-221 BCE) was the blossoming of the "hundred schools" when philosophy flourished. As theories were debated in the intellectual centers of the various states, esteemed texts like the *Zhouyi* were reinterpreted in line with the new ways of thinking. Confucian moralists concentrated on ethical issues they found in the social content of the text. Proto-Daoists were interested in the symbolic relations between the linear symbols. The result was a collection of seven different commentaries (in ten sections) called the *Shiyi* 十異, "Ten Wings," each of which attempted to picture the *Zhouyi* as a rational system of thought. Modern scholars are almost unanimous in rejecting Confucius as the author of any of the commentaries, although it may be true that his disciples initiated a tradition of *Yi* studies. Following is a brief outline of the four most important commentaries.

1 Tuan zhuan

The first commentary is the *Tuan zhuan* 彖傳, or "Commentary on the Hexagram." For each hexagram, the name is explained by providing a moral context. Then, using various linear relationships, the good or bad fortune of each hexagram is determined from its unique structure of lines. The hexagram symbol consists of six positions, half of which (the 1st, 3rd, and 5th places, counting from the bottom) are described as superior, and half of which (the 2nd, 4th, and 6th places) are described as inferior. When a strong *yang* line occupies a superior position, or when a weak *yin* line occupies an inferior position, order and therefore good fortune is suggested. The opposite suggests disorder and misfortune. With this in mind, the following hexagram is considered to be the most balanced in the entire *Yijing*:

Illustration 13. Hexagram 63, Across the Stream

According to the *Tuan* commentary, lines whose strength does not match their station represent disorder and thus misfortune. Here is a hexagram that is slightly out of balance. In this example, accompanying the hexagram symbol are excerpts from the *yaoci* line texts.

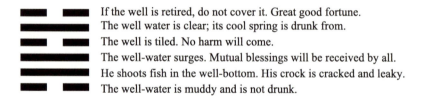

If the well is retired, do not cover it. Great good fortune.
The well water is clear; its cool spring is drunk from.
The well is tiled. No harm will come.
The well-water surges. Mutual blessings will be received by all.
He shoots fish in the well-bottom. His crock is cracked and leaky.
The well-water is muddy and is not drunk.

Illustration 14. Hexagram 48, The Well

The bottom two lines of Hexagram 48 do not conform to the ideal. Line 1 is a weak line in a superior position. Line 2 is a strong line in an inferior position. The text of each line indicates an unfortunate situation—a muddy well that can't be drunk from, and a cracked jar that can't be used for water. Lines 3-6, on the other hand, are appropriate to their position. Their texts all indicate good situations.

The hexagram symbol can also be divided into two separate trigrams. The corresponding lines of each trigram in a given hexagram (lines 1 and 4, lines 2 and 5, lines 3 and 6) attract each other if they are occupied by symbols of *opposite* character. In other words, a *yin*, or broken, line in position 1 of the lower trigram is attracted to a *yang*, or solid, line in position 4 of the upper trigram. This is perceived as auspicious. Finally, the second and fifth places in a hexagram, by virtue of their central position in each trigram, are perceived as the hexagram's rulers.

For example, Hexagram 37, "Home and Family," is composed of the trigram for wood over the trigram for fire:

Illustration 15. Hexagram 37, Home and Family

The *guaci* hexagram statement and its *Tuan* commentary read as follows:

> *Guaci*: Home and Family. A good omen for a girl.

> *Tuan*: Home and Family. The correct place of the woman is inside; the correct place of the man is outside. That man and woman have their proper places is the great model of Heaven and Earth. In home and family there are strict rulers called the parents. When the father is a father and the son a son, when the elder brother is an elder brother and the younger brother a younger brother, when the husband is a husband and the wife a wife, this is the proper way of the family. When the family is proper, then all under Heaven is secure. 家人: 利女貞. 象曰: 家人. 女正位乎內, 男正位乎外, 男女正, 天地之大義也. 家人有嚴君焉, 父母之謂也. 父父, 子子, 兄兄, 弟弟, 夫夫, 婦婦, 而家道正; 正家而天下定矣 (*Zhouyi zhengyi* 周易正義, 三, 家人, p. 121).

This passage is a good example of a commentary derived from the concept of the hexagram rulers. The lower or inner trigram is ruled by an *yin* line, representing the woman. The upper or outer trigram is ruled by a *yang* line, representing the man. The two rulers are opposite in nature, thus they attract each other. Heaven and Earth are opposite, with heaven above and earth below. Man and woman are opposite, with man above and woman below. Thus the *Tuan* says, "That man and woman have their proper places is the great model of Heaven and Earth."

2 Shuogua zhuan

The *Shuogua* 説卦, or "Explaining the *Gua* (Trigrams)," discusses the eight trigrams, and expands each of the general trigram categories into as many as twenty distinct terms. See tables 3 and 4, which organize the data from the *Shuogua* commentary.

Table 3. Trigram Attributes A

Gua	Name	Family Member	Animal	Direction	Season
☰	**Qian**	father	horse	north-west	early winter
☷	**Kun**	mother	cow and calf	south-west	early autumn
☳	**Zhen**	eldest son	dragon	east	spring equinox
☵	**Kan**	second son	pig	north	winter solstice
☶	**Gen**	youngest son	dog, rat	north-east	early spring
☴	**Xun**	eldest daughter	hen	south-east	early summer
☲	**Li**	second daughter	pheasant, turtle	south	summer solstice
☱	**Dui**	youngest daughter	sheep and goat	west	autumn equinox

Table 4. Trigram Attributes B

Gua	Elemental Forces	Person	Color	Body Part	Miscel-laneous
☰	Heaven	king	deep red	head	fruit, ice
☷	Earth	the people	black	abdomen	cloth, kettle, wagon
☳	Thunder	young men	dark yellow	foot	bamboo, giving orders
☵	Water	thieves	blood red	ear	a bow, wheels, moon
☶	Mountain	gate-keepers		fingers, hands	pebbles, a path
☴	Wood, Wind	merchants	white	thigh	plumb and square
☲	Fire	big-bellied men		eye	armor, a spear
☱	Lake	shaman, concubine		mouth, tongue	salty

3 Xiang zhuan

The *Xiang zhuan* 象傳, or "Commentary on the Images," breaks down each hexagram into its component trigrams and deduces the meaning of the former out of the latter. First, the name of the hexagram is deduced, and then a conclusion is reached of a social nature, based upon that deduction.

Here is an example. The trigram for thunder over the trigram for water forms Hexagram 40, *Jie* 解, "Loosening." The *Xiang* commentary for this hexagram's *guaci* statement reads as follows:

> After thunder, rain is produced. This is Loosening. Thus the lord for-
> gives errors and pardons crimes. 雷雨作，解；君子以赦過宥罪
> (*Zhouyi zhengyi* 周易正義, 四, 解, p. 20).

In other words, when the heavens are sufficiently dark and oppressive, lightning strikes, thunder roars, and the rain is released. The trigram for water is the symbol of the thief (see table 3), while that of thunder is the symbol of decisiveness and the giving of commands. In addition, the word *jie* literally means "to untie," so the *Xiang* hypothesizes in these two trigrams the image of the ruler issuing a command that the thief be released.

The correlation of natural image to social image is an important one in ancient Chinese thought which can be seen in many hexagrams of the *Yijing*. It is even more common in the *Book of Odes* 詩經 (#19): "Deep rolls the thunder on the sun-side of the southern hills./Why is it, why must you always be away?" 殷其靁在南山之陽何斯違斯 (*Maoshi zhengyi* 毛詩正義, 卷 2, "Guofeng Zhaonan" 國風召南, "Yin Qi Lei" 殷其靁, p. 175; Waley, 1937: p. 98).[6] These are examples of a holistic worldview that does not separate the human realm from the realm of nature.

4 Da zhuan

The most important commentary in the "Ten Wings" is called the *Da zhuan* 大傳, "Great Commentary," also known as the *Xici zhuan* 繫辭傳, "Appended Words." This work, unlike the other Wings, does not consist of line-by-line or hexagram-specific commentaries, but is an essay about the nature of the *Yijing*. Concepts in the *Da zhuan* are tantamount to a metaphysics of change.

As we learned before, the term *yi* itself means change, specifically the change of one hexagram into another. However, according to the *Da zhuan*, the sequence of hexagrams is a model of the cosmos ("heaven and earth"). In this context change is discussed from two different perspectives—change in the natural world, the macrocosm, and change in the hexagrams of the *Yijing*, the microcosm. Furthermore, this concept of change can be subdivided into two different notions—alternation and transformation. Alternation is ordered change—the reversal of bipolar opposites (like AC—alternating current). We

---

6   In citations from the *Book of Odes*, regardless of the translation quoted, the ode se-
    quence number (#) from the oldest surviving commentary, the *Mao Shi* 毛詩, will be
    given.

see it in the *Yijing* as the alternation of *yin* and *yang* lines. It occurs in nature as the alternation of day and night. Transformation, on the other hand, is random change, or chance. In the *Yijing* we see transformation in the random appearance of the changing line. In the real world it is manifested in the appearance of omens.

Time is also a factor of change. In the *Da zhuan* time is presented as a function of alternation and progression, just as the seasons alternate as the months progress. On the microcosmic level the hexagram is perceived as a model of seasonal time. We learned in the last chapter the two monograms combine to form the bigram representing the four seasons. Alternation here is manifested, for example, by an *yin* line encroaching upon a *yang* line, which mimics the change from hot to cold seasons, the change from day to night, the change from youth to maturity, etc. In the stalk-casting ritual, the microcosm and the macrocosm merge. As the hexagram progresses from the bottom upwards, replicating organic growth, each line captures a possible development in the world outside the diviner. So the chance appearance of a given line in a given position, which resulted in a given omen, was equivalent to a real-life occurrence of a portent. The hexagram omen, as such, was a microcosmic model of a unique moment in the life of the inquirer.

The philosophers who pondered the mysteries of the *Yi* in the final centuries of the Zhou dynasty and the first century of the Han had a difficult task before them: to take a collection of oracular texts and develop it into a coherent system of thought. In their attempt to make sense of a largely forgotten tradition, they managed to create a metaphysics that explained the order in the universe. Their task was so successful the theories proposed in the "Great Commentary" became the basis of Chinese philosophy down to the 20th century.

In 136 BCE, Emperor Wu 武帝 of the Han 漢 dynasty established academic chairs for each of the five Confucian texts: the *Changes* 易, *Odes* 詩, *Documents* 書, *Rites* 禮, and *Spring and Autumn Annals* 春秋. Henceforth these texts were called *jing* 經, or classics, and became the canon or curriculum of the Han Academy. From this point on the book was called the *Yijing* 易經, or *Classic of Changes*.

Part 2. The Hexagram Texts

In this section of the book—which includes the translation of each of the 64 hexagram texts—each separate hexagram is contained in its own table. The arrangement of the various aspects of each hexagram text proceeds as follows.

In the top register of each hexagram table (see the example in table 5) are three items above a row of words. On the left is the Chinese logograph(s) for the hexagram name written in the script current when the *Zhouyi* was written—that found on bronze artifacts of the late Shang and early Zhou dynasties.[1] This is followed by the hexagram number in the King Wen sequence. On the far right is the six-line hexagram symbol composed of solid and broken lines.[2] Below these items is the name of the hexagram in the *pinyin* spelling of its Mandarin pronunciation (in italics), followed by the English translation.

Table 5. How to read a hexagram table: Name, Number, and Hexagram Symbol

Da Chu, Greater Stock

In the bottom register (see table 6) are seven rows of text divided into three columns based on the three divination categories descussed in some de-

---

1   The images of the *jinwen* 金文 bronze script ideographs appearing in each hexagram table are taken from two reference works: the Han dynasty *Shuowen* dictionary (*Shuowen jiezi zhu* 說文解字注, edited by the Qing scholar, Duan Yucai 段玉裁), and the modern dictionary, *Hanzi shuti zidian* 汉字书体字典 (edited by the Japanese scholar Chikudo 竹堂).

2   The hexagram figures used in this book are the Mac OS X version of the Unicode symbols.

tail in section 1.2.3.5 *The Origin of the* Yijing *Line Texts*. In the original Chinese, *omen*, *counsel*, and *fortune* (or prognostication) texts are not distinguished, so these labels have been added for the reader's convenience. Below these headings, the first row of text is the *guaci*, or hexagram statement (enumerated with "0" to indicate that it precedes the six *yaoci*). The next six rows contain the *yaoci* texts 1 through 6 corresponding to the six lines of the hexagram symbol (counting from the bottom).

Table 6. How to read a hexagram table: Hexagram and Line Texts

	OMEN	COUNSEL	FORTUNE
0		A good omen.	There will be good fortune.
		These are not to be eaten at home.	
		Now is the time to ford the great river.	
1		It is time to make a sacrifice.	There is danger.
2	The carriage loses an axle box.		
3	Fine horses being chased.	A good omen in times of difficulty.	
	He said: "Circle the wagons in defense!"	It is time to go on a journey.	
4	The hobble of a young bull.		There will be great good fortune.
5	The tusks of a gelded boar.		Good fortune.
6	Bearing the course of Heaven.	Your plea is heard.	

A look at almost any hexagram text will show what appear to be empty cells scattered throughout the table. For example, in the example above (Hexagram 26), the hexagram statement has no omen text, three counsel texts, and one prognostication text, or fortune. Line 2 has an omen text but no counsel or prognostication. Line 3 has two omens, each followed by its own counsel, but no prognostications.

It is also important to know the order of the original text when consulting a statement or line text—the reader should proceed in a straight line from left to right across the row and down the column. For example, in table 6, the second counsel of the hexagram statement: "These are not to be eaten at home" leads to the prognostication: "There will be good fortune." In line 1, the prognostication: "There is danger" leads to the counsel: "It is time to make a sacrifice."

In the original text of the *yaoci*, each line is introduced by its order in the sequence: "bottom," "second," "third," "fourth," "fifth," and "top," along with its numerological character: "nine" (*yang*, or solid line) or "six" (*yin*, or broken line).[3] In my translation, I have indicated "sixes" (that is, *yin* lines) by shading in black the first cell in the corresponding rows. Conversely, "nines" (that is, *yang* lines) are indicated by leaving the first cell of the corresponding rows unshaded, or white. Thus, counting from the bottom of the hexagram symbol in the top register of table 5, lines 4 and 5 are broken, which therefore correspond to the shaded or black cells in the first column of the appropriate lines in the bottom register of table 6.

Following each hexagram table is a line-by-line commentary, beginning with an explanation of the hexagram name. The purpose of the commentary is to provide detailed background for the situations presented in the texts, to interpret metaphorical language, and to explicate technical syntax. Occasionally, a context for the contemporary diviner is also provided, so that the archaic language may be appropriated for contemporary use. Finally, the Chinese text of the hexagram is appended at the end of each commentary.

---

3   For an explanation of the meaning of the numbers 6 and 9, see 3.1, Casting the *Yijing*.

1

Qian, The Vigorous

	OMEN	COUNSEL	FORTUNE
0		Your primary plea is heard. A good omen.	
1	Hiding dragon.	Do not use this omen.	
2	See the dragon rising in the fields.	It is time to see the great one.	
3	The nobleman is vigorous all day and wary by night.	Omen of danger.	No harm will come.
4	Now it springs up from the deep.		No harm will come.
5	The dragon flies in the skies.	It is time to see the great one.	
6	Setting dragon.		There will be problems.
7	See the gathered dragon without a head.		There will be good fortune.

1. Qian, The Vigorous

Qian's meaning is derived from the lower right hand element in the graph depicting the "twist" of a newly emerged sprout. The full character means, "to shoot upwards," and refers to the vigor of new spring growth.

Hexagram statement: *Heng* 亨, "Your plea is heard," records the establishment of a link between diviner and ancestral spirit through a sacrifice or the casting of yarrow stalks. *Yuan* 元, "primary," means this is the first of more than one question. *Li zhen* 利貞, "a good omen" indicates the outcome of action based on the reading will be advantageous.

Line 1: The "dragon" of this hexagram is a composite constellation called *qinglong* 青龍 (or *canglong* 蒼龍), the Azure Dragon, which stretches across the southern sky at the peak of summer. It is a contiguous group of seven separate smaller constellations, including the Horn and Neck (in Virgo), as well as the Heart and Tail (in Scorpio). During the Western Zhou dynasty, the Horn appeared on the eastern horizon at dusk in late winter, the Heart was directly overhead on the summer solstice, and the Tail disappeared beneath the western horizon in autumn. In line 1 the Dragon is submerged beneath the eastern horizon at dusk. The time is the winter solstice, when animals hibernate and farming families confine themselves to their homes to twist rope and spin yarn. It is time to "lay low," to "take stock." Conserve your energies during this time of decline, and do not expose yourself. "Do not use this omen" means to refrain from action.

Line 2: The Horn of the Dragon (the star Spica in Virgo) rises at dusk in late winter. This was considered the beginning of the year by the ancient Chinese. Now is when the farmers emerge to hunt. It is also the time when the feudal lords trained the farmers in the arts of war. *Li jian da ren* 利見大人, "It is time to see the great one," means to seek advice from a superior before initiating action.

Line 3: Like the Dragon whose rise in the east signals the growth of *yang* energy as the seasons progress, and like the sprouting seeds and budding trees of spring, the lord is vigorous in his actions as he "rises to the occasion." But his wisdom comes partly from his realization that an undertaking is most susceptible to failure just as it is initiated. He is alert and watches for signs of breakdown. The diviner who encounters the counsel, "omen of danger," will be extremely cautious. If he is vigilant, the prognostication is good.

Line 4: In mid-spring the Heart of the Dragon will be rising in the east. To the ancient Chinese who believed that oceans surrounded the habitable world, the Dragon would appear to be leaping from the depths. This leap is essentially a positive image. Thus the prognostication, "no harm will come."

Line 5: As one faces south—when the Heart is directly overhead at dusk, the Horn is approaching the western horizon, and the Tail is above the eastern horizon—this is the summer solstice. The entire dragon constellation now appears to be flying across the southern sky. It will begin its decline as autumn approaches. Harvest of the early crops is imminent. The farmer will once again see his lord to deliver the grain. "It is time to see the great one" means to report progress to a superior.

Line 6: The setting or "necked" dragon indicates the Neck constellation has encountered the western horizon as the Dragon slowly moves across the southern sky. Autumn has arrived; winter is just around the corner. The harvest has begun. Soon the farmers will return to their village homes and prepare for the cold of winter. The setting of the Neck is essentially the decapitation of the Dragon, which is not a good image. Thus the prognostication, "there will be problems."

Line 7: The "gathered dragon" refers to the macro-constellation of the Dragon. When the Dragon is "necked," it is headless. But, as the seasons progress, the Dragon completely disappears beneath the western horizon where it fights for supremacy with the Heavenly Turtle (Corona Australis). The prognostication of "good fortune" portends victory for the Dragon and the rebirth of the year. When all six lines change, creating Hexagram 2, *Kun*, this is the omen.

乾：　元亨，利貞。

初九：潛龍，勿用。

九二：見龍在田，利見大人。

九三：君子終日乾乾，夕惕若。厲，無咎。

九四：或躍在淵，無咎。

九五：飛龍在天，利見大人。

上九：亢龍，有悔。

用九：見群龍無首，吉。

坤 2 ䷁

Kun, The Compliant

	OMEN	COUNSEL	FORTUNE
0		Your primary plea is heard.	
		The omen is favorable for a mare.	
		On a journey if the nobleman leads he will lose the way; if he follows he will gain a ruler.	
		Now is the time to find friends in the southwest; you will lose them in the northeast.	
		Omen of peace.	There will be good fortune.
1	Frost is underfoot.	A hard freeze is coming.	
2	Inspect the outlying lands.	It will be great. It should not be repeated.	All signs are favorable.
3	The pattern holds.	Omen of approval. One who serves the king has no expectations.	There will be a good end.
4	Tie up the sacks.		No harm will come, nor will there be praise.
5	Yellow robes.		There will be great good fortune.
6	The dragon fights beyond the fields. Their blood is dark and yellow.		
7		An omen of favor in the long-term.	

2. Kun, The Compliant

The graph for this hexagram is unique to the *Yijing*, and does not occur in texts prior to the Spring and Autumn period (770-475 BCE). We must therefore rely on early commentaries to derive its meaning. According to the "Explaining the *Gua*" commentary, "the attribute of *kun* is compliance." The Mawangdui version of the *Yijing* records the 2nd hexagram with a different graph, *chuan* 川, which means "river" or "flow," perhaps in the sense of *shun* 順 "to go with the flow." Mesker relates *shun* to *xun* 巡, "make an inspection tour," which accords well with the theme of the hexagram.

Hexagram statement: The counsel announces that a link has been established with the spirits, and then pronounces the omen to be favorable for a mare, a symbol of fertility. The diviner who obtained this hexagram was assured his herds would multiply. It is the productivity of the mare, her ability to foal, that represents *Kun*. Similarly, it is the follower and not the leader who gains, according to the counsel. The Zhou homeland was to the west and south of the Central Plain of the Yellow River, whereas the Shang capital was to the north and east. This hexagram is an omen of peace and tranquility, rather than of agitation. Those who "go with the flow" will gain good fortune.

Line 1: As with the previous hexagram, these line texts also record various stages in a "calendar." Whereas Hexagram 1 is an astronomical clock that turns from spring to autumn, Hexagram 2 is a "works and days" that narrates the agricultural activities of fall and winter. Together both texts complete the year (Gao Wence; in Kunst, "Notes," 2.1.1). The omen of line 1 is the sudden appearance of frost, an image of autumn and a sure sign of the hard freeze of winter. This line has two implications: it is a sign of impending harvest, since the reaping of millet, the staple of the Zhou farmers, begins when the stalks die in the first hard freeze, allowing the grain to dry. Metaphorically, it refers to the taking of a wife, which must be done before the ice melts (Chow Tsetsung; in Kunst, "Notes," 2.1.1). This interpretation links this hexagram to the next, which discusses marriage customs in ancient China.

Line 2: The omen is the arrival in the borderlands of the royal crop inspector (Li Jingchi, "Jiaoshi"; in Kunst, "Notes," 2.2v). The counsel states that the crop will be abundant, and that the inquirer should not consult the oracle again. In the earliest stage of Chinese society it was common for professional diviners to ask a question up to three times.

Line 3: The omen of "the pattern holding" means that the color of the grain is consistent, a sign of its ripeness. With the crop ready for harvest, the farmer's prospects improve considerably. The omen of approval indicates the yield is acceptable. Still, although natural disaster has been avoided, in the feudal society of ancient China, the farmer was at the mercy of the estate lord for whom he toiled. So expectations were low. But in this case, the end was favorable. For those who encounter this line, if you do not "count your chickens before they are hatched," your flock should flourish.

Line 4: This omen is a picture of the finished harvest, bagged and ready for transport to the manor. Perhaps because the yield was just barely sufficient, the prognostication is neutral—no punishment and no praise. If you encounter this line, understand the outcome of your labors will be no cause for celebration, nor will you have reason to grieve.

Line 5: Yellow robes are the clothes of the nobility. This agricultural year culminated with a grand celebration in the lord's manor hall. Great sacrifices were offered to the ruler, and his health was toasted. When the farmers rub shoulders with their lords, the prognostication is one of great good fortune.

Line 6: This line describes what happens to the dragon constellation when it disappears in the west. The ancient Chinese were not aware of the rotation of the Earth, believing instead that the celestial dragon, a water creature, emerged from and returned to the watery abyss at the ends of the earth. Following the Dragon into the abyss, and separated from its Tail by the Heavenly River (the Milky Way), is the Heavenly Turtle (Corona Australis). Dragon and Turtle battle throughout the winter. The rising of the Horn in spring signals victory and the birth of a New Year.

Line 7: When all six lines change, this is the omen.

坤：元亨，利牝馬之貞。君子有攸往，先迷後得主。利西南
　　得朋，東北喪朋。安貞，吉。

初六：履霜，堅冰至。

六二：直方，大不習。無不利。

六三：含章，可貞。或從王事無成，有終。

六四：括囊，無咎無譽。

六五：黃裳，元吉。

上六：龍戰於野，其血玄黃。

用六：利永貞。

3

Tun, A Bunch

	OMEN	COUNSEL	FORTUNE
0		Your primary plea is heard. A good omen. Do not use this omen to go on a journey. Now is the time to establish fiefdoms.	
1	Back and forth.	Good omen for occupying a home. Now is the time to establish fiefdoms.	
2	Bunching and bucking, horse carts are rumbling.	"No thieves here, only a wedding pair." Omen for a girl: if you don't conceive now, in ten years you will.	
3	He draws near, but there is no gamekeeper. The doe enters the forest.	A nobleman at risk would rather give up the chase. To go on will bring cause for regret.	
4	Horse carts are rumbling.	If you seek a wedding match, going on a journey will bring good fortune.	All signs are favorable.
5	Tallow in bunches.	For the minor query, a good omen. For the major query, a bad omen.	
6	Horse carts are rumbling. Tears and blood are flowing.		

3. Tun, A Bunch

When pronounced *tun*, the name of this hexagram means "to accumulate," or "to tie together (in bunches)." Note line 5 where this meaning is especially evident. When pronounced *zhun*, the graph means "difficult" and pictures a sprout before it breaks through the soil.

Hexagram statement: Diviners in the early history of this text determined that travel conducted as a result of this hexagram usually ended in misfortune. So they recorded the counsel, "Do not use this omen to go on a journey." Similarly, when the king divined the proper time to enfeoff his nobles and this hexagram was obtained, the result was usually favorable. So the diviners recorded the counsel, "It is good to install feudal officers."

Line 1: The omens of this hexagram describe an ancient marriage custom where the groom's family, masquerading as bandits, "abduct" the bride from her home village. Here the bandits parade back and forth in front of the bride or perhaps around and around. Ancient diviners determined that those who obtained this hexagram would be fortunate in their choice of a new settlement. This would be the time to ask for a promotion, since the ancient Chinese used this line to award fiefdoms to their nobles.

Line 2: The omen text refers to an ancient marriage custom in which the bride is abducted by the groom in a mock raid conducted on the village of the future in-laws. The horse carts of the wedding party are in disarray as the "bandits" surround them. The counsel exposes the masquerade, identifying the abductor and abducted as the wedding pair. Furthermore, the bride is assured that conception may be delayed, but will nevertheless come in ten years.

Line 3: This omen describes a hunt in the king's forest in the absence of a royal gamekeeper, which is tantamount to poaching. Here it symbolizes the seduction of a maiden by a knave. Normally a man would seek the offices of a go-between to arrange a marriage between the two families. A gentleman would break off the chase when the doe enters the king's realm. That is, he would not approach a maiden without the proper introductions. A man who pursues the deer, or seduces the maiden, will regret it. If you obtain this line in divination, and you are pursuing an illegal or improper alliance, you are advised to cease and desist.

Line 4: The omen text refers to an ancient marriage custom in which the bride is abducted by the groom in a mock raid conducted on the village of the future in-laws. The horse carts of the wedding party are rumbling on the road to the bride's village. If you obtain this line in divination, and you are pursuing a union, the prognostication is excellent.

Line 5: Bunches of tallow are a gift to the family of the bride. Made from the fat of cattle, tallow was used in ancient China for candles. The counsel identifies this omen as good for a minor question, and bad for a major question. Since tallow was rare in peasant families, we know that this omen is for the nobility who would have considered tallow insignificant. The proper wedding gift would have been silk. If your question is of great import, this is a bad omen. Otherwise, the outcome will be good.

Line 6: The omen text refers to an ancient marriage custom in which the bride is abducted by the groom in a mock raid conducted on the village of the future in-laws. The horse carts of the wedding party are rumbling. However, unlike line 4 where the same image appears, in line 6 there is the added image of flowing tears and blood. So, this omen may indicate that the wedding will not take place.

屯： 元亨，利貞。勿用有攸往，利建侯。

初九：磐桓。利居貞，利建侯。

六二：屯如邅如，乘馬班如。匪寇婚媾。女子貞不字，十年乃字。

六三：即鹿無虞，惟入于林中。君子幾，不如舍，往吝。

六四：乘馬班如。求婚媾，往吉，無不利。

九五：屯其膏。小貞吉，大貞凶。

上六：乘馬班如，泣血漣如。

4

Meng, **Ignorance**

	OMEN	COUNSEL	FORTUNE
0	"I do not beg of you, ignorant youth; it is you who beg of me. For the first cast of stalks I shall tell your fortune; if you continue by casting a second and third time, I will not tell."	Your plea is heard. A good omen.	
1	Letting go of ignorance.	Now is the time to use the punished. Remove the manacles and shackles so they can walk.	There will be regret.
2	Wrapping up ignorance.	Bring in a wife. Now the son will sustain the family.	Good fortune. Good fortune.
3	Seeing a bronze man without a body.	Do not use this omen to take a wife.	No signs are favorable.
4	Suffering ignorance.		There will be regret.
5	Youthful ignorance.		There will be good fortune.
6	Attacking ignorance.	It is not the time to be a bandit. It is time to ward them off.	

4. Meng, Ignorance

The graph of *meng* 蒙 means "to cover," and by extension, "to be in the dark" (that is, ignorant or blind). A phonetically similar word, *meng* 萌, means "sprout." By Confucian times, the latter was glossed for the former as if "sprout" (like the English word, "greenhorn") meant an ignorant youth. However, there are no early Zhou texts where *meng* has the meaning of "youth."

Hexagram statement: This quotation records a fortune-telling episode between a professional diviner and an inexperienced inquirer—*tong meng* 童蒙. In the earliest history of Chinese divination it was common for professional diviners to ask a question up to three times. If the prognostication repeated itself, it was considered more reliable (see for example line 2.2b). In this situation, however, the diviner is insulted by the arrogance or disrespect of the immature inquirer ("It is not I who beg of you"). "A good omen" indicates the outcome of action based on this reading will bring advantage.

Line 1: The omen depicts someone casting off his or her blinders. Ancient diviners who obtained this omen determined that it was now appropriate to unshackle the prisoners. That there is regret is because the prisoners may now more easily escape. If you obtain this line when divining, then you are advised to cherish your newly found knowledge.

Line 2: The omen depicts someone bundling up their ignorance, that is, containing it, and keeping it "under wraps." For that reason, the prognostication is good fortune. The counsels are reminiscent of Hexagram 3, *Tun*, A Bunch. The line texts of that hexagram dealt with the ancient marriage custom of "abducting" the bride from her home village. Whereas Hexagram 3 depicts the bride's point of view, here the omens describe the groom's situation. We see the unmarried son bringing home his new wife to sustain the greater family by providing descendants.

Line 3: The counsel advises you to refrain from taking a wife. It would be inadvisable to form any long-term union. The omen depicts what may be a bronze mask, probably of a warrior, but possibly of a spirit or shaman, which may explain why the prognostication is inauspicious.

Line 4: This omen shows someone whose inexperience is cause for suffering. If the distress overwhelms the individual, there will be cause for regret.

Line 5: This omen identifies the ignorance as that of youth. Young people who have yet to gain the experience of their elders may be excused for their lack of wisdom. The prognostication is good fortune.

Line 6: This omen shows someone attempting to counter his ignorance. The counsel of this line text refers again to the marriage "raid" of Hexagram 3.

The time is not right to conduct the marriage raid, because the prospective bride will be defending herself from such abduction.

蒙：亨。匪我求童蒙，童蒙求我，初筮告，再三瀆，瀆則不告。利貞。

初六：發蒙。利用 刑人，用說桎梏以往。吝。

九二：包蒙，吉。納婦，吉。子克家。

六三：勿用取女。見金夫，不有躬。無攸利。

六四：困蒙，吝。

六五：童蒙，吉。

上九：擊蒙。不利為寇，利禦寇。

5

Xu, A Drenching

	OMEN	COUNSEL	FORTUNE
0		That captives are taken is honorable. Your plea is heard. Omen of good fortune. Now is the time to ford the great river.	
1	Getting drenched in the suburbs.	By this omen it is time to persist.	No harm will come.
2	Getting drenched in sand.	There will be talk.	There will be good fortune in the end.
3	Getting drenched in mud.	This makes raiders come.	
4	Getting drenched in blood.	Get out of your lair.	
5	Getting drenched in wine and food.	Omen of good fortune.	
6		Enter your lair. Three guests arrive uninvited. Welcome them.	In the end good fortune.

5. Xu, A Drenching

The upper element of *Xu* 需 means "rain" (see also Hexagram 51). The graph originally meant, "to stop for the rain," and by extension, "to wait." However, the character *ru* 濡, "to wet, to immerse," is composed of *xu* with the addition of the "water" element, and in early texts the former character is sometimes borrowed for the latter. The context of this hexagram requires *xu* to be translated as "drenched, wet" (Li Jingchi 李鏡池, "*Zhouyi* shici kao"《周易》釋辭考; in Kunst, "Notes," 5.1).

Hexagram statement: Border raids were common in the ancient homeland of the Zhou people. The captives were enslaved and often used as sacrificial victims in the important rituals of the state. The counsel of this hexagram informs the diviner of the honor of such capture. That the honor is one of blood is likely, considering the subject of the hexagram. One context of "getting wet" is the sacrificial alter drenched in blood. "Omen of good fortune" indicates that the outcome of action based on the reading will bring good fortune. Regarding the last counsel, the act of crossing great bodies of water in ancient China was not to be taken lightly since boats were primitive. Diviners in the early history of this text determined that river crossings conducted as a result of this hexagram usually succeeded. So they recorded the counsel, "Now is the time to ford the great river."

Line 1: The omen shows a man getting caught in a storm outside the capital. If he had been more determined, perhaps he would have returned home in time. So the counsel advises you to be persistent.

Line 2: The omen shows a man getting wet on a sandbar while crossing a river. A sandbar may appear solid, but it can conceal quicksand. The counsel warns of gossip, which is sometimes harmless but at other times quite damaging. As long as one is aware of the danger, good fortune will prevail.

Line 3: This omen shows a man whose carriage is bogged down in mud. The counsel warns that bandits will take advantage of his distress to rob him. The person who encounters this line should realize his current situation is mired in difficulty. Others may take advantage of him.

Line 4: This omen shows someone wounded and bleeding profusely. The counsel warns the diviner to get out of his house to avoid injury. The ancestors of the Zhou people are said to have lived in kiln-like caves, where cave-ins must have been a threat. The person who obtains this line should realize that drastic measures must be taken to avoid a dire situation.

Line 5: This omen shows a celebration where someone is showered with feasts and libations. The counsel identifies it as an omen of good fortune.

Line 6: The situation of line 4 has returned to normal. The counsel advises you to re-enter your house. Once inside, three uninvited people will arrive, whom you should welcome as guests. If you do so, good fortune will prevail.

需：有孚，光。亨，貞吉，利涉大川。初九：需于郊，利用恒，無咎。

九二：需于沙，小有言，終吉。

九三：需於泥，致寇至。
六四：需於血，出自穴。
九五：需于酒食，貞吉。
上六：入於穴，有不速之客三人來，敬之，終吉。

Song, Litigation

	OMEN	COUNSEL	FORTUNE
0	There are prisoners, frozen with fear.	It is time to see the great one. It is not good to ford the great river.	There is good fortune now, but in the end there will be misfortune.
1	He did not prolong his service.	There will be talk.	In the end there will be good fortune.
2	He could not win the lawsuit. When he returned, in his township three hundred households had absconded.		Calamity is avoided.
3	He lived off old bounty.	Omen of danger. "One who serves the king has no expectations."	Good fortune will prevail.
4	He could not win the lawsuit. He returned to comply with the command.	There will be a change. Omen of peace.	There will be good fortune.
5	He won the lawsuit.		There will be great good fortune.
6	A leather belt of honor was conferred, but he was stripped of it three times in one morning.		

6. Song, Litigation

The graph of *song* 訟 is composed of the element "to speak" on the left, and the phonetic element, *gong*, which means, "duke." In feudal China, disputes among the nobility outside the jurisdiction of the clan could be heard by the county magistrate whose court was located in the walled capital city of the marquisate. The decision of this magistrate could be appealed to the duke's grand administrator, whose court was located in the provincial capital. This court's charge could only be appealed to the king. If one of the disputing parties held rank above the level of marquis, the case would be argued in the duke's court.

Hexagram statement: The omen shows prisoners so afraid they are comatose. Since the prognostication is for good fortune in the midst of litigation, but trouble in the end, the implication is to stop while you are ahead. The counsel advises you to see an important person (who would be the duke in the case of the nobleman's lawsuit). On the other hand, it would be dangerous to cross a river at this time, or perform any major maneuver.

Line 1:   The omen describes a nobleman who terminated his service to the king. The counsel indicates that there will be slander by his enemies ("belittling words"). But the prognostication is excellent. After suffering a period of difficulty, the nobleman will have good fortune.

Line 2:   The omen is quite specific. The nobleman who brought suit before the grand administrator was not successful. When he returned home from the capital, three hundred of his tenant households had absconded. In feudal China farmers were bound to the estate of their lord. The reality of their flight is evidence of the significance of his legal defeat. Contrary to the evidence of his loss, the prognostication is also quite specific: "Calamity is avoided." There is no counsel to advise the diviner how to proceed in order to avoid calamity, but the subsequent lines may be informative.

Line 3:   Lines 1 and 2 describe a nobleman who has quit the service of the king, has lost his lawsuit, and returns home to an abandoned estate. This omen continues to describe him. He has no choice but to live off of bounty gained in the past. The word that means "bounty" (*de* 德), is usually translated as "virtue," which is its fundamental sense. However, in Zhou dynasty texts the character is sometimes semantically equivalent to another character with the same pronunciation (*de* 得), meaning "to get" (Nivison; Li Jingchi, "Zai jieshi 再解釋"; in Kunst, "Notes," 6.3). That is the case here and with other instances of the word in the *Zhouyi*. The primary counsel warns of the danger of such a state of affairs. Still, the prognostication is excellent. When a person's bounty is not ill gained, he will prevail even when the situation is precarious. The final counsel reminds the diviner that the nobleman was wise to terminate his service, because "One who serves the king has no expectations."

Line 4:   Lines 1, 2 and 3 describe a nobleman who quit the service of the king, lost a lawsuit, returned home to an abandoned estate, and lived off his reputation. This omen continues to describe him. He was unable to win his initial lawsuit, so he returned to the capital to comply with the command.

Hoewever, the counsel advises that the situation will change (perhaps for the worse). On a good note, the omen predicts stability, and the prognosis is for good fortune.

Line 5: In the previous line the nobleman returned to the capital to answer the charge. Here we learn he won the lawsuit. His reputation remains intact, and his actions are vindicated. The prognostication could not be better: great good fortune.

Line 6: The omen informs us that the nobleman was awarded a leather belt, probably in honor of his successful lawsuit. But the feudal courts were full of slanderers, so he was stripped of it. Two more times he was awarded the belt, but it was withdrawn both times, all in the space of one morning. There is no counsel, nor prognostication. The omen text is sufficient to warn you to tread lightly in a den of vipers.

訟：　有孚，窒惕。中吉，終凶。利見大人，不利涉大川。
初六：不永所事，小有言，終吉。
九二：不克訟，歸而逋，其邑人三百戶。無眚。
六三：食舊德。貞厲，終吉。或從王事無成。
九四：不克訟，復即命。渝，安貞。吉。
九五：訟，元吉。
上九：或錫之鞶帶，終朝三褫之。

7

Shi, Army Troops

	OMEN	COUNSEL	FORTUNE
0		Omen of good fortune for an older man.	No harm will come.
1	The army troops march off in tune.	It will not be good.	There will be misfortune.
2	That he is in the army is fortunate. Thrice the king bestowed his commands.		No harm will come.
3	Someone in the army carts a corpse.		There will be misfortune.
4	The army camps to the left.		No harm will come.
5	They bag game in the hunt. The elder brother leads the troops; the younger carts the corpse.	Now is the time to question captives. Omen of misfortune.	No harm will come.
6	The great lord has the mandate. He founds states and sires clans.	This omen is of no use to the lowborn.	

7. Shi, Army Troops

A *shi* 師, or "army," was the largest unit of the military, which consisted of three brigades of 100 troops each (left, right, and central) for a total of 300 soldiers.

Hexagram statement: Here the older man refers to King Wu (whereas in Hexagram 17, the old man refers to King Wen, while the son refers to Wu). That the omen is auspicious means his campaign against Shang will succeed. No harm will come to the inquirer in this particular situation.

Line 1: The omen of this line shows the army of King Wu departing to do battle against the Shang realm. The phrase "in tune" paraphrases the Chinese expression *lü* 律 "pitch pipes," whose extended meaning is "in order" (Li Jingchi, "*Zhouyi* jiaoshi" 《周易》校釋; Kunst, "Notes," 7.1). These were panpipes of 12 standard lengths that were used by diviners to determine the outcome of battles (see Raphals, p. 91). According to the *Records of the Grand Historian*, when King Wu attacked Zhou Xin he personally blew the pipes and divined that his army would be harmonious (ch. 25). The *Records* does not tell us which attack this was, for King Wu supposedly twice led his troops east to conquer the Shang. On the first attempt his father, the posthumous King Wen, had just died and, instead of waiting the proper three years of mourning, the son carried his father off into battle, the account of which forms the omen of lines 3 and 5. This is probably why the counsel says that no good will come of this, and the prognostication is that misfortune will fall.

Line 2: The omen shows a military officer who is trusted by the king— probably Lü Shang, the Grand Duke. Three times the king sends his charges down to his commander, whose service brings good fortune. No harm will come if you have your superior's trust.

Line 3: The omen shows someone in the army carrying a corpse. It is probably King Wu carrying his father's body into battle (Wen Yiduo 聞一多, "Putang" 璞堂; Kunst, "Notes," 7.3). According to tradition, King Wen died waiting for the proper time to begin his campaign against Shang. His son, King Wu, by custom was required to mourn his father for three years. Instead, he carried his father's body into battle. Thus the omen portends misfortune. See line 1.

Line 4: This omen shows the troops camping on the left bank of the river, which is still within the realm (see line 13.0). After the river is crossed, the army is in enemy territory. Until then, hostilities are nil and no harm is forecast.

Line 5: The great hunt of winter was the training ground for military tactics. Here the farmers conscripted as infantry were taught how to coordinate with the gentry who commanded them from chariots. This omen shows a successful hunt, which foretells the capture of enemy troops. The counsel advises that the captives (the "seized") be interrogated, so that the adversary's intentions can be known. This is a good portent, foretelling that troops will be saved from harm. The second omen in this line depicts an elder and younger brother in battle. The older, King Wu, commands the troops, while the younger, the Lord of Kang, performs the task of transporting his father's corpse (Kunst, "Notes," 7.5v). King Wu, by custom, was required to mourn his father for three years; instead, he and his brother carried their father's body into battle. Thus the counsel is one of misfortune.

Line 6: The campaign to overthrow Zhou Xin was successful. King Wu (through his father, King Wen) received the Mandate of Heaven and founded the Zhou dynasty. The king then granted fiefdoms to his commanders where they established feudal houses. The army was composed of an officer corps chosen from the nobility and infantry conscripted from the rural populations. As in any feudal society, the commoners of ancient China were unsophisticated and untrained in the customs of polite society. From the perspective of the aristocrats these are the small-minded, or petty people, those who do not have the capacity to lead. They would never be granted titles and would have no use for such an omen.

師：　貞丈人吉，無咎。

初六：師出以律，否臧。凶。

九二：在師中吉，無咎。王三錫命。

六三：師或輿屍，凶。

六四：師左次，無咎。

六五：田有禽，利執言，無咎。長子帥師，弟子輿屍，貞凶。

上六：大君有命，開國承家，小人勿用。

8

Bi, Alliance

	OMEN	COUNSEL	FORTUNE
0	Hostile countries arrived. The latecomer met with misfortune.	The original cast of the stalks was superlative. The long-range prognostication is that no harm will come.	Good fortune.
1	He sides with those who have captives.		No harm will come.
	They fill the urns with captured goods.	In the end an unexpected threat will come.	There will be good fortune.
2	He sides with an insider.	Omen of good fortune.	
3	He sides with the non-human.		
4	He sides with an outsider.	Omen of good fortune.	
5	Illustrious alliance.	With this omen the king mounted a three-pronged chase, but lost the quarry ahead of him. The townspeople are not frightened.	There will be good fortune.
6	He forms an alliance without a leader.		There will be misfortune.

8. Bi, Alliance

The most primitive graph of *bi* 比 depicts two people standing "side-by-side," while later versions showed one person "following" another. From these literal meanings came the extended ideas, "to associate with," or "partisan." From the context of the hexagram I translate *bi* as a political or military "alliance." All hexagram lines cite types of alliance, while the hexagram statement recounts a legend of one of China's earliest dynastic alliances. Since line 5 mentions a king, the alliances mentioned in the line texts probably relate to early Zhou history.

Hexagram statement: The general prognostication is good fortune. However, the counsel for this hexagram is a record of two divinations. On the first casting of the milfoil stalks, the prognosis was excellent. On the second divination, the long-range prognostication was no misfortune. The omen statement recounts the story of Yu, the Great, founder of the Xia dynasty, who is most famous for his flood control of the Yellow River. After thirteen years of labor, when the floods were finally quelled, Yu assembled the chiefs of his tribal alliances to extract tribute. However, one recalcitrant leader was late to arrive, so Yu executed him (Gao Heng; in Kunst, "Notes," 8.0).

Line 1: The first omen shows Zhou forming an alliance with a tribe or state that has captured numbers of the enemy. According to the prognostication, the alliance will have no harmful effects. The second omen shows the tribe's coffers filled with the spoils of warfare. The counsel warns you to prepare for unanticipated trouble, literally "a snake appearing" 來有它. If you take the advice, there will be good fortune.

Line 2: This omen shows Zhou—perhaps Chang, the Western Earl, himself—allying with a state within the Shang federation. This probably indicates one of the Eastern Yi tribes who, although allied with Shang, began to rebel as the Zhou rose in the west. As an indication that the seeds of rebellion have been sown against the ruthless Shang king, this is an omen of good fortune.

Line 3: Here we see Zhou allying with non-Chinese tribes, perhaps the land known as Guifang. This particular country harassed the Shang for much of their history. As a vassal of Shang King Wen Ding, Ji Li, father of King Wen, led several military campaigns against the Guifang. The inhabitants of Guifang, or Ghost-land, that is, the "ghost" people, could very aptly be called "non-human," or perhaps "inhuman."

Line 4: This omen shows Zhou allying with a state outside the Shang federation. Any number of states qualifies here—perhaps what is meant are the Yu and Rui in southwest Shanxi (near Bin, where Danfu began his migration). As an indication that border states recognize the superiority of the Zhou against the Shang, this is an omen of good fortune.

Line 5: An illustrious alliance is one whose impact was widespread. The ally here was possibly Shaofang 召方, a strategic region west of the Shang domain and south of the original Zhou homeland. It is said that the alliance with Shao consolidated the western front of Shang and guaranteed the success of the push eastward. The king in this line is probably Chang, Western Earl. Here he organizes a great hunt to rally his subjects. His brush-beaters drive forward from three directions, but he loses the wild game ahead. The people are not worried about their king's disappointment. The prognostication for Zhou victory is excellent.

Line 6: Here we see Fa, eldest son of Chang, forming alliances after his father has died. Fearing that his new allies will perceive his father's death as a sign of Heavenly displeasure, he does not disclose the loss. Although the rebellion is eventually successful, and Fa (King Wu) founds the Zhou dynasty, the death of Chang (King Wen) is a major blow in the early campaign. Thus, the prognostication is bad.

比： 吉。原筮元，永貞無咎。不寧方來，後夫凶。

初六：有孚比之，無咎。有孚盈缶，終來有它，吉。

六二：比之自內，貞吉。

六三：比之匪人。

六四：外比之，貞吉。

九五：顯比。王用三驅，失前禽，邑人不誡。吉。

上六：比之無首，凶。

Xiao Chu, Lesser Stock

		OMEN	COUNSEL	FORTUNE
0		Dark clouds but no rain from our western environs.	Your plea is heard.	
1		Returning by the road.		What is the harm in that? There will be good fortune.
2		Returning on a leash.		There will be good fortune.
3		The wagon loses a wheel.	Husband and wife will avert eyes.	
4		There is capture, a bloody gelding, and cautious exit.		No harm will come.
5		There is capture on a tether.	You will prosper on account of your neighbor.	
6		It rains, and it clears.	You will still get your wagon-full. For a married woman, omen of danger.	
		The moon is almost full when the lords attack.		There will be misfortune.

9. Xiao Chu, Lesser Stock

The graph of *xiao* 小 is three "bits," which indicates smallness. *Chu* 畜 is the dark earth (on top) of a cultivated field (beneath). It means to raise crops or animals. Here the two words mean "smaller livestock." Sheep or goats, dogs, and fowls are the smallest of the six domestic animals. As the topic of the hexagram, the smaller barnyard animal represents the ease of domestication when compared to the difficulty of taming larger livestock such as horses (see hexagram 26).

Hexagram statement: The vassal state of Zhou was located in the west of the Shang kingdom. The storm brewing in the west represents the rebellion that originated there, eventually leading to the downfall of Shang. That the rain has yet to fall means that the revolt is still in its infancy.

Line 1: The small animal depicted in the line texts is probably the goat, an important commodity in a society that was separated from its nomadic roots by only a few generations. In this line lost animals return by the road on their own accord. The prognostication questions whether such a return is auspicious. Were these not domesticated goats, it would indeed be suspicious. Mountain goats would never have come back without being herded. Regardless, the fact of their return is cause for good fortune.

Line 2: Here we see the goats returning on a leash, indicating they are being returned by someone. This is cause for good fortune.

Line 3: The omen depicts a wagon wheel that has lost its spokes. The counsel predicts a domestic squabble: husband and wife will avoid looking at each other. The wagon's loss parallels the rift in the marriage. You are advised to prepare for breakdowns on the road and also in your personal life.

Line 4: Here we see goats being captured. Since kids must be castrated within three weeks of birth or the meat will be tainted, this is done. Then, the captors steal away with their livestock. The prognostication is that no harm will come. Presumably, the goats were being "stolen" by their original owners.

Line 5: This omen shows tethered goats being captured from a neighbor. The counsel may also indicate that the Zhou victory over Shang was partly due to the assistance of neighboring tribes or states.

Line 6: In this line we see that the dark clouds in the west have finally produced rain, after which the skies have cleared. The rebellion in the state of Zhou is gathering momentum, while the Shang court is still unconcerned. The counsel then returns to the image of the previous lines. The husband and wife will get their wagon-full of goats. You will finally get what belongs to you. The omen of rain means more battles. This is not good news for the wife since her husband may go to war. Sure enough, the lords attack when the moon is full. This is cause for misfortune.

小畜：亨。密雲不雨，自我西郊。

初九：復自道，何其咎？吉。

九二：牽復，吉。

九三：輿說輻，夫妻反目。

六四：有孚血去惕出，無咎。

九五：有孚攣如，富以其鄰。

上九：既雨既處，尚德載，婦貞厲。月幾望君子征，凶。

10

Lü, Walking

	OMEN	COUNSEL	FORTUNE
0	He walks on the tail of a tiger and doesn't get eaten.	Your plea is heard.	
1	He walks in plain silk shoes.	On a journey no harm will come.	
2	He walks the level road.	Omen of good fortune for a man in the dark.	
3	The weak-eyed can see, and the lame can walk. He walks on the tail of a tiger and gets eaten. All warriors act on behalf of our great lord.		There will be misfortune.
4	He walks on the tail of a tiger and is terror-stricken.		In the end there will be good fortune.
5	He walks in ruined shoes.	Omen of danger.	
6	He watches the walk, checks for good omens.		Great good fortune on your return.

10. Lü, Walking

The graph of *lü* 履 has the "body" radical (top and left) standing over a phonetic element, and means, "to step" or "to walk." By extension the word means, "what is under the feet," that is, shoes, although this is primarily a late Zhou usage (Duan Yucai 段玉裁; in Kunst, "Notes," 10.1).

Hexagram statement: The omen shows someone performing a very dangerous act without getting hurt. The tiger is the most ferocious beast in China, and thus represents the warrior. Upon the threshold of battle in the Wilds of Mu, with his three hundred chariots and three thousand "tiger warriors," King Wu addressed his troops, saying: "Display a martial bearing. Be like tigers and panthers!" 尚桓桓如虎如貔 (*Shangshu* 尚書, "Zhoushu" 周書, ch. 4, "Mushi" 牧誓, p. 17; Legge, *Chinese Classics, vol.* 3, p. 304). Stepping on the tail of the tiger symbolizes directly threatening the ruler.

Line 1: The humble farmers in general wore no shoes at all or wore woven grass sandals. The merchants and the gentry, those whose business required frequent travel, wore shoes made of hempen cloth (for the merchants) or leather (for the gentry). The royalty wore shoes fashioned of silk or brocade. The omen of unadorned silk shoes evokes the image of Chang, Earl of the West, who was very modest. The counsel says that such a man will meet with no harm.

Line 2: The word translated as "road" is *dao* 道. In this period of Chinese history the word had not yet evolved its abstract meaning of "the Way." Here the path being walked is level and open, as opposed to a crooked path vulnerable to ambush. The level road does not mean "the True Path," but something like "in plain sight." The counsel says this open road is favorable to the man in the dark. Such a man is either in hiding, or in a dungeon (Gao Heng, *Gujing jinzhu*; in Kunst, "Notes," 10.2). If hidden, you are advised to come out in the open. If you are in peril, the omen predicts that you will be safe. It might represent the Earl of the West who was imprisoned by the Shang king on suspicion of sedition. Upon his release, Chang did indeed begin the rebellion that would eventually result in the founding of a new dynasty.

Line 3: The omen that the weak-eyed can see and the lame can walk refers to the reversal of fortunes for the Zhou people when Chang—the man in the dark—was released from prison and began his rebellion against the Shang. The second and third omens in line 3 make explicit the images of tigers and warriors. Here, we see the consequences of waking the sleeping tiger—it will bite. And, unlike the army of Shang king Zhou Xin, which abandoned their lord, the tiger warriors of King Wu are united in the service to their lord. The inquirer who encounters this line will meet with misfortune if the warning is not heeded.

Line 4: This omen shows a person who is terrified of treading on the tiger's tail, but still proceeds, thinking his actions are justified. The prognostication for such an individual is eventual success.

Line 5: The omen shows someone walking in worn-out shoes. The counsel identifies it as an omen of danger, possibly because worn shoes will slow down the traveler.

Line 6: The final omen of the hexagram shows a person stepping wisely, and cautiously, looking for auspicious signs. The prognostication is excellent. King Wen saw the Mandate revealed in the heavens when the five planets gathered in the Beak of the Vermilion Bird. Yet, the battle to conquer Shang King Zhou Xin was not fought for thirteen long years, when Jupiter finally returned to the Beak. By then, King Wen had already died, leaving his son, King Wu, to return victorious to the Zhou capital.

履虎尾不咥人，亨。

初九：素履，往無咎。

九二：履道坦坦，幽人貞吉。

六三：眇能視，跛能履。履虎尾咥人，凶。武人為于大君。

九四：履虎尾愬愬，終吉。

九五：夬履，貞厲。

上九：視履考祥，其旋元吉。

11

Tai, Grandeur

	OMEN	COUNSEL	FORTUNE
0	The small departs and the great arrives.	Your plea is heard.	There will be good fortune.
1	Pull up the thatch grass and with it come the roots.		An attack will bring good fortune.
2	A bundle is discarded.	With this omen you may cross the river. It will not be left far behind nor be forgotten.	A boon will come en route.
3	"There is no plain that does not rise; there is no trip without return."	Omen of difficulty. Do not worry.	There will be no harm. There will be fortune in his capture at dinner.
4	He flutters about.	You will not prosper on account of your neighbor. You will be captured on account of negligence.	
5	King Di Yi joyfully gave his daughter in marriage.		There will be great good fortune.
6	The wall fell into the moat. From the city came the orders.	Do not use this omen to field troops. Omen of regret.	

11. Tai, Grandeur

The earliest function of the word *tai* was to name the great Mount Tai in Shandong province. In the *Book of Odes*, it appears in a sacrificial ode of the state of Lu, where the Duke of Zhou spent his final years. Its graphic form has "hands" holding "water" beneath the image of "greatness" (meaning "spreading everywhere") and is commonly understood to be the complex form of *da* 大, the standard word for "great" (see Hexagrams 14, 26, and 34).

Hexagram statement: The name of the hexagram is "Grand," or "Grandeur," and this omen shows the small departing as the great arrives. The content of the line texts implies that the grand state of Zhou has arrived to take the mandate of rule away from the wicked Shang. The prognostication for this change of mandate is good fortune.

Line 1: The omen depicts someone pulling up a handful of *mao* 茅, or cogon grass. This plant was commonly used to thatch houses in China, but, more importantly, was a common wrapping for sacrifices. In medieval China cogon grass was also used in divination similar to yarrow stalks (Rong Zhaozu 容肇祖; in Kunst, "Notes," 11.1av). In this omen, the *ru* 茹 "interlaced roots," come along with the plant when it is pulled, which is considered to be a good omen (see also 12.1).

Line 2: Here we see a discarded (or perhaps "rejected") *bao* 包, or bundle. With the cogon grass of the previous line, and considering the omen text of the next hexagram (12.2), "bundled offering" and "bundle and proffer," this bundle is most likely a sacrifice, especially since the counsel text recommends crossing the river. However, although the sacrifice is discarded, it is not far behind and will not be forgotten (reading 弗忘 for 朋亡, according to the Mawangdui ms.). The prognostication indicates that in the midst of such a journey a reward will come.

Line 3: This omen speaks of the inevitability of cyclical change. What goes up must come down. The prediction is that even when the situation appears thorny, the outcome will not be disastrous. The inquirer here is concerned about the capture of his leader. This may be Chang, Earl of the West, who was imprisoned by Zhou Xin when he traveled to the Shang capital to present tribute. The counsel advises he will be well cared for.

Line 4: The omen depicts an elegant court dandy, the silk sleeves and sashes of his brocade gown fluttering as he moves about. An image of the corrupt court of the Shang grandees, this omen does not bode well. The counsel says that such people will not profit at the expense of a neighbor. In truth, they will lose their freedom because of their own carelessness.

Line 5: Di Yi, second to the last ruler of the Shang dynasty, married his daughter to Chang, Earl of the West. Yi realized that Chang's popularity and power were increasing. He wanted to consolidate that power by joining the two clans in marriage. The prognostication could not be better. See Hexagram 54 The Young Bride for a more detailed account of Di Yi's daughter.

Line 6: The image of the city wall collapsing into the moat is unlucky for most situations, especially military maneuvers. The counsel warns the inquirer to refrain from using the omen to dispatch an army. Instead, orders come from the city to recall troops needed to defend the city.

泰：　小往大來，吉。亨。

初九：拔茅，茹以其彙。征吉。

九二：包荒，用馮河，不遐遺朋亡。得尚於中行。

九三：無平不陂，無往不復。艱貞，無咎。勿恤，其孚於食有福。

六四：翩翩。不富以其鄰，不戒以孚。

六五：帝乙歸妹以祉，元吉。

上六：城復於隍，勿用師。自邑告命，貞吝。

12

Pi, **Wrongdoing**

	OMEN	COUNSEL	FORTUNE
0	Wrong are the non-human.	Not a good omen for the nobleman. The great departs and the small arrives.	
1	Pull up the thatch grass and with it come the roots.	Omen of good fortune. Your plea is heard.	
2	Bundle the offering. Your plea is heard.		For the lowborn there will be good fortune. For the great one it is wrong.
3	Bundle and proffer it.		
4	We have a mandate. A pair of lia-birds.		No harm will come. Blessings are bestowed.
5	He ceases wrongdoing. No more! No more! Tie it to a bundled mulberry.		There will be good fortune for the great one.
6	Overthrow the wrong-doer.		First there is wrongdoing. Later there is joy.

12. Pi, Wrongdoing

The graph consists of the negative adverb *bu* 不 above a "mouth" 口. When pronounced *fou*, it simply means "not." When pronounced *pi*, however, it means "bad" or "wrong."

Hexagram statement: In a previous hexagram (see line 8.3) the "non-human" are the nomadic non-Chinese known as the Ghost people. Here it probably refers to the Shang king, Zhou Xin, who is known for his cruelty to his subjects. For this reason, *pi* might be more appropriately translated "wicked," as in "Wicked is the inhuman Zhou Xin." This is not a good omen for upright noblemen such as Bi Gan 比干, who reprimanded their monarch and paid for it with their lives. Whereas the previous hexagram shows the great Zhou state conquering the wicked Zhou Xin, this hexagram marks the eclipse of the good by the bad. The diviner should take proper measures to counteract this trend.

Line 1: The omen depicts someone pulling up a handful of cogon grass (used to thatch houses in Asia). If the roots come along with the grass, that is a good omen (see also 11.1).

Line 2: This omen depicts a common form of sacrificial offering: steamed food wrapped in leaves. While appropriate for the common man, it would be inappropriate for the nobility, especially someone as great as a ruler whose offerings were presented to his ancestors in bronze caldrons. If the diviner must make a present of something, he must be sure that his package is appropriate to its recipient.

Line 3: This omen depicts a *bao* or bundle being presented as a sacrifice. Those familiar with the Dragon Boat Festival will recognize the *zongzi* 粽子— a glutinous rice ball wrapped in bamboo leaves and steamed. These delicacies were originally sacrificial offerings to the river god.

Line 4: The mandate is Heaven's command to rule, which the Zhou nation received upon their defeat of the Shang. As an omen, it represents the triumph of righteousness over wrongdoing. The second omen shows the auspicious appearance of a pair of lia-birds (see Hexagram 30). In Chinese mythology, the appearance of the *fenghuang* 鳳凰, or phoenix, is said to foretell the ascent to the throne of a new emperor. The failure of the bird to appear in the time of Confucius was cause for his lament, according to the *Analects* (9.9).

Line 5: The wrongdoing of this line is that of the last Shang king. The prognostication shows good fortune for the great one, in this case, the Zhou leader, King Wu. The exclamation "No more!" must have been screamed from the rooftops after Shang king Shou was confirmed dead. The mulberry tree, aside from furnishing leaves for the silk worm, was considered sacred in ancient myth. A bundled mulberry may have been a sacrifice like the bundles of lines 2 and 3. In this case, something is tied to the bundle, presumably, before it is burned. On the other hand, "bundled mulberry" might also be translated as "bushy mulberry," and attaching something bad to a tree may also represent a "tying ritual" such as the scapegoating ceremony of Hexagram 25 (Kunst, "Notes," 12.5).

Line 6: Here the omen clarifies the actions of the preceding two lines. The wrongdoer (the Shang king) is overthrown. After his transgressions cease, there was rejoicing. If you encounter this line, be assured that the guilty will be punished and the innocent will rejoice.

否之匪人，不利君子貞。大往小來。

初六：拔茅，茹以其彙，貞吉。亨。

六二：包承，小人吉，大人否。亨。

六三：包羞。

九四：有命，無咎。疇離，祉。

九五：休否，大人吉。其亡其亡，系于苞桑。

上九：傾否。先否，後喜。

13

Tong Ren, Assembled Men

	OMEN	COUNSEL	FORTUNE
0	Assemble men in the backcountry.	Your plea is heard. Now is the time to ford the great river. A good omen for the nobleman.	
1	Assemble men at the gate.		No harm will come.
2	Assemble men at Zong.		There will be regret.
3	Rong troops hide in the thicket.	If you climb that lofty range, there will be no uprising for three years.	
4	Mount the walls, and they cannot be taken.		There will be good fortune.
5	The assembled men first howl and yowl, and then they laugh.		The great armies will be able to rally.
6	Assemble men in the suburbs.		There will be no problems.

13. Tong Ren, Assembled Men

The character *tong* 同 shows an opening in a tube fitted with a cover, which implies "to fit together," or "to assemble." By extension, it means "to agree," or "to accord." *Ren* is the pictograph for "person." The phrase *tong ren* means literally "assemble the people," or, by extension, "people in agreement," or "comrades."

Hexagram statement: The "backcountry," or *ye* 野, is uncultivated land lying outside the civilized territory of a state (often translated as "wilderness"). If men are being assembled in these wilds, it is likely for the purpose of surprise attack. Since this omen is advantageous for the nobleman, it is not bandits who are assembling. Uninhabited territory is the safest location to assemble a great number of people with a subversive purpose. Possibly, this hexagram depicts King Wu calling together his allies in preparation for the attack on Shang. The day prior to arriving at Muye 牧野, the Wilds of Mu, his armies successfully crossed the Yellow River at Mengjin 孟津. Thus, the omen is favorable for the armies of the Zhou nobles to cross the great river.

Line 1: This omen is the image of men assembling at the gate of the city to initiate action. Since the army has progressed this far, the prognostication is that no trouble lies ahead.

Line 2: This omen shows men assembling at Zong 宗, which is normally understood to mean *zongmiao* 宗廟, the ancestral temple. There can be only one purpose for assembling at the temple—to enlist the ancestors in the enterprise for which the men are gathering. However, this omen could also refer to Zongzhou 宗周, the Ancestral Capital of Zhou, the name that King Wu gave to his new capital at Hao 鎬. If there is assembly at Zong, then it may be enemy troops (see next line), which would be reason for the counsel to advise regret.

Line 3: In this omen the enemy is the Rong 戎, one of the non-Chinese tribes in the northwest. They lie hidden in the underbrush, ready to ambush the unsuspecting troops. The counsel advises the divining party to climb to the highest point and make camp. There they will be safe for three years.

Line 4: The walls in this omen are the fortified walls of the city. Although the walls were successfully scaled, the battle for the city is not yet complete. However, the prognostication will be good fortune for a successful conclusion.

Line 5: When the forces were scattered, and the danger of ambush was greatest, the troops were fearful. However, the military leaders were able to muster the separate bands and rally their forces. There was cause for joy.

Line 6: The *jiao* 郊 "suburbs" is the cultivated land of the rural district surrounding a city. This indicates the assembly of the troops at the suburban altar after the conclusion of the battle so that sacrifices could be made to thank the spirits for victory. There is no reason for worry.

同人於野。亨，利涉大川，利君子貞。

初九：同人於門，無咎。

六二：同人于宗，吝。

九三：伏戎於莽。升其高陵，三歲不興。

九四：乘其墉，弗克攻，吉。

九五：同人先號咷，而後笑。大師克相遇。
上九：同人於郊，無悔。

Da You, Possessing Greatness

	OMEN	COUNSEL	FORTUNE
0	Possessing greatness.	Your primary plea is heard.	
1		Have no relationship with what is injurious, and you will be without harm.	In case of difficulty, no harm will come.
2	A great carriage for an undertaking.	There is a journey to go on.	No harm will come.
3		The duke used this omen to pay tribute to the Son of Heaven. The lowborn cannot do so.	
4	It is not his self-importance.		No harm will come.
5	His confidence was mutual and awe-inspiring.		There will be good fortune.
6	From Heaven come his blessings.		There will be good fortune.

All signs are favorable. |

14. Da You, Possessing Greatness

Da 大 is the pictograph of a man with his arms stretched out indicating great size. *You* 有 shows a hand holding something, perhaps "meat," a common possession of the nobleman. Together they mean "possession in great measure."

Hexagram statement: The context of the hexagram lines indicates this phrase describes the Tianzi 天子, or Son of Heaven, who is "possessed of greatness."

Line 1: The Duke of Zhou was serving as regent in the place of his young nephew, the future King Cheng, who ascended the throne upon the unexpected death of King Wu. There were those who did not trust the regent, thinking he was about to usurp the throne for himself. Taking advantage of the period of instability, three of his brothers joined in a revolt. The Duke of Zhou had nothing to do with such treasonous acts. After this difficult time, he managed to defeat the rebels and successfully returned control of the government to his nephew.

Line 2: The *da che* 大車, or "great carriage" was the limousine of the royalty. As an omen, it is a symbol of a journey, perhaps the journey east taken by the Duke of Zhou to subdue the rebels. On such a journey no harm will come.

Line 3: Two years after the victory over Shang, King Wu contracted an illness and was close to death. His son, the Duke of Zhou, prayed to his immediate ancestors, King Wen, Wang Ji, and Tai Wang, and offered his own life for that of the dying king. This is the tribute that the duke offers to King Wu, the Son of Heaven. Only the Tianzi and his descendants could pray to their ancestors, the deceased kings. The common people could not communicate with the spirits of the royal ancestors.

Line 4: When the Duke of Zhou prayed to his ancestors, offering his life for that of King Wu, he rather arrogantly stated that his brother "has not so many abilities and arts as I and is not so capable of serving spiritual beings" 不若旦多材多藝不能事鬼神 (*Shangshu* 尚書, "Zhoushu" 周書, ch. 8, "Jinteng" 金縢, p. 17; Legge, *Chinese Classics,* vol. 3, p. 354). It was only a feigned self-importance, however, stated in order to convince the spirits to take him instead of his brother. For someone so magnanimous, no harm will come.

Line 5: This omen describes the confidence of the Duke of Zhou, and probably refers to the assurance he had that the king's illness would be cured if he offered to sacrifice himself in his brother's place. For the diviner whose confidence is total, the prognostication is good fortune. The graph translated as "confidence" is *fu* 孚, which depicts a "claw" or "hand" above a "child," and literally means "to hatch," or "hatchling," and by extension, the "trust" of the hatchling for its mother. If the "person" element is joined to this graph 俘, the new word means "captives" or "the catch" (of game in a hunt). In the *Zhouyi* all thirty instances of the graph *fu* are missing the "man" element, yet this instance is the only one that retains the original meaning of "trust" or "confidence."

Line 6: When the Duke of Zhou addressed his prayer to his ancestors on behalf of King Wu, he said: "You three kings have in heaven the charge of (watching over) him, (Heaven's) great son" 若爾三王是有丕子之責于天

(*Shangshu* 尚書, "Zhoushu" 周書, ch. 8, "Jinteng" 金滕, p. 17; Legge, *Chinese Classics,* vol. 3, p. 354). This omen describes that relationship, the possession of which ensures good fortune in the future. For the person who receives Heaven's assistance, anything is possible.

大有，元亨。

初九：無交害，匪咎。艱，則無咎。

九二：大車以載。有攸往，無咎。

九三：公用亨于天子，小人弗克。

九四：匪其彭，無咎。

六五：厥孚交如，威如，吉。

上九：自天祐之。吉，無不利。

Qian, The Wedwing

	OMEN	COUNSEL	FORTUNE
0		Your plea is heard. For our lord there will be completion.	
1	Taking wing.	Our lord used this omen to cross the great river.	There will be good fortune.
2	A calling wedwing.	Omen of good fortune.	
3	Toiling wedwings.	For our lord there will be completion.	There will be good fortune.
4	Parted wedwings.		All signs are favorable.
5		You will not prosper on account of your neighbor. By this omen it is time to launch an attack.	All signs are favorable.
6	A calling wedwing.	By this omen it is time to field troops against cities or states.	

15. Qian, The Wedwing

The graph of *Qian* contains 言, the "speech" element, on the left and the *jian* 兼 phonetic (a hand holding two arrows) on the right. Its ancient meaning is "respectful" or "modest." However, the context of the lines require that the hexagram designate an animal of some kind, especially lines 2 and 6, which depict a "calling" or "crying" animal (see Hexagram 16.1, the "trumpeting elephant"; and Hexagram 36, the "calling arrow-bird"). Kunst interprets *qian* as a type of rodent, based on the Mawangdui manuscript whose *qian* graph has the "mouth" 口 radical rather than the "speech" element. The more likely possibility is the graph with the "bird" radical, which is the name of a mythical bird called the *jian* 鶼, or *biyi'niao* 比翼鳥 "wedwing bird" (Li Jingchi 李鏡池, "*Zhouyi* jiaoshi" 周易校釋; Kunst, "Notes," 15.1). The description of the bird first appears in the *Classic of Mountains and Seas*, purportedly written by Yu, the Great. There is also a record in the *Yi Zhoushu* 逸周書, the *Lost Book of Zhou*, that wedwing birds were presented in tribute to King Cheng, son of King Wu (ch. 59, "Wang Hui Jie" 王會解). The wedwing had only one wing and could fly only if it bonded with its mate. For this reason, in later ages it became a symbol of wedded bliss.

Hexagram statement: To have "completion" means that the job will be successfully concluded. This counsel, which occurs again verbatim in line 3, probably describes the accomplishments of King Wen and his son, Fa. That is, it took two of them to complete the task of overthrowing Shang.

Line 1: Literally, *qian qian* 謙謙 (*jian jian* 鶼鶼), this is the name of a pair of wedwing birds, a phrase which first appeared in the *Erya* 爾雅, purportedly written by the Duke of Zhou, as a gloss on the *Mountains and Seas* description cited in the Hexagram name above (南方有比翼鳥焉, 不比不飛, 其名謂之鶼鶼: *Erya* 爾雅, "Shidi" 釋地, ch. 9 第九, p. 61). The implication of the phrase is "taking wing" or "winging," which is evidently a good omen for crossing a river.

Line 2: A calling wedwing is seeking its mate in order to fly. If you encounter this line you are assured of good fortune.

Line 3: This omen depicts a pair of wedwing birds with joined wings struggling to fly. Especially when King Wu carted his dead father into battle (see Hexagram 7, lines 3 and 5), joining with King Wen to conquer Shang was a struggle. The prognostication for the outcome of an action initiated as a result of this line is excellent.

Line 4: The omen depicts a pair of wedwing birds perching and thus not flying. The word translated as "parting" (撝 *hui*) appears only this one time in early Zhou texts. The earliest definition of the term is "to split," which appears in the Han dynasty *Shuowen* dictionary. For any action initiated as a result of this line, all signs are favorable.

Line 5: This line implies that Zhou was unable to prosper because of its powerful neighbor to the east. Only when King Wen allied with his neighbors and launched an attack against Shang did he profit at the expense of Shang. All signs are favorable for a successful consequence of such a strike.

Line 6: A calling wedwing bird is seeking its mate in order to fly. As with the omen of the wedwing birds taking wing in line 1, this crying bird is a good omen for toppling kings. When the ancient diviner obtained this omen, he advised the inquirer to field troops for a campaign to overthrow a state.

謙：　亨。君子有終。

初六：謙謙。君子用涉大川，吉。

六二：鳴謙，貞吉。

九三：勞謙。君子有終吉。

六四：無不利，撝謙。

六五：不富以其鄰，利用侵伐。無不利。

上六：鳴謙。利用行師征邑國。

Yu, The Elephant

	OMEN	COUNSEL	FORTUNE
0		It is good to establish feudal officers and to field troops.	
1	A trumpeting elephant.		There will be misfortune.
2	Wall it off with rocks, but not all day long.	Omen of good fortune.	
3	A wistful elephant.	Problematic.	If you wait, there will be problems.
4	Using an elephant.	Do not doubt that friends will soon join you.	There will be a bountiful harvest.
5		Omen of illness.	It will be long, but the patient does not die.
6	An elephant in the dark.	If completed, there will be change for the worse.	No harm will come.

16. Yu, The Elephant

The standard translation of the character *yu* 豫 is "enthusiasm," or "joy." However, the context of the lines require that the hexagram designate an animal, especially line 2, which depicts a "calling" animal (see hexagram 15.2, 6: the "calling wedwing bird"). The left hand component is phonetic, while the right hand portion of the graph is the pictograph for "elephant." The Han dynasty *Shuowen* dictionary defines *yu* as "the size of an elephant," which is the meaning that seems most appropriate for the context of this hexagram. With the hexagram name identified with the elephant, there is also the likelihood that the subject of the hexagram is a mythical elephant (Kunst, "Notes," 16.1v). Sage-king Yao 堯 discovered his successor Shun 舜 in the wilderness, where he was using elephants to plow (舜葬蒼梧, 象為之耕: *Lunheng* 論衡, 卷第三 "Ouhui" 偶會, p. 103; Forke, vol. 2, p. 246). Furthermore, Shun's half-brother was named Xiang 象, which means "elephant."

Hexagram statement: There is no omen text, so the counsel must derive solely from the character of the hexagram name, "the elephant." The Asian elephant was indigenous to China and was common in the late Neolithic (Elvin, p. 9). The elephant was best known as the source of ivory, an important tribute commodity to early feudal courts. To the ancient diviner who obtained this hexagram, the elephant conjured up the image of exotic borderlands and belligerent southern tribes. Thus the counsel, "It is good to establish feudal officers and to field troops."

Line 1: The omen of a trumpeting elephant was probably frightening to the ancient Chinese, since the elephant was related to thunder (Eberhard, p. 258). Thus the prognostication was one of misfortune.

Line 2: The ancient Chinese, or their tribal forbears, domesticated the Asian elephant. This omen may be a vestige of one method by which elephants were tamed. While a stockade would not be adequate to fence in an elephant, perhaps a rock wall could succeed, but only for a short period of time. The rocks may also refer to the attempt by Xiang (elephant), brother of Shun, to kill him by directing him to dig a well and then throwing stones in after him. Shun escaped by digging a tunnel. The counsel for such a domestication procedure is good fortune.

Line 3: The elephant, after being tamed, remains loyal to its master. A "wistful elephant" can die of sadness (Eberhard, p. 263). Thus, the counsel foretells problems, especially if the inquirer delays before taking action.

Line 4: Shun was rejected by his father and his stepmother, who favored her own son, Xiang (elephant). After surviving three attempts to kill him by his family, Shun fled to the wilds and became a farmer. He later returned to help his mother in a time of need, at which time she realized her error and accepted him back into the family. Sage-king Yao abdicated in his favor due to this exemplary filial piety. Shun then crowned his brother Xiang prince of Bi. Modern scholars speculate that Shun, who "tamed" his arrogant brother Xiang, in actuality, tamed the elephant to clear the jungle. Thus the counsel reads, "do not doubt that friends will soon join you."

Line 5: The ancient diviner who obtained this line must have had reason to suspect the onset of illness. Fortunately, the prognostication for illness is that, although protracted, it will have a good end. You should take all precautions to avoid contagion.

Line 6: Here we see another vestige of elephant taming. If an elephant's eyes are shielded with blinders, it will not frighten as easily. This omen may also be an allusion to the father of Shun and Xiang (elephant), who was blind. Xiang and his birth mother conspired to murder Shun behind his father's back, but Shun survived three attacks. In the end his family accepted him. The prognostication for such change is that no harm will come.

豫： 利建侯行師。

初六： 鳴豫，凶。

六二： 介於石，不終日。貞吉。

六三： 盱豫，悔。遲有悔。

九四： 由豫，大有得。勿疑朋盍簪。

六五： 貞疾，恒不死。

上六： 冥豫，成有渝。無咎。

17

Sui, Pursuit

	OMEN	COUNSEL	FORTUNE
0		Your primary plea is heard. Good omen.	No harm will come.
1	There was a change of residence.	Omen of good fortune. Associating with others outside will bring results.	
2	Tie up the son and lose the old man.		
3	Tie up the old man and lose the son. In pursuit, he got what he wanted.	Good omen for occupying a settlement.	
4	In pursuit, there was a catch.	Omen of misfortune. If captives are taken on the road, will it be harmful to use them for a covenant?	
5	Captured at the celebration.		There will be good fortune.
6	They seized and bound him. Then they loosened his ropes.	With this omen the king sacrificed to the spirit of West Mountain.	

17. Sui, Pursuit

The graph for *sui* 隨 is composed of the "walking" element on the left, and the phonetic element *sui* 隋 on the right. It means, "to follow" or "to pursue."

Hexagram statement: This hexagram probably pertains to various stages of the pursuit of King Wen for the Mandate of Heaven and the throne of Shang.

Since that was a successful pursuit, this is a good omen. If you pursue a well-defined goal, no harm will come in that pursuit.

Line 1: In his pursuit of the Mandate of Heaven, King Wen moved his residence from Mount Qi and established a new capital at Feng, some one hundred miles eastward. He was attempting to consolidate his control of the river valleys east of the Zhou homeland and extend his influence. The ancient diviner who encountered this line thus identified it as an omen of good fortune. The second counsel pictures someone crossing your path as soon as you leave the gate of your house. This omen predicts success in your venture.

Line 2: The omen possibly describes a predicament faced by Zhou Xin, the last Shang king, when he sought to restrain his vassal to the west. Should he take the eldest son of Chang as a hostage to guarantee allegiance? This was a common procedure for feuding states later in Chinese tradition. For example, in 644 BCE, Duke Mu of the state of Qin 秦穆公 took Prince Yu 圉, son of Duke Hui of Jin 晉惠公, hostage in ransom for his father. However, by so doing Zhou Xin risked losing forever the loyalty of the Western Earl.

Line 3: The omen describes the predicament faced by Zhou Xin, the last Shang king, when he sought to restrain his vassal to the west. Should he take Chang prisoner and put an end to his encroachment eastward? By doing so he risked encountering the wrath of the Western Earl's ten sons. The ancient diviner who obtained this line was aware that Zhou Xin did indeed capture King Wen and imprison him at Youli 羑里. Wen's son, Fa, eventually overthrew him and established a new dynasty. Thus the omen, "In pursuit, he got what he wanted." King Wu established his capital at Hao, across the river from Feng. Thus the counsel says, "good omen for occupying a settlement."

Line 4: The society of the waning years of the 2nd millennium BCE was so complex that oaths were no longer sufficient to bind parties over in a negotiation. Instead, covenants were drawn up on bamboo slips. Three copies were made, a sacrifice was offered, and all copies were smeared with sacrificial blood. One copy of the covenant went to each side and the third copy was buried at the spot where the contract was drawn. The omen of this line shows captives taken while on a journey. The counsel marks it as an omen of misfortune, and then—rare in the *Yijing*—asks if it appropriate to use such captives to make the sacrifice for the covenant.

Line 5: This line may indicate that a celebration was held by Shang King Zhou Xin for his vassal, and the Western Earl was tricked into letting down his guard. The ancient diviner who recorded the prognostication realized King Wen was eventually released. Thus the prediction is for good fortune. For more on the capture of Chang, see the commentary on Hexagram 47.

Line 6: This omen depicts King Wen being tied up, and eventually let go. West Mountain was another name for Mount Qi, the cradle of the Zhou people. The ancient diviner recorded here a sacrifice to their sacred mountain by a Zhou king. If you encounter this line you will eventually be extricated from a precarious situation and will have occasion to thank the gods.

隨： 元亨，利貞。無咎。

初九：官有渝，貞吉。出門交有功。

六二：系小子，失丈夫。

六三：系丈夫，失小子。隨有求得，利居貞。

九四：隨有獲，貞兇。有孚在道，以明何咎？

九五：孚于嘉，吉。

上六：拘系之，乃從維之。王用亨于西山。

18

Gu, Curse

	OMEN	COUNSEL	FORTUNE
0		Your primary plea is heard. On the third day before and the third day after the first day of the week, it is good to cross the great river.	
1	A curse of the departed father.	There is a son, so the deceased father will be blameless.	There will be danger, but in the end good fortune.
2	A curse of the departed mother.	Omen of disapproval.	
3	A curse of the departed father.		There will be small problems, but no great harm.
4	A curse of the enriching father.		Going to visit will be cause for regret.
5	A curse of the departed father.	Use this omen for praise.	
6	He serves neither king nor feudal lord. Higher still does his service go.		

18. Gu, Curse

The graph of *gu* 蠱 shows three insects in a bowl, which was described in the Han dynasty *Shuowen* dictionary as "worms in the belly," presumably food poisoning. By the Han dynasty, the concept of *gu* was understood as something akin to voodoo. Several poisonous creatures (such as lizards and scorpions) were placed in a closed container in hopes that one would emerge as victor. Such a creature was thought to have acquired the strength of the vanquished, and could then be ground up and used as a magic potion. In this hexagram the *gu* is apparently an affliction assumed to be caused by ancestral spirits, and is thus translated "curse."

Hexagram statement: The ten days of the Shang dynasty week were given names as sequential designations which are now called the "Heaven Stems." The first day of this ten-day week was called *jia* 甲. Three days after *jia* (day 4, named *ding* 丁), and three days before *jia* (day 8, named *xin* 辛), were often considered auspicious days. The counsel for this hexagram says those two days are lucky for crossing the great river.

Line 1: In the Shang dynasty, the personal names of deceased kings were taboo. Once a king died, he received a stem designation based on certain kinship relationships, plus an honorific title such as Wen, "cultured," which together became his ancestral name. For example, the Shang king who reigned when Zhou vassal Ji Li governed the western regions was Wen Ding 文丁 (the cultured king of the 4th line). On oracle bone inscriptions he is addressed as Fu Ding 父丁—Father Ding. In this and subsequent hexagram lines, the omen resembles a standard oracle bone query about the cause of an illness: "Is the curse due to Father X?" (where X represents the stem of the deceased ancestor). The literal expression "stem father" in lines 1, 3, and 5, will therefore be rendered as "departed father" (and similarly with "stem mother" in line 2) in order to simplify the understanding of this technical language. As to which deceased father is referred to in this hexagram, Kunst speculates that it is the stem of the day on which the divination was performed ("Notes," 18.1c). In other words, if this is a *ding* day, then is it Father Ding's curse? Aside from that possibility, just as likely the "departed father" of line 1 is King Wen. If so, the prognostication recognizes that his son, Fa, succeeded him as King Wu, and so his line endured. There will be many dangers before the kingdom of Zhou is secure, but in the end there will be good fortune.

Line 2: The "departed mother" here may refer one of the "Three Virtuous Mothers of the Zhou Temple," that is, Tai Jiang 太姜, the wife of Ancient Duke Danfu 古公亶父, Tai Ren 太任, the wife of Ji Li 季歷 and mother of King Wen, or Tai Si 太姒, the wife of King Wen and the mother of King Wu. Tai Ren and Tai Si were both Shang royalty. Since King Wu's campaign sought to overthrow the Shang, perhaps they could not be counted on to confer good fortune. The counsel indicates any action taken as a consequence of this line will not be acceptable.

Line 3: The "departed father" here may refer to King Wen. Since we know that King Wen was succeeded by his son, Fa, who overthrew the tyrant, Zhou Xin, this was considered a good omen. Thus, the prognostication is for small problems, but no great harm.

Line 4: Rather than a "stem" father—that is, a deceased forefather with a designated sacrifice day—this line shows someone taking advantage of the curse of an "enriching" father (*yufu* 裕父). This also likely refers to King Wen, who was said to have "enriched the people" (*yumin* 裕民: *Shangshu* 尚書, "Zhoushu" 周書, ch. 11, "Kanggao" 康誥, p. 42). The prognostication indicates the inquirer will regret traveling to see someone.

Line 5: The "departed father" here probably refers to King Wen, who was the most praiseworthy of all the ancestors of the Zhou people. This omen predicts praiseworthiness for the diviner.

Line 6: Here the omen depicts paragons of virtue such as King Wen, who did not serve the king of Shang, and was vassal to no one. Instead, he served Heaven, who chose him to receive the mandate of rule. This line was used as a slogan in later ages by recluses who refused to come out of hiding to serve a king.

蠱：　元亨。利涉大川，先甲三日，後甲三日。

初六：幹父之蠱。有子，考無咎。厲終吉。

九二：幹母之蠱，不可貞。

九三：幹父之蠱。小有悔，無大咎。

六四：裕父之蠱。往見，吝。

六五：幹父之蠱，用譽。

上九：不事王侯，高尚其事。

19

Lin, Wailing

	OMEN	COUNSEL	FORTUNE
0		Your primary plea is heard. Good omen.	 There will be misfortune until the eighth month.
1	Bitter tears of wailing.	Omen of good fortune.	
2	Bitter tears of wailing.		There will be good fortune. All signs are favorable.
3	Sweet tears of wailing.		No signs are favorable. When grieving is done, no harm will come.
4	Wailing to the extreme.		No harm will come.
5	Mastering the rites of wailing for the great lord's sacrifice.		There will be good fortune.
6	Ernest wailing.		There will be good fortune. No harm will come.

19. Lin, Wailing

The standard translation of the Hexagram name, *lin* 臨, is "to approach," or "to oversee." However, the same character can mean "ceremonial wailing," which was its original meaning—witness the three "mouths." From the line texts of the hexagram, it appears that the proper method of funereal wailing is the topic (Kunst, "Notes," 19.1).

Hexagram statement: Mourning rites in ancient China were very complex and included, among other things, rules governing proper dress and length of mourning periods. The reference to the eighth month probably refers to the seasonal sacrifices taking place in the autumn. Once the deceased became an ancestor, annual sacrifices were conducted at the death or the renewal of the agricultural year—propitiation in the spring and gratitude in the autumn. The *yi* 宜, or "great lord's sacrifice" in line 5, specifically honors the earth god, whose phallic altar stands next to the ancestral temple.

Line 1: Reading *xian* 鹹, "salt, salty" for the phonetically and structurally equivalent character *xian* 咸, meaning "unite," this phrase may be translated "bitter (tears of) wailing." This interpretation also complements the "sweet" of line 3. The grief of the mourner and thus his wailing is most intense when he returns from attending the grave and realizes the deceased is no longer to be seen. At this point the Zhou custom was that formal condolences be offered. Thus it is an omen of good fortune.

Line 2: As in line 1, the prognostication for actions taken as a result of this omen is good fortune.

Line 3: Sweet (tears of) wailing are tears of joy. After the body is buried, the mourners return and continue wailing. The spirit of the departed leaves the flesh and bones when the corpse is interred and is given a permanent resting-place in a wooden tablet placed in the ancestral shrine. A sacrifice of repose formally conducts the spirit from grave to shrine. On that day wailing ends and sadness turns to joy. During the time between burial and the sacrifice of repose, the spirit might be anywhere. It is a dangerous period for the living. Thus, the prognostication "no signs are favorable." Once the spirit resides in the tablet and the mourning ceases, the prognostication is a positive one: no harm will come.

Line 4: Line 4 reads literally *zhilin* 至臨 "extreme wailing." According to the *Book of Rites*: "The rites of mourning are the extreme expression of grief and sorrow" 喪禮哀戚之至也 (*Liji* 禮記, 卷 4, "Tan Gong xia" 檀弓下, p. 118; Legge, *Li Ki*, 2.2.1:21). Until such expressions exceed the proper limits, no transgression has occurred. Thus, the prognostication, no harm will come.

Line 5: Here is pictured a sacrifice for the royal ancestors, led by the king of Zhou. The *yi* 宜, or "great lord's sacrifice," specifically honors the earth god, whose phallic altar stands next to the ancestral temple. The prognostication for such an important ceremony is good fortune.

Line 6: Line 4 reads literally *dunlin* 敦臨 "earnest wailing." The *Book of Rites* says: "to do earnestly what is good, and not become weary in so do-

ing—these are the characteristics of him whom we call the *junzi*" 敦善行而
不怠謂之君子 (*Liji* 禮記, 卷 1, "Qu Li shang" 曲禮上, p. 47; Legge, *Li Ki,*
1.1.1.4: 3). Ernest sentiment in the mourning rite has two consequences. The
spirit of the deceased is gratified, and the mourner is mortified. The more the
mourner undergoes mortification, the more gratified is the spirit, and the more
likely the spirit is to visit good fortune on his descendants.

臨： 　元亨，利貞。至於八月有凶。

初九： 咸臨，貞吉。

九二： 咸臨，吉無不利。

六三： 甘臨，無攸利。既憂之，無咎。

六四： 至臨，無咎。

六五： 知臨大君之宜，吉。

上六： 敦臨，吉，無咎。

Guan, Observation

	OMEN	COUNSEL	FORTUNE
0	There is ablution but no sacrifice. There are captives standing tall.		
1	The young boy watches.		For the lowborn no harm will come. For the nobleman there is cause for regret.
2	A clandestine observation.	Good omen for the young woman.	
3	Watching our sacrifices presented and withdrawn.		
4	Behold the glory of the state.	By this omen it is time to be a guest of the king.	
5	Watching our sacrifices.		For the nobleman no harm will come.
6	Watching their sacrifices.		For the nobleman no harm will come.

20. Guan, Observation

The graph of *guan* 觀 combines a phonetic element on the left, and on the right, an element meaning "to see." In the context of this hexagram *guan* means "to observe the sacrifice" (Wang Bi; Kunst, "Notes," 20.1). Observation was crucial during the sacrifice because omens, and thus important communication from the gods, could be derived from every facet of the ceremony.

Hexagram statement: The first omen shows a priest having washed his hands in preparation for the ceremony. Although the sacrificial animal is not offered up, it is not for lack of victims. The second omen claims that there are captives *yongruo* 顒若 "majestic-like." This probably describes horses captured in a raid, since the word describing the captives here also depicts horses in a song from the *Book of Odes* (其大有顒: *Maoshi zhengyi* 毛詩正義, 卷17, "Xiaoya Tonggong zhi shi" 小雅彤弓之什, "Liuyue" 六月, p. 49; Ode #177). This hexagram contains no counsel or prognostication. But, given the great importance of sacrifice in ancient China, the cancellation of a ceremony for a reason other than a lack of victims is not an auspicious image.

Line 1: Here we see the image of a child watching a sacrificial ceremony. In ancient China, the folk rhymes of children were said to be free of artifice and thus a reflection of nature. For this reason, children's verses were sometimes the subject of divination. A child, therefore, might be a more trustworthy observer. However, it was improper for someone "uncapped" (a boy) or "unpinned" (a girl) to participate in such rituals. Since commoners were not as constrained by ritual as were the nobles, such an omen is harmless to them.

Line 2: Here, we see someone watching the sacrificial ceremony in secret. The character for "clandestine," *kui* 窺, literally means "peeping through the door." Since the women of the aristocratic household were confined to the inner chambers of the compound, the only way they could see what was going on elsewhere was by stealth. The counsel for this line is the recognition by the ancient diviner that such spying was a good sign for a maiden.

Line 3: This omen depicts an audience observing "our" sacrificial victims. The graph *sheng* 生, "life," is the proto-graph for *sheng* 牲, "sacrificial victim," which appears in lines 3, 5, and 6 (Waley, "Changes"; Kunst, "Notes," 20.3). The victims are presented on the altar and then withdrawn. The audience here is presumably the king and his clan.

Line 4: Those who observe the grand imperial ceremonies in which, for example, hundreds of slaves, horses with their chariots, cattle, etc., were sacrificed, would have been awed by the majesty. Such an image is the omen for this line. The visit advised by the counsel is the *bin* 賓 ceremony, where the king welcomes his ancestors as guests to partake of the sacrificial ceremony. K.C. Chang identifies such rituals as shamanistic since they involved the descent of spirits (Chang, 1983: p. 55).

Line 5: This omen depicts an audience observing "our" sacrificial rites. There are only two legitimate audiences for a sacrificial rite: the nobility conducting the sacrifice ("us") and the spirits who partake. In this case, the audience is the king and his clan. For a nobleman, such an omen is a good sign.

Line 6: This omen depicts the observation of "others" conducting sacrifices. There are only two legitimate audiences for a sacrificial rite: the nobility conducting the sacrifice ("us") and the spirits who partake. In this case, the audience is the ancestral guests. For a nobleman, such an omen is obviously a good sign.

觀：　盥而不薦，有孚顒若。

初六：童觀。小人無咎，君子吝。

六二：闚觀，利女貞。

六三：觀我生進退。

六四：觀國之光，利用賓于王。

九五：觀我生，君子無咎。

上九：觀其生，君子無咎。

嚙嗑 21 ䷔

Shi He, Bite and Chew

	OMEN	COUNSEL	FORTUNE
0		Your plea is heard. It is time to take legal action.	
1	With his ankles shackled, his toes are cut off.		No great harm.
2	He takes a bite of fresh meat, and his nose is cut off.		No great harm.
3	He takes a bite of cured meat, and gets a taste of poison.		There will be some regret, but no great harm.
4	He takes a bite of dried meat on the bone, and gets a bronze arrowhead.	A good omen in times of difficulty.	There will be good fortune.
5	He takes a bite of dried meat, and gets a piece of bronze.	Omen of danger.	No harm will come.
6	With his head in a cangue, his ears are cut off.		There will be misfortune.

21. Shi He, Bite and Chew

Shi 嚙 means to bite into, while *he* 嗑 means to close the mouth around. Four line texts of the *Shi He* hexagram depict a person biting off and chewing a piece of meat. On the other hand, three line texts and the hexagram statement all depict the seemingly unrelated topic of justice and harsh punishments. Only one line deals with both.

Hexagram statement: The person who obtains this hexagram is advised that the time is right to seek justice for his grievances.

Line 1: In a society whose main institutions are based on the veneration of ancestors, it is not surprising that the greatest insult to the ancestors is the mutilation of the body they bequeathed to you. So the greatest punishment that can be inflicted is the amputation of body parts—the nose, ears, fingers, toes, and finally, castration. In this line text, the prisoner has his toes amputated while his ankles are shackled. The prognostication of "no great harm" describes future actions undertaken by the inquirer. The ancient diviner who made this determination probably came to this conclusion because the criminal avoided execution.

Line 2: The subject of this line was forbidden to eat meat and was punished for his transgression. The punishment was not execution, but merely amputation. The prognostication of "no great harm" describes future actions undertaken by the inquirer. The ancient diviner who made this determination probably came to this conclusion because the criminal avoided execution.

Line 3: The subject of this line bit into cured meat and immediately tasted the presence of poison. The prognostication of "some regret" means there will be some adverse reaction, like a mouth sore perhaps. But, since the eater did not swallow the poison, "no great harm" (that is, death) will occur.

Line 4: The subject of this line bit into dried meat and found a bronze arrowhead. The presence of the bronze arrowhead implies that it was a nobleman who shot it (because only aristocrats would own bronze arrowheads). Furthermore, the fact that the meat is dried or cured would usually indicate it was obtained from a hunt (venison, wild boar, etc.). The large quantities bagged in a royal hunt could not be eaten immediately and had to be preserved. Fresh meat from domestic animals could be eaten as needed and did not need to be preserved. In ancient China bronze was as valuable as gold, so the discovery of a bronze arrowhead in ancient times would be like finding a gold nugget now. The counsel indicates that the ancient diviner considered this a time of difficulty for the person depicted in the omen. Perhaps he was on a journey, or was participating in a military campaign. Regardless, the bronze arrowhead was a good omen, and it predicted good fortune.

Line 5: The fact that the meat is dried would usually indicate that it was obtained from a hunt. The large quantities bagged in a royal hunt could not be eaten immediately and had to be preserved. In this omen we see someone who bites down on a piece of bronze. How the bronze got into the jerky is a mystery, so the ancient diviner who encountered this omen interpreted it as dangerous. But since bronze was a valuable commodity at that time, the prognostication was still good.

Line 6: Here we see a person having his ears cut off while he is wearing a cangue (a wooden collar worn by criminals). Such an omen foretells bad luck for the person encountering this line text. Perhaps the inquirer feels that the current situation is like being choked. If so, then a failure to disengage may result in decapitation.

噬嗑：亨，利用獄。

初九：屨校，滅趾。無咎。

六二：噬膚，滅鼻。無咎。

六三：噬臘肉，遇毒。小吝無咎。

九四：噬乾胏，得金矢。利艱，貞吉。

六五：噬乾肉，得黃金。貞厲，無咎。

上九：何校滅耳，凶。

22

Bi, Adornment

	OMEN	COUNSEL	FORTUNE
0		Your plea is heard. There is some advantage in going on a journey at this time.	
1	His feet bejeweled.	Leave the carriage and go on foot.	
2	His beard festooned.		
3	Elegant and sleek.	Omen of good fortune in the long term.	
4	Fancy and fair, white horse and mare.	"No thieves here, only a wedding pair."	
5	Bedecked up the hill, scanty bolts of silk.		There will be regret, but good fortune in the end.
6	Trimmed in white.		No harm will come.

22. Bi, Adornment

The oldest form of the graph *bi* 賁 was the picture of a flowering plant and meant "brilliant, ornate." Later versions added the element for "cowry shell," an early form of money, with the extended meaning, "to adorn, ornament." In each line text below, the incidence of *bi* is translated according to a somewhat different context, depending on where the adornment occurs. In all cases, the decorations accompanying a wedding are described (Li Jingchi, *Tanyuan*; Kunst, "Notes," 22.1a). However, the customs depicted are not what we normally would expect in a traditional Chinese wedding where red is the dominant color. Gao Heng believes line 1 describes the non-Chinese custom of tattooing (*Gujing jinzhu*: Kunst, "Notes," 22.1).

Hexagram statement: This hexagram describes the adornments of the groom, just prior to his wedding. The counsel anticipates the wedding journey taken by the groom to meet his bride.

Line 1: Here, we see the groom with his feet adorned. He may simply be wearing embroidered shoes or shoes made of silk brocade rather than hempen cloth. The counsel advises the groom to descend from his carriage in order to greet his bride and her chaperone.

Line 2: Here, we see the groom with an ornamented beard, perhaps braids festooned with ribbons. A beard is unusual since the Han Chinese have sparse facial hair in their youth. However, the close relationship of the early Zhou people to nomadic border tribes may be a factor.

Line 3: We are not told who or what is "elegant and sleek," but this line may describe the horses of the bridal carriage. After the groom has left his carriage to greet his bride and her family, the bride and groom together mount her carriage and the groom drives it three times around the yard. The counsel pledges good fortune for the new couple, "until death do they part."

Line 4: This line text describes the pair of horses drawing the bridal carriage. The counsel describes an ancient marriage custom where the groom's family, masquerading as bandits, "abduct" the bride from her home village (see Hexagram 3).

Line 5: Here, we see the train of the carriage decorated with flowers and streamers, parading through the hills on the trip from the home of the bride's parents. The counsel describes the groom's wedding gift of silk as meager, which is not a good omen. Thus, the prognostication calls first for regret. However, in the end good fortune will prevail.

Line 6: The use of white for wedding trim in this image is not to be confused with later Confucian funereal traditions where white represented the color of mourning. Here, white represents purity, which serves as a counterpart to the overt ornamentation of the wedding ceremony.

賁： 亨，小利有攸往。

初九： 賁其趾，舍車而徒。

六二： 賁其須。

九三： 賁如濡如，永貞吉。

六四： 賁如皤如，白馬翰如。匪寇，婚媾。

六五： 賁於丘園，束帛戔戔。吝，終吉。

上九： 白賁，無咎。

23

Bo, Cutting

	OMEN	COUNSEL	FORTUNE
0		Now is not a good time to go on a journey.	
1	They cut up the bed together with his feet.	Omen of destruction.	Misfortune.
2	They cut up the bed together with his knees.	Omen of destruction.	Misfortune.
3	They cut it up.		There will be no regret.
4	They cut up the bed together with his skin.		Misfortune.
5	The palace ladies are favored with a stringer of fish.		Unfavorable for nothing.
6	The plump fruits are not eaten. The nobleman gained a carriage. The lowborn man cut down his hut.		

23. Bo, Cutting

The graph of *bo* 剝 is composed of the "knife" element on the right, and another element which pictures a ritual vessel. Its meaning is "to cut, flay, peel." With the pronunciation *pu*, it also means "to strike." In this hexagram it is the body of Wang Hai 王亥, ancestor of the Shang kings, who is being systematically slaughtered (Kunst, "Notes," 23.1b). King Hai is said to be the first domesticator of cattle and sheep in ancient China. He and his brother Heng 恆 were pasturing their herds across the river in the neighboring country of Yi 易

(see Hexagram lines 34.5 and 56.6). When the Chief of Yi learned of the brothers, he invited them to his court and treated them like dignitaries. Soon the luxurious life had fattened them. But the chief's consort developed a prurient interest in the two stalwart youths. She first caroused with Heng, the younger, and then seduced Hai, the elder. When jealous Heng discovered his brother's deeds, he informed a guard, who proceeded to the brother's bed and chopped the body of Hai into eight pieces. The unfaithful consort had already conveniently vacated the bedroom. When the death of Hai was announced, the chief banished Heng, who fled to his homeland. He reported only that his brother had been murdered and the herds were lost. Heng was made king, and he pledged to return and recover the livestock. Arriving across the river, he found the chief had forgiven him, so he stayed and resumed his intemperate lifestyle. When he did not return home with the cattle, his people installed Shang Jia Wei 上甲微, the son of Hai, as king. Wei crossed the river and destroyed the kingdom. His line endured, and the kings of Shang are descended from him (Field, *Tian Wen*: pp. 114-15).

Hexagram statement: Three of the six line texts depict the object of the hexagram's "cutting" as a *chuang* 床, "bed" or, more specifically, the body of King Hai as it lay on the bed. Since Hai was murdered while he was visiting a neighboring land, this hexagram statement counsels against going on a journey.

Line 1: Here, we see the bed being cut at its foot, together with (以, following Shaughnessy) the feet of Wang Hai. The ancient diviner who obtained this omen identified it as a sign of destruction.

Line 2: Here, we see the bed being cut, dismembering the legs at the knee in the process. The ancient diviner who obtained this omen identified it as a sign of destruction.

Line 3: Here, we are not specifically shown what is being cut. Presumably it is just the bed, thus the line is not perceived as an omen of destruction. Furthermore, since the consort of Yi managed to escape the bed before its destruction, she suffered no harm. For an action undertaken when this line is encountered, the prognostication is "no regrets."

Line 4: Here, we see the bed being cut, taking the skin and flesh of Wang Hai. The inquirer who obtains this line is advised to cease all questionable activity, or misfortune will result.

Line 5: Here, the king's harem is being presented with a stringer of fish as a sign of favor. Since the fish is a sexual symbol in ancient China, this may be an indication that the consort of Yi is now cavorting with younger brother, Heng. Chances are that you will be favored with a gift.

Line 6: This omen pictures fruit, plump with ripeness, but uneaten. If the fish of line 5 represents Heng, then the uneaten fruit of line 6 must represent the consort of Yi. The nobleman, Shang Jia Wei, would then gain the carriages of war, while the small man, the Chief of Yi, lost his kingdom.

剝：　不利有攸往。
初六：剝床以足。蔑貞，凶。
六二：剝床以辨。蔑貞，凶。
六三：剝之，無咎。
六四：剝床以膚，凶。
六五：貫魚，以宮人寵，無不利。
上九：碩果不食，君子得輿，小人剝廬。

復 24 ䷗

Fu, Return

	OMEN	COUNSEL	FORTUNE
0	A friend arrives without difficulty and returns by the same path—a round trip of seven days.	Your plea is heard. When coming in or going out there will be no sickness. Now is the time to go on a journey.	
1	Returning from a short journey.	There will be no harm or trouble.	Great good fortune.
2	A lucky return.		Good fortune.
3	Returning from the brink.		Dangerous, but no harm will come.
4	Returning alone in the middle of a journey.		
5	Urged to return.		There will be no problems.
6	Losing the way back.	If this omen is used to marshal troops, great defeat is assured, reaching to ruler of the state.	Misfortune. There will be accidents. Misfortune. For ten years the army cannot attack.

24. Fu, Return

The graph is composed of the "step" element on the left, and a component that means "to take the former road" on the right. *Fu* therefore means "to walk back the way you came," or simply "to return."

Hexagram statement: This hexagram is concerned with the way in which a person returns from a journey. Is the return journey fraught with difficulty, or free of trouble? For the most part, the hexagram depicts positive images of return. The counsel for this text is three-fold. There will be no fear of illness if you must enter or exit a locale. A friend will arrive on his journey having encountered no problems, and then he will return home. The round trip will have taken seven days. Finally, if you need to go on a journey, it will be advantageous.

Line 1: The subject of this line text has returned from a journey that was not considered long. He encountered no difficulties along the way.

Line 2: The subject of this line text has taken a journey. Unknown to him his return could have been complicated, but he was spared the difficulty through a stroke of luck. It is not advisable to depend on luck, but if you are prepared, fortune is more likely to shine on you.

Line 3: The subject of this line text has taken a journey that required crossing a river. However, he encountered a steep river bank. Because there was no way around this path, the factor of danger increased. However, he was able to return without incurring injury. If you are pressed to retrace your steps or repeat some aspect of your business, despite the increased risk, there will be a good end.

Line 4: The subject of this line text returns alone in the middle of his journey. For some reason his journey has been cut short, while his fellow travelers continued on without him. His absence is apparently no cause for concern.

Line 5: The subject of this line text returns urgently from his journey. Although his traveling companions did not return with him, this was not an issue. There will be no problems if you are required to back out of a venture.

Line 6: This omen shows a person who has lost his way back. If you find yourself in such a situation, not only is it unfortunate, but there is a great possibility of disaster. Immediately seek assistance. In the early Zhou, if a king sought to mobilize troops and encountered this omen, the counsel advised against it. Such foolishness would result in sure defeat. Not only would this defeat reach all the way to the king, the army would be unable to march for ten years.

復：亨，出入無疾。朋來無咎，反復其道，七日來復。利有
　　攸往。
初九：不遠復，無祇悔，元吉。
六二：休復，吉。
六三：頻復，厲無咎。
六四：中行獨復。
六五：敦復，無悔。
上六：迷復，凶，有災眚。用行師，終有大敗，以其國君。
　　凶，至於十年不克征。

25

Wu Wang, Pestilence

	OMEN	COUNSEL	FORTUNE
0		Your primary plea is heard. A good omen. It is not the right time to go on a journey.	His misconduct brings disaster.
1	Pestilence.		Going on a journey will bring good fortune.
2	"Do not plow, and reap a crop. Break no ground, and the land is tilled."	So now is the time to go on a journey.	
3	The pestilence disaster.	If tied to an ox, what the traveler will gain is what the townspeople will lose.	
4		Omen of approval.	No harm will come.
5	The pestilence disease.	Without medicine there will be a joyous recovery.	
6	Pestilence.	There will be disaster in traveling.	No signs are favorable.

25. Wu Wang, Pestilence

The meaning of *wu* 无 is "without." *Wang* 妄 means "fault" or "reckless." *Wu wang* therefore means "faultless" or actions not due to recklessness or negligence. However, the character *wang* does not appear in any texts earlier than the Warring States period, which leads some scholars to replace it with the character *wang* 望 meaning "hope, expect." As a hexagram name, "The Unexpected" is a logical choice, especially in lines such as "unexpected disaster" and "unexpected illness." However, there is no record of this character ever having been loaned for the original, and the binome, "unexpected," does not appear until the Warring States period. Another interpretation has been offered by Arthur Waley, the British translator of the *Book of Odes* (Waley, 1934: pp. 131-32). According to him, *wu wang* is the name of a pestilence, which is expelled from the community by a scapegoating ceremony. Although there is no record of such a pestilence, similar unseen monsters occur in Warring States texts (such as the *wang liang* 罔兩, "which resembles a three-year-old child in form and is reddish black in color, with red eyes, long ears and beautiful hair" [Bodde, 103; Kunst, "Notes," 25.3a]). Edward Shaughnessy, the most discriminating of all contemporary translators of the *Yijing*, also accepts this interpretation of the *wu wang* (Shaughnessy, 1996: p. 51).

Hexagram statement: "A good omen" indicates that the outcome of action based on the reading will bring advantage. However, the prognostication for the hexagram text is that someone's improper behavior may be the cause of calamity. For this reason, the counsel advises not to go on a journey.

Line 1: The omen shows the pestilence appearing in one's locale. One's only recourse is to leave on a journey.

Line 2: This omen is likely a saying of antiquity indicating bounty from Heaven. The occurrence of such fortune is a sign that any action undertaken will have a good outcome. The counsel advises the inquirer to go on a journey as a consequence of receiving this omen.

Line 3: Here, we see pestilence having arrived in a community. Arthur Waley cites a passage from the *Book of Rites* that depicts a Chinese version of the scapegoating ceremony, in this case using clay oxen: "He issues orders to the proper officers to institute on a great scale all ceremonies against pestilence... to send forth the ox of earth to escort away the (injurious) airs of the cold" (Legge, *Li Ki,* 1.4.4.3: 6). In line 3, the pestilence is tied to an ox, which is then picked up inadvertently by a traveler, thus ridding the townspeople of the calamity.

Line 4: The line has no omen text. The counsel advises that the outcome of current actions is acceptable. Regardless, no harm will come from those actions.

Line 5: The omen indicates that the pestilence is capable of spreading disease. The counsel predicts that the disease will be cured without medicine as long as the pestilence is led out of the town attached to an ox.

Line 6: This omen shows the pestilence appearing in a locale. However, now that it is attached to an ox, traveling is no longer recommended.

無妄：元亨，利貞。其匪正有眚。不利有攸往。

初九：無妄，往吉。

六二：不耕獲，不菑畬，則利有攸往。

六三：無妄之災。或系之牛，行人之得，邑人之災。

九四：可貞，無咎。

九五：無妄之疾，勿藥有喜。

上九：無妄，行有眚，無攸利。

26

Da Chu, Greater Stock

	OMEN	COUNSEL	FORTUNE
0		A good omen.	
		These are not to be eaten at home.	There will be good fortune.
		Now is the time to ford the great river.	
1		It is time to make a sacrifice.	There is danger.
2	The carriage loses an axle box.		
3	Fine horses being chased.	A good omen in times of difficulty.	
	He said: "Circle the wagons in defense!"	It is time to go on a journey.	
4	The hobble of a young bull.		There will be great good fortune.
5	The tusks of a gelded boar.		Good fortune.
6	Bearing the course of Heaven.	Your plea is heard.	

26. Da Chu, Greater Stock

The original text reads *da chu* 大畜, "large domestic animals" (as opposed to small—see Hexagram 9). Horses, oxen, and swine are the remaining six domestic animals. Each of these three are specifically referred to in line texts of this hexagram.

Hexagram statement: "A good omen" indicates that the outcome of action based on the reading will bring advantage. The three large domestic animals: the stallion and mare, the bull and cow, and the boar and sow, were raised by the royal stockbreeders for state sacrifices. They were seldom eaten by the common people, and rarely at home. What little meat the peasants ate was wild game or the smaller domestic animals: dogs, fowl, and goats. Thus, the counsel: "these are not to be eaten at home." The prognostication for a hexagram dealing mainly with the chief sacrificial victims is good fortune. When the ancient diviner encountered this hexagram he determined that the counsel was good for crossing the great river.

Line 1: There is no omen for line one, but the prognostication is a clear warning. Whatever you are doing is dangerous. The counsel advises conducting a sacrifice, probably a grand sacrifice with one of the large animals of the hexagram name. The graph translated as "sacrifice" is most likely a loan character. Originally *ji* 己 ("self"), some scholars emend to *yi* 已 ("cease"), or *si* 巳. I side with Li Jingchi, who believes the character should be read, *si*, which he believes is a loan for *si* 祀, "to offer sacrifice" (Li Jingchi; Kunst, "Notes," 26.1).

Line 2: The omen of this line pictures a damaged carriage. The carriage was the standard transportation of the nobility. In times of war, the lords and knights could use their carriages and chariots to move rapidly across the battlefield and outflank their enemies. A broken-down carriage is dangerous because the lord is now afoot and completely at the mercy of the enemy infantry.

Line 3: Line three depicts a lord catching his runaway steeds. In such times of difficulty this is a good omen. When the lord returns to the battlefield with his fine horses, he gives the order to "circle the wagons," thereby saving the day. This image inspired the ancient diviner to declare the time appropriate for a journey. If you are in the midst of a crisis you might expect the appearance of a "white knight."

Line 4: When a young bull grew horns a board was fastened across the tips to protect other cattle and their breeders from injury. These bulls were raised for use in the greater sacrifices, where horn shape and the color of the coat were very important. It was imperative that neither coat nor horns be damaged. This omen depicts the process by which such livestock was raised. The prognostication for actions conducted on behalf of this omen is excellent.

Line 5: Young boars were gelded to keep them from developing aggressive behavior and growing large tusks. Since the omen depicts a gelded pig with tusks, this is a rare enough occurrence to foretell good fortune.

Line 6: This omen depicts someone accepting the course of Heaven, just like the domesticated animals bear their constraints. The counsel for such a man is that Heaven will listen to his plea.

大畜：利貞。不家食，吉。利涉大川。

初九：有厲，利巳。

九二：輿說輹。

九三：良馬逐，利艱貞。曰：閑輿衛，利有攸往。

六四：童牛之牿，元吉。

六五：豶豕之牙，吉。

上九：何天之衢，亨。

27

Yi, **Jawbones**

	OMEN	COUNSEL	FORTUNE
0	Eye the mandible to see for yourself what the mouth has to say.	Omen of good fortune.	
1	Discard your sacred turtles; behold my racks of mandibles.		Misfortune.
2	Turn a jawbone upside down; touch the firebrand to the crown.		Attacking will bring misfortune.
3	Touch the mandible.	Omen of misfortune. For ten years you cannot act.	No signs are favorable.
4	Turn a jawbone upside down. The tiger's gaze is piercing, its prey so far away.		There will be good fortune. No harm will come.
5	Touch the firebrand.	Omen of good fortune for occupying a settlement. It is not possible to ford the great river.	
6	Follow the mandible.	Dangerous. Now is the time to ford the great river.	There will be good fortune.

27. Yi, Jawbones

The graph of *yi* 頤 is composed of the "head" element on the right, and the pictograph for "chin" on the left. The chin is connected to the head by the "jaws," which is what the full graph means. In this hexagram the jaws refer to jawbones or mandibles of sacrificial victims used for divination. Note the pattern of the hexagram symbol, which resembles two rows of teeth set in the jawbone. While the mandible was less utilized for divination than the bovine scapula or the turtle plastron, the pig mandible was clearly important in Neolithic religion, considering the number discovered in Longshan burials (Shelach-Lavi, p. 141).

Hexagram statement: The counsel identifies this hexagram as a good omen. This is because its subject—the oracular jawbone—is numinous. The omen invites the observer to conduct a divination ritual with a diviner's numinous mandibles to see what "truth" will be "mouthed" by the spirit.

Line 1: Here, the omen text specifically is a charge by one diviner to another to partake of his hanging collection of jawbones. Consequently, he abandons the turtle plastrons he normally uses for divining. This is perceived as unlucky, because the turtles are still sacred objects.

Line 2: This omen is the record of the actual technique for cracking the jawbone. First the mandible must be inverted so that the teeth are on the bottom. Then a burning ember of brier (*jing* 荆) is touched (*fu* 拂) to the crown (*qiu* 丘) or hinge of the jawbone. This will produce a crack, which then may be read by the diviner. In the original text, the word *jing* 經, meaning "warp, rule," is probably a loan for the *jing* 荆 meaning "brier." In Han dynasty descriptions of oracle bone cracking, it was branches of the *jing* shrub that were burned to produce the firebrand for scorching. For example, the *Baihu Tong* 白虎通 asks: 龜以荆火灼之何 "Why is a briar ember used to scorch the turtle?" (*Baihutong delun*, vol. 2, 卷 6, "Shigui" 蓍龜, p. 36). Incidentally, the technical jargon referred to here as *fu* 拂 "touching" is attested in a line from a *Chuci* 楚辞 poem: 詹尹乃端策拂龜: "Zhan Yin accordingly arranged his stalks and prepared his turtle" (*Chuci*, 卷 6, "Buju" 卜居, p. 121).

Line 3: This omen would appear to be an abbreviation of the second half of the omen of line 2, which reads in full: "*Touch* the firebrand to the crown of *the mandible.*" However, since this is an image of misfortune, it likely is not a short version of the full ritual of "scorching the mandible." Instead, it simply means to touch or brush the jawbone, which by itself is not sufficient to "see what the mouth has to say."

Line 4: This omen is the first step in the bone-cracking ritual—the upending of the jawbone to expose the plane of the crown. The inspection of oracular jawbones by the diviner is a good sign. The second omen depicts the king in his capital (the "tiger"), pondering the enemy ("its prey") in a far-away land.

Line 5: This omen is the second step in the bone-cracking ritual—applying the ember to the prepared bone to elicit the crack. Although this is a good omen for breaking new ground, the good fortune is limited. Do not attempt to cross the great river.

Line 6: If not conducted by an experienced diviner, following the counsel of the oracular jawbone can be dangerous. For the diviner who puts aside his turtles and follows the advice of the experienced mandible diviner, good fortune is the prognostication, even including the crossing of rivers.

頤：　貞吉。觀頤，自求口實。

初九：舍爾靈龜，觀我朵頤，凶。

六二：顛頤，拂經於丘頤，征凶。

六三：拂頤，貞凶。十年勿用，無攸利。

六四：顛頤，吉。虎視耽耽，其欲逐逐，無咎。

六五：拂經，居貞吉。不可涉大川。

上九：由頤，厲。吉，利涉大川。

28

大過

Da Guo, **The Old Surpass**

	OMEN	COUNSEL	FORTUNE
0	A sagging ridgepole.	Now is the time to go on a journey. Your plea is heard.	
1	For the offering mat use white thatch grass.		No harm will come.
2	A dried-up willow sprouts a new limb.	An old man will get his young wife.	All signs are favorable.
3	A sagging ridgepole.		There will be misfortune.
4	A crowning ridgepole.	Dangerous.	Good fortune. There will be cause for regret.
5	A dried-up willow begins to bud.	An old woman will get her young husband.	No harm, but no praise.
6	Fording the shallows, he sinks to his crown.		Unfortunate, but no harm will come.

28. Da Guo, The Old Surpass

Da is a picture of a man with his arms outstretched, and means "big, great." *Guo* means "to pass through, to pass by," or "fault, mistake." Here *da* and *guo* combine to mean what is great in years manages to surpass the young.

Hexagram statement: The hexagram text introduces the image of the sagging ridgepole, the main roof beam against which the rafters are fixed. A sagging ridgepole is a sign that the roof is weak. While disaster may not be imminent, nevertheless, a sagging ridgepole is an old ridgepole, and not an ideal situation. The ancient diviner who encountered this omen determined that now was a good time to go on a journey.

Line 1: This omen shows an offering being presented on a mat of common white cogon grass. Like the leaf-wrapped offerings of lines 12.2-3 this is a sacrificial offering of the common people. What you have given to the situation may not be substantial, but it is still significant. The prognostication is that no harm will come.

Line 2: Here, we see a striking image from the natural world: the withered tree growing a new limb. The counsel recognizes the omen as a symbol of the old man who finds a young bride. In a patriarchal society this is considered a positive image. Thus, the prognostication predicts no harm.

Line 3: Here, we see the image of a sagging ridgepole, the main roof beam against which the rafters are fixed. A sagging ridgepole is an aging ridgepole and a sign that the roof is weak. Disaster is imminent.

Line 4: A crowning ridgepole is the opposite of a sagging ridgepole. No wooden beam is completely straight. There is always a slight bowing in the virgin wood. When the roof beam is laid atop the two main pillars, it is placed with the bow arching upwards. So a crowning ridgepole represents a new roof. This predicts good fortune. However, you still must be on guard. *Fengshui* masters, for example, always recommend a bed never be placed under a roof beam. Regardless of the apparent condition of the beam, there still might be cause for regret.

Line 5: Here, we see a curious image from the natural world. What appears to be a dead tree begins to bud. The counsel recognizes the omen as a symbol of the old woman who finds a young husband. In a patriarchal society this is not considered a positive image, but neither is it negative. Thus, the prognostication predicts no harm but also no praise.

Line 6: This omen depicts a man wading across a stream. Unfortunately, he falls into a hole and sinks to his head. Although this is not a good situation, the man does not drown. If you are treading on thin ice and fall in, all is not lost.

大過：棟撓，利有攸往，亨。

初六：藉用白茅，無咎。

九二：枯楊生稊，老夫得其女妻，無不利。

九三：棟橈，凶。

九四：棟隆，吉。有它吝。

九五：枯楊生華，老婦得其士夫，無咎無譽。

上六：過涉滅頂，凶無咎。

Kan, The Pit

	OMEN	COUNSEL	FORTUNE
0	There is a capture.	Consider offering the heart in sacrifice. A trip will be rewarded.	
1	Pit within a pit. He plunges down the pitfall.		There will be misfortune.
2	The pit has a drop.	Expect to gain a little.	
3	Bring him here and thump him down. Steep and deep, he plunges down the pitfall.	Do not use this omen.	
4	A flask of wine, tureens—a pair—in earthenware, handed through the window, bound.		No misfortune in the end.
5	The pit is not filled, though all around is level.		No misfortune.
6	Tie him up with braids and cords. Throw him into a thorny keep.	For three years he is not bagged.	Misfortune.

29. Kan, The Pit

The graph combines the "earth" element on the left with a component meaning "to yawn." Together they imply a yawning hole in the ground, that is, a "pit."

Hexagram statement: The pit (or ditch) has been used since the beginning of Chinese society for defensive purposes. However, from this text it is clear that pits were also used for other purposes, including tombs and dungeons. The omen says that a capture has occurred, while the counsel advises that the heart be offered in sacrifice. This hexagram may describe the predicament of Chang, Earl of the West, who did his best to restrain himself when the Lords of Gui 鬼 侯 and E 鄂侯 were murdered by Shang King Zhou Xin. When Chang heard that the heart of the wise minister, Bi Gan 比干, was cut from his body, his heavy sighs betrayed him. He was subsequently captured and thrown into prison, which is the pit of Hexagram 29.

Line 1: The pit within a pit is probably describes the court of King Zhou Xin. While Chang managed to refrain from directly criticizing the king's wicked actions, he ran afoul of the Marquis of Chong who reported his sighs to the king. Nothing bodes well for the person who falls into a pit.

Line 2: This omen depicts a pit with a steep drop-off like that of a tomb, as opposed to sloping sides like a ditch or moat. If you gain anything from encountering this omen, it will be modest.

Line 3: The omen shows a captive thrown down at the edge of a pit, where he sees a steep drop-off before plunging in. This counsel instructs the inquirer to refrain from action.

Line 4: The earthenware dishes of this omen indicate that it is prison fare handed through the window of the dungeon (Wen Yiduo, "*Zhouyi* yizheng leizuan"; Kunst, "Notes," 29.4). However, the presence of wine indicates that the prisoner is being enticed. This line may metaphorically describe Chang. Since he is eventually released, and even begins work on the text of the *Yi* while imprisoned, the prognostication is that the misfortune will not last. At least one scholar believes that "bound" in this omen refers to "the bound one," an allusion to King Wen (Gerhard Schmitt; Kunst, "Notes," 29.4v).

Line 5: Here, the omen depicts a pit being refilled, as if someone was being entombed, but there is not enough soil to fill the hole. The burial was unsuccessful. The prognostication is that no misfortune will come.

Line 6: This omen shows the captive tied up with braids and cords and thrown into a thorny enclosure. The counsel attests that the captive will not be "bagged" (that is, converted) for three years. While the omen is bad, the implication is not. After three painful years, the prisoner is still not broken. Eventually—after three more years, Chang was released from prison.

「習」坎： 有孚，維心亨，行有尚。

初六：習坎，入於坎窞，凶。

九二：坎有險，求小得。

六三：來之坎坎，險且枕入於坎窞，勿用。

六四：樽酒簋貳，用缶，納約自牖，終無咎。

九五：坎不盈，祗既平，無咎。

上六：系用徽纆，置於叢棘，三歲不得，凶。

30

Li, **The Lia-Bird**

	OMEN	COUNSEL	FORTUNE
0		A good omen. Your plea is heard.	Raising cows will bring good fortune.
1	He walks in a tangle.	Take care of him.	No harm will come.
2	A yellow lia-bird.		Great good fortune.
3	The setting sun's lia-bird.	Unless you beat an earthen pot and sing, your elders' lamentations will be substantial.	Misfortune.
4	Suddenly it alights, like blazing up, like snuffing out, like casting off.		
5	Tears flow like a river as they moan and grieve.		There will be good fortune.
6	It is good that heads are lopped off. The catch was not just of enemies.	The king used this to launch an attack.	No harm will come.

30. Li, The Lia-bird

The graph of *li* 離 (pronounced *lia* in archaic Chinese) is composed of the "short-tailed bird" element on the right and a "mountain demon" on the left. *Li* is defined as a *huang canggeng* 黃倉庚, or yellow oriole in the Han dynasty *Shuowen* dictionary. In early texts it can also indicate the horned owl or a type of pheasant. Here, it seems to be a bird of ill omen.

Hexagram statement: The founders of the Zhou dynasty may have originally been a nomadic people for whom livestock was a symbol of wealth and power. Diviners in the early history of this text determined that keeping cows brought good fortune.

Line 1: This omen pictures someone whose walking is crisscrossed as if he is confused. The counsel advises that he be respected and taken care of. If this advice is taken, no harm will come.

Line 2: The appearance of a golden yellow bird is a good omen in a poem in the *Book of Odes* (#156): 倉庚于飛熠燿其羽之歸 "The oriole is in flight,/Oh, the glint of its wings!/A girl is going to be married" (*Maoshi zhengyi* 毛詩正義, 卷 15, "Guofeng: Binfeng" 國風豳風, "Dong Shan" 東山, p. 93; Waley, 1937: p. 117). The prognostication is great good fortune.

Line 3: The lia-bird in this line may be the three-legged raven, which lives in the sun (Kunst, "Notes," 30.3a). Scholars theorize that this mythical bird is an explanation for sunspots, which are visible as the sun sets. The appearance of a dark spot on the sun prompts the villagers to attempt to frighten it away with noise-making and ritual singing. The counsel warns that the elders' cries will be substantial unless the bird is driven away.

Line 4: This omen text describes the abnormal appearance of the lia-bird as seen in line 3. Its arrival is sudden, like a brushfire or a flash flood, like an accidental death or unexpected illness, or like abandonment. Such an abrupt change is bound to instill fear in the people. Be aware of sudden changes.

Line 5: The elders' lamentations have turned to tears of grief because the lia-bird has not flown away. If it is a sunspot, then as soon as the sun sets the bird will also disappear, thus the prognostication of good fortune.

Line 6: This counsel text records that the king launched an attack based on this line. This may refer to King Wen's raid on Chong, described in some detail in the *Book of Odes* (#241). One stanza is particularly descriptive: "The wheeled towers advanced, and rams, steady and serried./ Chong's walls rose above, unperturbed and immense./ --Their seized chiefs came in lines, to be put to the question,/And in calm, awesome, fashion we axed off their heads" 臨衝閑閑崇墉言言執訊連連攸馘安安 (*Maoshi zhengyi* 毛詩正義, 卷 23, "Daya: Wenwang zhi shi" 大雅文王之什, "Huang Yi,"皇矣, p. 162; Elvin, p. 91). This battle was one of the turning points of the rebellion. The Marquis of Chong was the man who slandered King Wen and suggested his imprisonment. Some speculate that the city of Chong was rebuilt as King Wen's capital of Feng. The "catch," in addition to prisoners, was the construction of a new capital; thus, the prognostication that no harm will come.

離:　利貞，亨。畜牝牛，吉。

初九：履錯然，敬之，無咎。
六二：黃離，元吉。
九三：日昃之離，不鼓缶而歌，則大耋之嗟，凶。
九四：突如其來如，焚如，死如，棄如。
六五：出涕沱若，戚嗟若，吉。
上九：王用出征，有嘉折首，獲匪其醜，無咎。

31

Xian, Chopping Off

	OMEN	COUNSEL	FORTUNE
0		Your plea is heard. A good omen for taking a wife.	There will be good fortune.
1	Chop off his big toe.		
2	Chop off his leg at the calf.		Misfortune. For settlements, there will be good fortune.
3	Chop off his leg at the thigh. Hold up the marrow.	To go on a journey will bring regret.	
4	"If you dither back and forth, a friend is thinking of you."	Omen of good fortune.	Problems cease.
5	Chop off the loin.		There will be no problems.
6	Chop off his jowl, cheeks and tongue.		

31. Xian, Chopping Off

The oracle bone version of the graph, *xian* 咸, shows an axe standing upright over a mouth, which implies chopping off the head. No dictionary defines it as such, and only a couple of isolated passages in Zhou dynasty texts use the character in this meaning, combining *xian* 咸 with the graph *liu* 劉, meaning "to hack." One of them occurs in the *Book of Documents*: "There were still four of those men who led on King Wu to the possession of the revenues of the kingdom, and afterwards, along with him, in great reverence of the majesty of Heaven, chopped and hacked all his enemies" 後暨武王誕將天威咸劉厥敵 (*Shangshu* 尚書, "Zhoushu" 周書, ch. 18, "Jun Shi" 君奭, p. 93; tr., Legge, vol. 3, 482).

Hexagram statement: This hexagram describes the ritual dismemberment of a sacrificial victim (Kunst, "Notes," 31.1v). It is clear from the line texts that the victim is a person, and humans were used only for major sacrifices, such as sanctifying imperial tombs and the construction of royal palaces. The fact that a human sacrifice is being performed indicates an important event is being consecrated. Therefore, the omen is good for all ceremonies, including the taking of a wife, for which the prognostication is good fortune.

Line 1: This omen shows the big toe of the victim being cut off. The toes are the least significant appendages on the body, so this omen has no counsel attached.

Line 2: This omen shows the lower leg of the victim being cut off. The flesh of the calves would be stripped off and shredded. The shredded sacrifice would then be buried. The prognostication for any action undertaken as a consequence of this omen is misfortune. An exception would be the consecration of a new settlement, for which the prediction is good fortune.

Line 3: The omen shows the legs of the victim being cut off at the thigh. The flesh of the legs would be stripped off and shredded. The remaining bone and marrow would then be held up and presented to the gods. The ancient diviner who encountered this omen determined that the inquirer would regret taking a trip.

Line 4: The omen text here is likely a proverb that links a person's indecision to the superstitious belief that a friend is therefore thinking of them (Waley, 1934: p. 123). This is an omen of good fortune. All problems associated with the decision will cease to exist.

Line 5: The omen shows the spine of the victim being cut out. The flesh on either side of the spine would be stripped off and shredded. The shredded meat would then be buried as a sacrifice. This was the most prized flesh of the victim and would have been reserved for the most important sacrifices. The prognostication is that there will be no problems.

Line 6: The omen shows the cheeks and tongue of the victim being cut off. As with the toe, the tongue is an appendage of lesser significance, so this omen has no counsel attached.

咸： 亨，利貞取女，吉。

初六：咸其拇。
六二：咸其腓，凶。居吉。
九三：咸其股，執其隨，往吝。
九四：貞吉，悔亡。憧憧往來，朋從爾思。
九五：咸其脢，無悔。
上六：咸其輔、頰、舌。

32

Heng, Constancy

	OMEN	COUNSEL	FORTUNE
0		Your plea is heard. A good omen. Now is the time to go on a journey.	No harm will come.
1	His dredging was constant.	Omen of misfortune.	No signs are favorable.
2			Problems disappear.
3	Their bounty is not constant.	Perhaps a savory offering is made. Omen of regret.	
4	In the hunt there is no game.		
5	Their bounty is constant.	Omen of good fortune for the wife, misfortune for the husband.	
6	His movement was constant.		Misfortune.

32. Heng, Constancy

The graph of *heng* 恆 is composed of the "heart" element on the left, and on the right a rising and setting crescent moon meaning "to wane." As such, the character means "recurrent, persistent" or "constant."

Hexagram statement: For the inquirer who obtains this hexagram, any action undertaken as a result will bring no harm. "A good omen" indicates that the outcome of action based on the reading will bring advantage. Ancient diviners who encountered this hexagram determined that a journey would be advisable.

Line 1: According to the *Shiji*: "Yu dredged the rivers, thereby calming all the Nine Provinces" 維禹浚川九州攸寧 (史記, 卷130, "Liezhuan" 列傳, "Taishigong zi xu" 太史公自序, p 117). This omen describes the mythical hero known as Yu, the Great, queller of the floods (see Hexagram 39 Stumbling). For thirteen years he labored, traveling the length and breadth of the land, never pausing even when he passed his home and heard the cries of his son. Inheriting the task from his father whose dams and dikes had failed to stop the flooding Yellow River, Yu dredged channels to drain the inundating waters. Although Yu's constancy benefited the people whose lives were being devastated by the floods, the counsel advises against such constant digging. There are limits to the depths you should go, and constant dredging is likely to bring misfortune.

Line 2: Inquirers who obtain this line will see an end to their problems.

Line 3: This omen depicts a people whose livelihood is dependent on hunting. The word that means "catch, bounty" pronounced *de* 德, is usually translated as "virtue," which is its fundamental sense. However, in Zhou dynasty texts the character is sometimes substituted for another character with the same pronunciation 得 meaning "to get." That is the case here and with other instances of the word in the *Zhouyi*. In this particular setting, the catch from the hunt is not constant. In other words, there are times of plenty and times of need. The counsel advises that a sacrificial offering of savory delicacies might be appropriate to insure an increased catch. Otherwise, there may be regret.

Line 4: The situation depicted in line 3 continues. Here, a supply of game formerly described as inconstant is depicted as nonexistent. If you are seeking something, you will probably not find it.

Line 5: The situation depicted in line 3 is finally remedied. The catch from the hunt is now constant. This is an omen of good fortune for the wife, for she now has a sufficient supply of game to cook and feed her family. On the other hand, it spells misfortune for the husband whose labors simultaneously increase.

Line 6: In this omen we see a man who is constantly in motion. The word translated as "moving" also means "fear." Perhaps this is because the livelihood of a hunter, who must constantly put himself in harm's way, is so precarious. The prognostication for such a life is misfortune.

恒：　亨，無咎。利貞，利有攸往。

初六：浚恒，貞凶，無攸利。

九二：悔亡。

九三：不恒其德，或承之羞，貞吝。

九四：田無禽。

六五：恒其德。貞婦人吉，夫子凶。

上六：振恒，凶。

Dun, A Suckling Pig

	OMEN	COUNSEL	FORTUNE
0		Your plea is heard. Omen of slight advantage.	
1	The tail of a piglet.	Omen of danger. Do not use this omen to go on a journey.	
2	Tether it with the hide of a yellow ox.	There is no way it can succeed in getting loose.	
3	A tied-up piglet.	There is danger of illness. Tend to your servants.	 Good fortune.
4	A fine piglet.		Good fortune for the nobleman, bad for the lowborn.
5	A festival piglet.	Omen of good fortune.	
6	A plump piglet.		All signs are favorable.

33. Dun, A Suckling Pig

The graph combines the element for "walking" on the left with a component on the right that means "piglet." Together they mean, "to withdraw," in the sense of going into hiding. However, the context of the hexagram line texts demands that the "walking" element be removed, leaving the piglet (Gao Heng; Kunst, "Notes," 33.1). Pigs were probably the most important and most popular of all types of livestock. Domestic swine bones have been found in virtually all of the archaeological digs of Neolithic Chinese settlements. The same cannot be said for poultry, horses, or cattle.

Hexagram statement: "Omen of slight advantage" indicates the outcome of action based on the reading will bring some small advantage.

Line 1: In this line text we learn the tail of the young pig is a symbol of danger. Aggressive piglets have the tendency to bite their pen mate's tails to establish a "pecking order." Once blood has been drawn, further biting may result, sometimes leading to more serious injury, even death. For this reason, swine breeders dock the tails of their piglets to protect them from harm.

Line 2: Young swine are hobbled to keep them from wandering off. Tethers made of rawhide are the strongest, as opposed to rope woven of hemp. Use leather thongs and your pigs will not be able to escape.

Line 3: In this line a tied-up piglet is an omen of disease. The inquirer should be careful he is not "tied-up" by an illness. In addition, as pigs are tied up prior to being served in sacrifice to the ancestors, the nobleman must also be careful that his servants and slaves do not abscond before they serve him. If he properly dispenses discipline, he will have good fortune.

Line 4: A fine piglet is probably being offered as a gift or sacrifice. This is appropriate for a nobleman but not so for a commoner. The former can afford it while the latter cannot. If one must give a gift or make a sacrifice, he or she should be sure it is worth the expense.

Line 5: The image of a spitted, whole pig in a barbecue, or the roasted pig served with an apple in its mouth at a Hawaiian luau are familiar symbols of opulent celebration, which is the image of this line text.

Line 6: A plump piglet is appropriate for sacrificial offerings, gifts to feudal princes, and feasts of the aristocracy. The nobleman who makes such use of a fatted pig is assured of gaining benefit, whether sacred or profane. The inquirer who obtains this omen is assured all signs are favorable if the gift is "fat" enough.

遯：　　亨，小利貞。

初六：　遯尾，厲，勿用有攸往。

六二：　執之用黃牛之革，莫之勝說。

九三：　系遯，有疾厲，畜臣妾，吉。

九四：　好遯，君子吉，小人否。

九五：　嘉遯，貞吉。

上九：　肥遯，無不利。

Da Zhuang, The Strongman

	OMEN	COUNSEL	FORTUNE
0		Good omen.	
1	Strength in the feet.	Attacking will bring misfortune. There will be captives.	
2		Omen of good fortune.	
3	The lowborn uses strength; the nobleman uses wiles. A ram butts the hedge and entangles his horns.	Omen of danger.	
4	The hedge breaks and the ram is untangled. The strength of the great carriage resides in its axles.	Omen of good fortune.	Problems disappear.
5	He loses his sheep in the land of Yi.		There will be no trouble.
6	A ram butts the hedge. It cannot withdraw, and it cannot follow through.		No signs are favorable. After difficulty there will be good fortune.

34. Da Zhuang, The Strongman

Da 大 is the pictograph of a man with outstretched arms and means "big," or "great." *Zhuang* 壯 is composed of a phonetic element on the left and the pictograph for "warrior" on the right. It means "strong" or "great." Together *da zhuang* means "the stalwart" or "the strongman."

Hexagram statement: In this hexagram the strongman is not a bully but a giant of a man. Therefore, it is a good omen. The strongman who is the subject of this line is probably Wang Hai, domesticator of livestock and progenitor of the Shang people. See the commentary for line 5 below.

Line 1: If the strength of a strongman resides in his feet, this means his talent lies in his ability to stop rather than his ability to go. While this is an admirable skill for those intent on retreat, it is not needed when one is about to attack. Thus, the counsel advises that attack will bring misfortune. In this case, the captives are probably from the strongman's troops.

Line 2: There is some speculation that the counsel, "There will be captives," from line 1, may somehow have become separated from the text of line 2. That is because there is no omen in the line text upon which to base the counsel, "Omen of good fortune."

Line 3: The counsel indicates the common man uses strength to get ahead, while the nobleman uses his wits. That the omen is one of danger may stem from the context of the "net" which is the root meaning of "wits, wiles." Those who get ahead by trying to outwit the competition sometimes end up outsmarting themselves. The omen of line 3 begins a three-line narrative that pictures a ram butting a hedge. In this line, the ram entangles his horns. If you are attempting to break through into new territory, there is some likelihood you will become entangled. The characters in this drama are probably the shepherds, Hai and Heng. See the commentary for line 5 below.

Line 4: The omen of line 4 predicts good fortune and the end of problems. It pictures the hedge breaking open and the ram disentangling itself. What could have been a thorny situation has resolved itself. The omen continues by stating an adage about the strength of a carriage. The state is the corollary to the carriage whose axle represents the leader. See the commentary for line 5 below.

Line 5: Hai and his brother Heng were pasturing their herds across the river in the country of Yi. The King of Yi welcomed them to his realm and invited them to his palace where he treated them like dignitaries. But the queen developed a sexual interest in the two stalwart youths. First she caroused with Heng, the younger, and then seduced Hai, the elder. When jealous Heng discovered his brother's deeds, he informed a palace guard, who proceeded to the brother's bed and chopped the body of Hai into pieces. When Hai's death was announced, the king banished Heng, who fled to his homeland. He reported only that his brother had been murdered and the herds were lost. Heng returned to Yi with an army. Finding that the king had forgiven him, he stayed and resumed his intemperate lifestyle. When he did not return with their herds, the people installed a new king, Shang Jia Wei, son of Hai, who crossed the river and massacred the citizens of Yi (Field, *Tian Wen*: pp. 114-15).

Line 6: This omen text depicts a ram butting the hedge. It is unable to break through and is unable to withdraw. This image is a metaphor for Hai and Heng, ancestors of the Shang people, who were unable to resist the enticements of Yi, and were unable to escape. For these two stalwart men no signs were favorable. While both of these brothers lost their lives, Wei was able to save the herds and punish the immoral Yi. Thus after a period of great difficulty, Wei triumphed, his line endured, and the kings of the Shang dynasty are descended from him.

大壯：利貞。
初九：壯於趾。征凶，有孚。
九二：貞吉。
九三：小人用壯，君子用罔，貞厲。羝羊觸藩，羸其角。
九四：貞吉，悔亡。藩決不羸，壯於大輿之輹。
六五：喪羊于易，無悔。
上六：羝羊觸藩，不能退，不能遂。無攸利，艱則吉。

35

Jin, Advance Against

	OMEN	COUNSEL	FORTUNE
0	The Lord of Kang was presented with horses numerous and fine, the spoils of three victories in a single day.		
1	He advances like a scythe. Prisoners are abundant.	Omen of good fortune.	There will be no problems. No harm will come.
2	He advances in strength. He receives a tremendous blessing from the Queen Mother.	Omen of good fortune.	
3	The people are sincere.		Troubles disappear.
4	He advances like a lemming.	Omen of danger.	
5		Don't worry about losses and gains.	Troubles disappear. Going on a journey will bring good fortune. All signs are favorable.
6	He advances his horns.	Only use this to take a town. Omen of regret.	Dangerous, but there will be good fortune. No harm will come.

35. Jin, Advance Against

The graph shows two birds over the sun. Earlier versions of the character show two arrows on a stand, representing a gift "brought forward" to present to a lord.

In this hexagram a particularly military meaning is suggested: the sense of the "forward movement" of an attack, assault, or offensive.

Hexagram statement: Feng, the Lord of Kang 康侯封, was the ninth son of King Wen who was enfeoffed in the state of Kang upon the Zhou victory over Shang. King Wu (second son of Wen) made Feng the Director of Crime in his new court. After the Shang nobles rebelled in the east under the leadership of Guanshu Xian 管叔鮮 (third son of Wen), the Duke of Zhou (fourth son of Wen) led the six armies east to suppress the rebellion. Feng was the commander of one of the armies. Although the day of the triple-victory in this hexagram has been forgotten, we do know that after the three-year rebellion was put down, Kang was given a new fief in Wei 衛.

Line 1: Here, we see the Lord of Kang's attack compared to the cutting of fodder, mowing down the enemy like a scythe. Thus, the omen is one of good fortune. The prognostication statement: "There will be no problems," inserts the character *hui* 悔, "trouble," into the sentence, based on the Mawangdui version of the text. Otherwise, the sentence would read: "There are no prisoners abundant," which makes no sense. The second omen thus shows great numbers of prisoners taken by Kang. If you obtain this line you will come to no harm.

Line 2: In this line appears the only instance in early Zhou texts of the character for "grieve" (*chou* 愁). Some scholars therefore replace it with a character of similar pronunciation, *qiu* 逎, meaning "to press" (Gao Heng; Kunst, "Notes," 35.2). With that in mind, here we see the Lord of Kang advancing forcefully. The second omen in this line shows that the Lord of Kang receives a tremendous blessing from his mother. Kang's mother was a Shang princess, given to King Wen in marriage by Shang king Di Yi (see lines 11.5 and 54.4). The great blessing Kang received was the fiefdom of Wei, which is where the former Shang nobles were relocated after the rebellion was quelled.

Line 3: This omen refers to the people of the state of Wei 衛, the new home of the displaced Shang nobles whose rebellion was suppressed by Zhou. Kang received the blessing of his mother, a former Shang princess. In being true to their new lord the people of Wei were, in a sense, swearing allegiance to their princess. Once the Lord of Kang had the trust of his people, trouble between the Zhou and Shang nobles disappeared. Peace reigned in the kingdom for the next several decades.

Line 4: The *shishu* 鼫鼠 rodent can fly, but no further than across the room; it can climb, but not to the top of a tree; it can swim, but not across a river; it can dig, but not deep enough for a burrow; and it can run, but no faster than a man. The person who advances like the *shishu* will always be short of its goal. Therefore, the counsel identifies this as an omen of misfortune. The rendering of *shishu* as "lemming" is because of that rodent's reputation for migrating, a type of advancing.

Line 5: With no omen text in this line, the counsel and prognostications are to be taken at face value.

Line 6: This omen depicts a military tactic similar to a pincer movement, where two military forces converge on opposite sides of an enemy position. The ancient diviner advised that this tactic be used only to take an enemy town. Although such a movement is dangerous, the prognostication is for good fortune to result and no harm. However, there may be some regrets.

晉：　康侯用錫馬蕃庶，晝日三接。

初六：晉如、摧如，貞吉。[悔] 罔，孚裕，無咎。

六二：晉如，愁如，貞吉。受茲介福于其王母。

六三：眾允，悔亡。

九四：晉如鼫鼠，貞厲。

六五：悔亡。失得勿恤，往吉，無不利。

上九：晉其角，維用伐邑。厲，吉。無咎，貞吝。

明夷 36 ䷣

Ming Yi, The Calling Arrow-Bird

	OMEN	COUNSEL	FORTUNE
0		A good omen in times of difficulty.	
1	A calling arrow-bird in flight locks its wings. The nobleman on a journey does not eat for three days.	If there is a journey to make, the ruler will have something to say.	
2	A calling arrow-bird is wounded in the left thigh.	If this omen is used to geld a horse, it will grow strong.	There will be good fortune.
3	A calling arrow-bird is wounded on the southern hunt. They got the big chief.	This omen is not appropriate for an illness.	
4	Entering the belly on the left, taking the heart of the calling arrow-bird.	He will exit the gate from the courtyard.	
5	Jizi's calling arrow-bird.	A good omen.	
6	It is not bright, it is dark. First it rises up to heaven, then it plunges into the earth.		

36. Ming Yi, The Calling Arrow-Bird

Both graphs that name this hexagram have more than one meaning. *Ming* 明 is composed of a "sun" and "moon" and means "light, bright." Another graph with a similar pronunciation in archaic Chinese, 鳴, means "the call of a bird."

Just like the English word "crow" can be both a noun and a verb, so can the word *ming* in Chinese; that is, it "crows" (to *ming*) at first "light" (*ming*). *Yi* 夷 is a pictograph of a retrievable dart for hunting birds and means, "to wound." A related character, 雉, composed of the element for "bird" and a similar tethered arrow, means "pheasant." Originally, both characters were pronounced the same (*zhi*). Kunst speculates that the *zhi*-pheasant is the "arrow-bird" (because its feathers were used for fletching), which I have adopted here ("Notes," 36.1av).

Hexagram statement: Because of the subject of the text of line 5 below, this hexagram has always been associated with Jizi, the Viscount of Ji, and uncle of Shang king Zhou Xin. Imprisoned by his nephew for admonishing the king, Jizi was freed by King Wu after the overthrow of Shang. Thus, the counsel for this hexagram acknowledges the hardship faced by Jizi.

Line 1: The pheasant flies only when startled—giving an abrupt *karch-karch* cry while rapidly flapping its wings to achieve altitude, before locking its wings and finally gliding to cover. The locked wing glide in this omen is depicted literally as "drooping." This omen is thus the image of someone fleeing out of fear. The counsel harmonizes with a parallel scene from the human realm. A nobleman on a journey does not eat for three days. He is so intent on the object of the journey that he cannot stop to eat. The counsel warns the inquirer that should he plan on making a journey, his ruler will complain.

Line 2: The omen pictures a pheasant wounded in the left thigh. For the hunter this is a good sign. If a tethered arrow was used, then all that the hunter had to do was pull it in like a fish (see line 62.5). The ancient diviner who obtained this omen determined it was an appropriate sign for gelding a horse, another type of "wound." Just like the hunter who profited from the wounded pheasant, the horse breeder profited from the gelded horse. The prognostication for the person encountering this omen is good fortune.

Line 3: Here, the pheasant is wounded on the southern hunt (emending the text by adding the graph, *yi* 夷, "to wound," after the Mawangdui ms.), and the big chief is captured or killed. The big chief and the Calling Arrow-bird (or Singing Arrow) may be one and the same. The *yi* of *Ming Yi*, in addition to meaning "to wound," is also the name of a tribe of non-Chinese who sided with the Shang in the rebellion against the Zhou. The *Yi* were defeated by the Zhou when the rebellion was quelled. If you suffer from an illness, it is not possible to determine appropriate action.

Line 4: Here, the omen describes the bird's belly being opened and the heart being removed. It is likely that the heart being taken here belongs to the chief of the previous line. It was not unusual, up to the last century, for the conquering general to rip out the heart of the vanquished leader and devour it in front of his men. In this manner, he ingested the courage of his enemy. The ancient diviner who received this omen determined that the inquirer would exit the gate of his courtyard.

Line 5: Jizi, uncle of Shang king Zhou Xin, was enslaved by his nephew when he admonished the king for his cruelty and immorality. As such, his admonition was like the *karch-karch* cry of a startled pheasant. Jizi was freed by King Wu after the overthrow of Shang. Thus, it is a good omen.

Line 6: Here the omen may describe the heavenly lights since the sun and the moon are bright when they rise up to heaven and are dark when they enter the earth. Conversely, the omen depicts the flight of an arrow. Archer Yi (夷羿) of myth and legend shot down nine of the ten sun-birds when their flight threatened to burn up the earth. Archer Yi was also a chieftain from the Eastern Yi tribes who usurped the thrown of Xia (Field, *Tian Wen*: pp. 109-11).

明夷： 利艱貞。

初九： 明夷於飛，垂其翼。君子于行，三日不食。有攸往，
　　　 主人有言。

六二： 明夷，夷于左股，用拯馬壯，吉。

九三： 明夷于南狩，得其大首，不可疾貞。

六四： 入于左腹，獲明夷之心，於出門庭。

六五： 箕子之明夷，利貞。

上六： 不明晦，初登於天，後入於地。

Jia Ren, Home and Family

	OMEN	COUNSEL	FORTUNE
0		A good omen for a girl.	
1	He guards his home.		Troubles disappear.
2	There is no other place but inside preparing meals.	Omen of good fortune.	
3	The family squawks and bellyaches. Mother and child giggle and titter.	There is trouble. It will be dangerous.	There will be good fortune. In the end there will be regret.
4	A wealthy family.		There will be great good fortune.
5	The king approaches his family.	There is nothing to fear.	Good fortune.
6		There will be captives terror-stricken.	In the end there will be good fortune.

37. Jia Ren, Home and Family

The first graph is composed of the element for "roof" over the pictograph of a pig. In parts of Asia today there are still rural homes where the first floor is a stable for the livestock and the second floor is for human habitation. A practical configuration, the livestock could be more easily protected from wild animals, and the heat from the stable helped warm the home in the winter. The second graph is the pictograph for "people." Thus, the name of the hexagram is literally, "the people of the home." In particular, the term refers to the women and children who, in general, are confined to the home, as opposed to the husband (and father) who works away from home.

Hexagram statement: In traditional societies all over the world the woman's place was at home. This was every girl's aspiration—to get married, have children, and nurture the family. Thus, the omen for this hexagram is good for a girl.

Line 1: From the hexagram statement above we saw how it was a girl's aspiration to marry and have children. Here, the husband and father aspire to have a home to protect. The use of *you* 有, "to have," as an adjective is unusual, but occurs twice in this hexagram: in lines 1, and 5. Its meaning is "the one there being." The family that has a man to defend them is not as troubled as the family without a head.

Line 2: The woman is expected to stay within the home taking care of domestic tasks, such as preparing meals. Except for venturing to the market to purchase produce for the daily repast, there is no reason for her to proceed beyond the gate. Since this is the image of the traditional family, it is thus a good omen.

Line 3: This omen is the picture of domestic behavior. First, we see the family members moaning and groaning because discipline is too severe. Then we see mother and children giggling because discipline is too lax. The former conduct is troubling, even dangerous if the discipline is too strict. But in the end a disciplined family is a fortunate family. On the other hand, the latter conduct will cause regret.

Line 4: A wealthy family is the universal symbol of good fortune.

Line 5: In this omen we see the king taking time to interact with his family members. The king is the father to his subjects, and the father is the king of his family. The image of the king approaching those who make up his family is the symbol of domestic and public happiness. Just like the wife and children have nothing to fear from the caring husband and father, the subjects of the realm have nothing to fear from the compassionate ruler. The prognostication for such an ideal family is good fortune.

Line 6: This image of captives cowering in fear is the symbol of the harsh ruler and strict father. While such a situation is an unfortunate one, such behavior insures that negligence will not destroy the order of the family. Good fortune will triumph in the end.

家人：利女貞。

初九：閑有家，悔亡。

六二：無攸遂，在中饋，貞吉。

九三：家人嗃嗃，悔厲，吉。婦子嘻嘻，終吝。

六四：富家，大吉。

九五：王假有家，勿恤，吉。

上九：有孚威如，終吉。

38

Kui, A Sighting

	OMEN	COUNSEL	FORTUNE
0			In small matters there will be good fortune.
1	A lost horse.	It will return by itself without a search.	Problems disappear.
	Seeing a hideous man.		No harm will come.
2	Meeting the master in the lane.		No harm will come.
3	Seeing a wagon dragging, its oxen held back, its man branded with his nose cut off.		What has no beginning will have an end.
4	Sighting the fox. Meeting the headman.	You will exchange captives.	Dangerous, but no harm will come.
5			Problems disappear.
	Their ancestor bites into the flesh.	What harm will there be in going on a journey?	
6	Sighting the fox, he sees pigs covered in mud and a cartload of ghosts. At first he draws his bow, and then he releases it.	"No thieves here, only a wedding pair."	If you go on a journey and meet with rain, there will be good fortune.

38. Kui, A Sighting

The graph of *kui* 睽 is a pictograph of an "eye" on the left, combined with the phonetic element *kui* on the right. The earliest dictionary interprets the word as "seeing something that others don't see." In particular, *kui* can mean, "to spy," or "to set one's sights on." However, in the context of this hexagram, it specifically means to observe the sky. The constellations observed in the following line texts rise in the east in each of the four seasons. In autumn appears *Tian Shi* 天豕, or the Heavenly Boar (in Pisces and Andromeda) and *Tian Ma* 天馬, or the Heavenly Horse (in Cassiopeia). In winter appears *Yu Gui* 輿鬼, or the Cart of Ghosts (in Cancer), and *Hu Shi* 弧矢, or the Bow and Arrow (in Puppis and Canis Major). In spring appears *Zhen* 軫, or the Wagon. In summer appears *Qian Niu* 牽牛, or the Ox Being Led (or the Led Ox, in Capricorn). Thus, the line texts of the hexagram, like that of Hexagram 1, record various stages in a "calendar." Wen Yiduo was the first to recognize the astronomical import of these lines, followed by Edward Shaughnessy ("Composition," pp. 211-220) and finally Richard Rutt (pp. 331-32).

Hexagram statement: For the most part, the images depicted in the line texts are constellations in the Chinese sky. Since none of the prognostications are unlucky, we can assume that the astronomical images are not ominous. The general prognostication for the hexagram is that there will be good fortune in small matters.

Line 1: The observation of this line text is twofold. The horse you expect to see is gone; instead you see the image of "a hideous man" (or "evil man"). The horse is the constellation Heavenly Horse. When the Heavenly Horse disappears beneath the western horizon in spring ("a horse is lost"), the Wagon is rising in the east. The Wagon does not appear in the hexagram until line 3. But we do see its "hideous man" who is "branded with his nose cut off." Since the horse is a constellation, it will rise again in the autumn. There is no need to search for it. Problems disappear of their own accord.

Line 2: The image here is the sighting of the master in the street. This is likely to be the ruler, which suggests one interesting interpretation. Lines 4 and 6 may be cryptic references to famous Archer Yi who usurped the throne from the profligate third ruler of the Xia dynasty, Tai Kang. According to Richard Kunst, this line may depict the archer's sighting of the future king in a town lane ("Notes," 38.2).

Line 3: Here, we see the Wagon constellation "trailing," that is, descending in the western sky where it is about to set. The time is summer, and the Led Ox is rising in the east. In ancient China criminals were sometimes branded on the forehead (the meaning here of *tian* 天) or tattooed, and other times disfigured by the amputation of noses, ears, etc., depending on the crime. Furthermore, the Cart of Ghosts was the constellation governing executions, according to Richard Rutt (p. 331). The prediction is that "all's well that ends well." In other words, while it may look ominous in the beginning, it is certain that the outcome will be promising.

Line 4: In the winter, when the Led Ox sets in the west, the Cart of Ghosts rises due east. Just a few degrees south of the Cart, Sirius, or the Dog Star, is simultaneously rising. The Chinese call Sirius *Tian Lang* 天狼, the Heavenly Wolf Star, and sometimes the Fox (Shaughnessy, "Composition," p. 217). According to the omen text, the rise of Sirius accompanies a meeting with the headman. The headman may be the master of line 2, or it may indicate Archer Yi. Yi's wife was named Chun Hu 純狐, Sable Fox. Following Kunst, *gu* 孤 "orphan," is a loan for *hu* 狐 "fox."

Line 5: Problems disappear because this line depicts a sacrificial rite. This omen pictures the spirit impersonator (embodying the ancestor) partaking of the sacrificial meat at an ancestral rite. In the rare instance of a counsel text in the form of a rhetorical question, the ancient diviner who interpreted this omen asks "what harm is there in going on a journey?"

Line 6: When the Heavenly Boar rose in the east in autumn, it marked the beginning of the monsoon season in ancient China (Shaughnessy, "Composition," p. 214). This is the significance of the omen of muddy pigs. By the time the Fox and the Cart of Ghosts rise in the east in winter, the Heavenly Pig is directly above. In the next few weeks, the Arrow will slowly rise above the eastern horizon, aimed directly at the Fox. Then will come the Bow. By spring, the Bow will begin to disappear beneath the southern horizon. This is probably the phenomenon described in the omen text as the drawing and releasing of a bow. The counsel here borrows a conventional allusion from other hexagram line texts (see lines 3.2 and 22.4). The prognostication of rain follows directly from the appearance of the Heavenly Pig. Since the Bow and Arrow constellations are not attested before the Han dynasty, the drawing and releasing of the bow is just as likely an allusion to Archer Yi, the mythical demi-god who shot down nine of the ten suns (see also line 36.6).

睽： 　　小事吉。

初九：悔亡。喪馬，勿逐，自復。見惡人，無咎。

九二：遇主於巷，無咎。

六三：見輿曳，其牛掣，其人天且劓。無初有終。

九四：睽孤，遇元夫。交孚，厲，無咎。

六五：悔亡。厥宗噬膚，往，何咎？

上九：睽孤，見豕負塗，載鬼一車。先張之弧，後說之弧。
　　　匪寇婚媾。往，遇雨則吉。

39

Jian, Stumbling

	OMEN	COUNSEL	FORTUNE
0		The south and west are favorable; the north and east are not. It is time to see the great one. Omen of good fortune.	
1	He stumbles ahead and is praised coming back.		
2	The king's minister stumbles and falls, through no fault of his own.		
3	He stumbles ahead and tumbles back.		
4	He stumbles ahead and comes back in a carriage.		
5	Great is his lameness.	Friends will arrive.	
6	He stumbles ahead and is prominent coming back.	It is time to see the great one.	Good fortune.

39. Jian, Stumbling

The graph of *jian* 蹇 is composed of a phonetic on top and the element for "foot" on the bottom. It means, "lame," as an adjective or "to stumble," as a verb. In this hexagram, the subject of each line is a lame man who somehow overcomes his disability. The most famous lame man in ancient China was Yu, tamer of floods, and this hexagram may be about him. The Daoist classic *Liezi* describes him as follows: "The Great Yu did not keep even his body for his own benefit; he worked to drain the Flood until one side of him was paralysed" 大禹不以一身自利一體偏枯 (*Liezi* 列子, 卷 7, "Yang Zhu" 楊朱, p. 46; Graham, p. 148). Steve Marshall believes that two other verses in the *Zhouyi* that depict a hobbling disease describe the Great Yu: "No flesh on his thighs, his steps are hobbled" (43.4) and "No flesh on his buttocks; his steps are hobbled" (44.3).

Hexagram statement: The Zhou homeland was to the west and south of the Central Plain of the Yellow River, which is why the counsel for this hexagram says these are favorable directions. To the north was the land of non-Chinese nomads, and to the east was the Shang domain. This is why those directions were unfavorable. The counsel advises on two occasions to "see the great one," which in this hexagram is the Great Yu, himself.

Line 1: According to the *Lüshi chunqiu*: "When Yu ascended the throne he toiled and labored on behalf of the world. He rested neither day nor night, opening up the great streams, cutting through obstructions and blockages, boring out the Dragon Gate, and circulating the flowing waters by guiding them to the Yellow River…. At this, Yu commanded Gaoyao to compose all nine movements of the 'Xia Flute' in order to celebrate his achievement" 禹立勤勞天下日夜不懈通大川 決壅塞鑿龍門降通瀿水以導河…於是命皋陶作為夏籥九成以昭其 (*Lüshi chunqiu* 呂氏春秋, 卷5, "Zhongxiaji" 仲夏紀, "Guyue" 古樂, p. 134; Knoblock and Riegel, p. 561).

Line 2: According to the *Lüshi chunqiu*: "Shun, thereupon, had [Gun] executed at Mount Yu and dismembered the corpse with a knife from the state of Wu. Yu, Gun's son, dared not harbor resentment against Shun but, on the contrary, served him, being appointed minister of works in charge of clearing the water courses" 舜於是殛之於羽山副之以吳刀禹不敢怨而反事之官為司空以通水潦 (卷 20, "Shijunlan" 恃君覽, "Xinglun" 行論, p. 151-52; Knoblock and Riegel, p. 532).

Line 3: According to the *Lüshi chunqiu*: "His complexion turned black, he developed a limp, his bodily vital ethers would not flow" 顏色黎黑步不相過竅氣不通 (卷 20, 行論, p. 152; Knoblock and Riegel, 532). Furthermore, "No one has suffered more than Yu in exerting himself and toiling for the people" 勤勞為民無苦乎禹者矣 (卷21, "Kaichunlun" 開春論, "Ai Lei" 愛類, p. 19; p. 561).

Line 4: According to the *Lüshi chunqiu*: "This time was called the 'Deluge.' In consequence of this, Yu dredged the Yellow River and channeled the Yangzi, he built the dike at Pengli Marsh, solved the problems of the eastern lands, and rescued the eighteen hundred states—this was Yu's achievement" 名曰鴻水禹於是疏河決江為 彭蠡之障乾東土所活者千八百國此禹之功也 (卷 21, "Kaichunlun" 開春論, "Ai Lei" 愛類, pp. 18-9; Knoblock and Riegel, 561).

Line 5: According to the *Lüshi chunqiu*, "In his search for worthy men and his desire to exploit fully the benefits of the land, he worked until his face turned black, the seven facial openings and five organs of the body were clogged, and he walked with a limp. These are extreme examples of making the greatest effort. In the end, Yu won the assistance of five men" 不有懈墮憂其　黔首顏色黎黑竅 藏不通步不相過以求賢人欲盡地利至勞也...五人佐禹 (卷 22, "Shenxinglun" 慎行論, "Qiuren" 求人, pp. 142-3; Knoblock and Riegel, 580).

Line 6: According to the *Lüshi chunqiu*, "While Yu was digging channels for the rivers and streams, the common people were still futilely piling up potsherds for a dam. When Yu's task was completed and success achieved, a myriad of generations benefited" 禹之決江水也民聚瓦礫事已成功已立為萬世利 (卷 16, "Xianshilan" 先識覽, "Le Cheng" 樂成, p. 114; Knoblock and Riegel, 389).

蹇： 利西南，不利東北。利見大人。貞吉。

初六： 往蹇，來譽。

六二： 王臣蹇蹇，匪躬之故。

九三： 往蹇，來反。

六四： 往蹇，來連。

九五： 大蹇，朋來。

上六： 往蹇來碩，吉。利見大人。

Jie, Loosening

	OMEN	COUNSEL	FORTUNE
0		The south and west are favorable.	If there is nowhere to go, his arrival and return will bring good fortune. If there is somewhere to go, early morning will bring good fortune.
1			No harm will come.
2	Bagging three foxes in the hunt and getting bronze arrowheads.	Omen of good fortune.	
3	Being mounted, yet with loaded backs, lured the bandits down.	Omen of regret.	
4	They loosen his thumbs. Friends arrive and capture them.		
5	The nobleman's rope is loosened.		Good fortune.
		There will be captives among the lowborn men.	
6	The duke used archers and falcons on the top of a great wall and bagged them.		All signs are favorable.

40. Jie, Loosening

The graph of *jie* 解 is composed of a "knife" above a "bull" on the right and a "horn" on the left, and depicts the dehorning of cattle. In early Zhou texts it meant "to be loose," or "to loosen."

Hexagram statement: The Zhou homeland was to the west and south of the Central Plain of the Yellow River, which is why the counsel for this hexagram says these are favorable directions. The prognostication outlines two prospects regarding travel—with no trip in mind, the visit of another will bring good fortune. If you have travel plans, it is best to leave in the early morning.

Line 1: Action taken as a result of obtaining this line will result in no harm.

Line 2: The text of this hexagram quite likely refers to an historical event that has been forgotten. This line begins the description of a major hunting expedition conducted by a duke and presumably made up of nobles and their servants. Here, three foxes are captured. The hunters who bagged them are presented with bronze arrowheads as a reward, since bronze was equivalent to gold in ancient China. For these reasons—a successful hunt, a valuable reward—the omen is one of good fortune.

Line 3: Here, we see the hunting party mounted on horses or riding in carriages, yet with their backs laden with game. From out of the hills comes a gang of bandits. They are drawn by the loaded backs of the servants and carts of the expedition. This is an omen of regret because losses are suffered.

Line 4: In this omen a nobleman, captured by the bandits, has his thumbs untied by his friends who save him and capture the bandits.

Line 5: Here, we see the nobleman's rope being loosened, for which the prognostication is good fortune. The counsel for the nobleman's release is the capture of lowborn men, presumably those bandits who had originally ambushed him.

Line 6: Here, we see the duke chasing the bandits (or game) beyond the great wall of a city. He sends his archers and falconers to the top of the wall where they are able to shoot and kill them. If you obtain this line, all signs are favorable.

解：　利西南。無所往，其來復，吉。有攸往，夙吉。

初六：　無咎。

九二：　田獲三狐，得黃矢，貞吉。

六三：　負且乘，致寇至，貞吝。

九四：　解而拇，朋至斯孚。

六五：　君子維有解，吉。有孚於小人。

上六：　公用射隼于高墉之上，獲之，無不利。

41

Sun, Decrease

	OMEN	COUNSEL	FORTUNE
0	What to use? Two tureens can be used for the plea.	There will be captives. Omen of approval. Now is the time to go on a journey.	Great good fortune will come and no harm.
1	The sacrificial service goes with haste. As for libations, reduce them.		There will be no harm.
2	They will not be diminished; it increases them.	A good omen.	Attacking will bring misfortune.
3	Three people walking will be decreased by one. One person walking will gain a friend.		
4	It shortened the illness, and accelerated the prospect of joy.		No harm will come.
5	If increased by a turtle worth ten *peng*, you cannot oppose.		There will be great good fortune.
6	They will not be diminished; it increases them.	Omen of good fortune. Now is the time to go on a journey. You will gain a servant without a home.	No harm will come.

41. Sun, Decrease

The graph of *sun* 損 includes a "hand" element on the left next to a component that means, "to return." In this hexagram *sun* means "to decrease," and is a counterpart to Hexagram 42, which means, "to increase." Both terms occur throughout the hexagram, but are translated somewhat differently depending on context.

Hexagram statement: The omen for this hexagram is a rare occurrence of a question: "What is the appropriate sacrifice?" It represents the realistic predicament faced by ancient priests: what type of offering and what amount will impress the spirits to whom they plea for guidance? The omen asks and answers the question, showing that for the sacrifice in question the priest determined two bowls of grain to be proper. Omen statements in line 1 also concern sacrificial procedures.

Line 1: As with the hexagram statement above, here the omen also deals with the performance of the sacrificial ritual (reading 已 as 巳/祀; see line 26.1). In addition to the amount of offering, this line text is concerned with the length of the ceremony. In this particular case, the priest who is conducting the rite finishes the ceremony quickly, for which the prognostication is no harm. Presumably, to shorten the service libations were reduced. If you encounter this omen and are engaged in any ritualized activity it would be best to speed up and spend less.

Line 2: Here, we see a good omen, predicting that most activities will end in success, except for attacks on neighboring states. You should refrain from taking the offensive for the moment. The omen states that they will not be diminished by your attacks, but will be enlarged.

Line 3: Confucius once said when traveling in the company of just two other men he could learn something from at least one of them. When this omen shows a group of three travelers being decreased by one, it means that the two remaining become friends. Although three men may share company, inevitably, they are each traveling alone until they become friends.

Line 4: The omen of line 4 shows that the sacrifice has decreased the nobleman's illness, and hastened the cure. If you are suffering a physical ailment, a sacrifice may lessen the impact and speed up your recovery.

Line 5: Since the Neolithic era, the Chinese divined by reading the cracks in scorched turtle shells. In the early period shells were imported from neighboring countries and were quite precious. Ten *peng* 朋 is ten double-strings of cowrie shells, which would represent a considerable amount of wealth in the late Shang or early Zhou. It would be very difficult to oppose such an offer. As such, the omen predicts great good fortune.

Line 6: Here again we see the subject of the omen advising that belligerent states will not be decreased by your attack, but will be increased. No harm will come if the attack does not occur. The second omen depicts a double gain: the subject of the line increases his household by one person, and the servant who had no home gains a household.

損：　有孚，元吉，無咎。可貞，利有攸往。曷之用？二簋可用享。

初九：巳事遄往，無咎，酌損之。

九二：利貞，征凶。弗損，益之。

六三：三人行則損一人，一人行則得其友。

六四：損其疾，使遄有喜，無咎。

六五：或益之，十朋之龜，弗克違，元吉。

上九：弗損，益之，無咎。貞吉，利有攸往，得臣無家。

42

Yi, Increase

	OMEN	COUNSEL	FORTUNE
0		Now is the time to go on a journey. Now is the time to ford the great river.	
1		By this omen it is time to accomplish great works.	There will be great good fortune. No harm will come.
2	If increased by a turtle worth ten *peng*, you cannot oppose.	Omen of good fortune in the long term. The king used this omen to sacrifice to the Lord.	Good fortune.
3	Increase him. There was a capture reported en route.	Use this omen in times of misfortune. The duke used this omen to present the jade mace.	In serving, no harm will come.
4	It was reported en route.	The duke concurred. By this omen it is time for Yin to move the capital.	
5	There was a capture. There was a capture.	It should be of hearts. Do not question it. The bounty should be ours.	There will be great good fortune.
6	No one increased him, and someone struck him.	Be steadfast in your heart.	To be inconstant will bring misfortune.

42. Yi, Increase

The graph of *yi* 益 shows a "bowl" on the bottom being filled with "water" on top. It means "to add to," or "to increase." In this hexagram it describes the increasing fortunes of the Zhou people, probably based on the heroic feats of Danfu, Ancient Duke of Zhou 古公亶父. This is according to Gao Heng, who believes the text of line 4 refers to the moving of the capital of the Shang state at Yin across the Yellow River to the north (*Gujing jinzhu*; Kunst, "Notes," 42.4).

Hexagram statement: This hexagram recommends that journeys be taken and the great river be crossed. Both actions were perilous in ancient China. The exodus undertaken by Danfu, ancestor of the Zhou kings and founder of the Zhou capital at Mount Qi, required many such crossings.

Line 1: There is no omen here, but the counsel recommends using the line to accomplish great works. In the hexagram statement, the diviner is advised that river crossing and journeys will be successful. In this line we learn that there will be great good fortune if great works are undertaken, such as establishing new capitals (see line 4).

Line 2: This omen is the same as that of line 5 of the previous hexagram. Ten *peng* 朋 is ten double-strings of cowrie shells, which would represent a considerable amount of wealth in the late Shang or early Zhou. It would be very difficult to oppose such an offer. When the king obtained this omen, he took it as a sign of approval. That is, a sacrifice to the Lord on High was sanctioned by his ancestors. The king in this line may be Wuyi 武乙, the Shang king who reigned when Danfu migrated to Mount Qi.

Line 3: The omen of "increase" in this line is to be used in times of misfortune, and the prognostication is good for one serving his superior. The second omen is quite detailed, and begins a narrative that continues into line 4. Unfortunately, it is not known what lost story these events pertain to. As an omen, it prompted the duke to make a sacrifice, presenting his jade mace of office to his ancestors.

Line 4: The narrative here continues from line 3. The significance of the capture was acknowledged by the duke. This prompted King Wuyi to move his capital to the north of the Yellow River, perhaps due to the floods (Huang, p. 9). In the same year, according to the *Bamboo Annals*, Danfu was confirmed as Duke by King Wuyi and his city at Mount Qi was officially conferred to him (*Zhushu jinian* 竹書紀年, "Di Yi" 帝乙, 卷上, p. 65; Legge, *Chinese Classics*, vol. 3: "Prolegomena," p. 138).

Line 5: In ancient China prisoners-of-war were used as slaves or sacrificial victims if transportation was convenient. Otherwise, heads or hearts were taken. The counsel advises the diviner not to question this outcome. The report of capture promises great good fortune. The omen of capture also portends further catches by the duke's troops.

Line 6: The tribe of Danfu was not large, about two or three thousand men, women and children. As the belligerent tribes moved closer he tried to appease them with gifts. But they continued to encroach. There were no friendly tribes to fortify or strengthen the duke's position. So, his enemies struck harder. Had he not remained steadfast and been willing to migrate, his tribe would have been swallowed up by the nomads, and the Zhou would never have been founded. The prognostication for those of steadfast heart is good; for those whose loyalty is inconstant, there will be misfortune.

益：　利有攸往，利涉大川。

初九：利用為大作，元吉，無咎。

六二：或益之十朋之龜，弗克違，永貞吉。王用享于帝，吉。

六三：益之，用凶，事無咎。有孚，中行告，公用圭。

六四：中行告，公從，利用為依遷國。

九五：有孚，惠心，勿問，元吉。有孚，惠我德。

上九：莫益之，或擊之。立心，勿恒凶。

43

Jue, Haste

	OMEN	COUNSEL	FORTUNE
0	On view in the courtyard of the king, the captives cry out. From a town comes a report of danger.	This is not the time to regulate the Rong tribes. It is the time to go on a journey.	
1	His strength is in stopping beforehand.	Going will not bring victory.	It will be harmful.
2	Cries of alarm. Attacks come in the night.	Fear not.	
3	His strength is in his face. The nobleman heads out alone hurry-scurry. He meets with rain and gets wet.		There will be misfortune. There is displeasure, but no harm.
4	No flesh on his thighs, his steps are hobbled.	If he leads a sheep his problems will disappear. He will hear talk but it is not reliable.	
5	The mountain goat leaps, helter-skelter, down the middle of the road.		No harm will come.
6	There are no cries.		There is misfortune in the end.

43. Jue, Haste

The graph of *jue* 夬 depicts a hand holding an archer's thimble, a device for grasping the string of the bow. This character was sometimes borrowed for another character of the same pronunciation, 決, which adds the "water" element on the left. It means "to breach a dam" and "to break out" or, by extension, "to rush, to gallop," or "in haste."

Hexagram statement: While captives are being punished publicly in the courtyard of the Zhou palace, an alarming report arrives from an outlying town. However, even if border tribes are attacking in the west, the counsel advises the king against mounting a campaign of retaliation. His dispute is not with the barbarians to the west. The time is right for a journey east.

Line 1: In this line, the character translated as "stopping," is based on the variant reading, *zhi* 止, in the Mawangdui manuscript, for the graph meaning, "foot" 趾, in the received manuscript. This omen depicts the king as a commander who knows how to stop before disaster befalls. For the diviner who obtains this line, if all action ceases, you will escape calamity, although some harm is inevitable.

Line 2: Cries of alarm indicate that an assault from western border tribes has come in the night. The ancient diviner who encountered this omen realized the outcome was not a disaster; thus his counsel, "Fear not!"

Line 3: The omen of a man with a strong or vigorous face is a sign of misfortune. Perhaps his cheeks are flushed from physical exertion, since we learn in the second omen that he is a nobleman traveling alone in great haste, an indication that his action was rash or impulsive. Otherwise, his entourage would have accompanied him. That he meets with rain and gets wet is a sign he was ill equipped or unprepared for this journey. The phrase translated "hurry-scurry" is the first instance in the line texts of the hexagram name, *jue*, which is doubled here.

Line 4: This omen shows a man who is gaunt and haggard, but who is still able to hobble along. It is the image of someone close to collapse. Some scholars think this omen refers to the Great Yu, queller of the floods, who dredged the rivers and opened channels to drain the inundating waters. One clue that strengthens this interpretation is the fact that the hexagram name means, "to breach a dam" (Marshall, p. 148). As for the custom of leading a sheep, this is something akin to waving a white flag. In a passage from the *Commentary of Zuo*: "with his flesh exposed and leading a sheep [a nobleman surrendered his city to the conquering army]" 肉袒牽羊以逆 (*Chunqiu Zuozhuan zhengyi* 春秋左傳正義, 卷 23, "Xuangong 12th Year" 宣公十二年, p. 6; Qu Wanli, "Xisu"; Kunst, "Notes," 43.4). A leader willing to sacrifice himself in such a manner is bound to hear disparaging words. They are not to be listened to.

Line 5: The image of a mountain goat leaping, hell-bent, down the middle of the road, symbolizes flight from harm. In the translation, "helter-skelter" is another rendition of the phrase, *juejue*, which appeared for the first time is line 3. The inquirer who heeds the warning and flees in great haste is assured no harm will come.

Line 6: In line 1, the omen showed captives in the royal court "crying out." The omen of line 6 indicates that no cries of warning were heard. Thus, no one was aware that danger was near. Since you will not be warned before calamity falls, in the end you cannot avoid misfortune.

夬：　揚于王庭孚號，有厲告自邑。不利即戎，利有攸往。

初九：壯於前趾，往不勝，為咎。

九二：惕號，莫夜有戎，勿恤。

九三：壯於頄，有凶。君子夬夬獨行，遇雨若濡。而慍，無咎。

九四：臀無膚，其行次且。牽羊悔亡，聞言不信。

九五：莧陸夬夬中行，無咎。

上六：無號，終有凶

Gou, Encounter

	OMEN	COUNSEL	FORTUNE
0	The girl is strong.	Do not use this omen to take a wife.	
1	Tied to a bronze spindle. Bound pigs and captives buck and balk.	Omen of good fortune.	If there is somewhere to go, you will see misfortune.
2	There is a fish in the bundle.	It is not the time to be a guest.	No harm will come.
3	No flesh on his buttocks; his steps are hobbled.	Danger.	No great harm will come.
4	There is no fish in the bundle.		Rising up will bring misfortune.
5	Bundle the gourd in willow. The pattern holds.	Something will fall from heaven.	
6	Encountering its horn.		Regret, but no harm will come.

44. Gou, Encounter

The graph of *gou* 姤 combines the element for "woman" on the left with a phonetic element on the right. The character appears nowhere else in early Zhou
texts, but has been defined as "to meet with, encounter" since the earliest

commentaries. From the context of the hexagram and line statements, it probably indicates a "rendezvous."

Hexagram statement: The hexagram statement shows a strong-minded young woman, not a good omen in a patriarchal culture like China. If the man who obtains this hexagram is inquiring about the feasibility of marriage, the answer is an unqualified no.

Line 1: In the patriarchal society of ancient China, the proper place for a young woman was in the inner chambers of the palace spinning silk from the silkworms raised by her clan. This omen depicts a woman "tied" to a bronze spindle. Since she is in her proper place, it is an omen of good fortune. It was improper for a woman to leave the inner palace in traditional Chinese society. If she left the compound, she would likely meet with misfortune. The second omen shows tethered pigs and captives bucking and balking. This is a metaphor for the strong woman who rejects her traditional role.

Line 2: This line has stumped scholars for centuries due to the difficulty of translating *bao*, which occurs in four different hexagrams: "a bundle of sprouts" (Hexagram 4); "a bundle is discarded" (Hexagram 11); "a bundled offering" and "a bundled present" (Hexagram 12). Scholars are hesitant to translate this line as a "fish in the bundle" because of its seemingly sexual connotation. So, it could also mean, "a fish in the kitchen" (Gao Heng—describing a household with sufficient food stocks), or "a fish in the womb" (Kunst—describing a dismembered sacrificial victim), etc. However, in pre-Confucian rural China apparently some type of sexual rendezvous was sanctioned in the spring when fertility rites were held. According to the *Rites of Zhou*: "In the month of mid-spring there is no prohibition on couples who run away" 中春之月令會男女於是時也奔者不禁 (*Zhouli shuzhu* 周禮述註, 卷 9, "Diguan Situ" 地官司徒, p. 50), While this rite may simply describe those couples that marry without go-betweens, nevertheless there is an undercurrent of sexual attraction. Thus, the prognostication for such an omen is that no harm will come. The counsel for this line says the time is not right for the ritual of *bin* 賓, whereby the new bride "visits" the husband's ancestors where she is formally introduced as his wife (Marshall, p. 114).

Line 3: This omen, a variation of the omen in line 4 of the previous hexagram, shows a man who is gaunt and haggard, yet is still able to hobble along. It is the image of someone starved and worked to death. The counsel warns of danger. Some harm is predicted for the inquirer. Some scholars think this omen refers to Yu, the Great, queller of the floods (Marshall, pp. 144-48).

Line 4: This omen uses the same imagery of line 2 to inform the diviner that the rendezvous has not been consummated. The prognostication warns against rising to action. In the Mawangdui manuscript, the graph for "rise up," *qi* 起, is replaced by that for, *zheng* 正, "upright," in the sense of "correct."

Line 5:   This omen collects another image that seems to describe metaphorically the consummation of a sexual rendezvous. "Bundle the gourd in willow" literally describes the process by which a gourd is shaped for use as a bottle. The image of the willow tree was also used as a sexual metaphor in lines 28.2 and 28.5. A variation of "the pattern holds" was used in line 2.3 to indicate fertility and ripeness. The counsel, "Something will fall from heaven," may pertain to anomalies such as rocks falling from the sky, but more likely refers to falling stars.

Line 6: This omen, while also seemingly sexual in nature (the third person possessive pronoun could also be translated "his"), may literally describe the rising of the Horn of the composite constellation, Azure Dragon. As seen in line 2 of Hexagram 1, the Dragon's Horn (the star Spica in Virgo) rose in early March in 800 BCE.

姤：　女壯，勿用取女。

初六：系于金柅，貞吉。有攸往，見凶。贏豕孚蹢躅。

九二：包有魚，無咎，不利賓。

九三：臀無膚，其行次且，厲，無大咎。

九四：包無魚，起凶。

九五：以杞包瓜，含章，有隕自天。

上九：姤其角，吝，無咎。

45

Cui, Suffering

	OMEN	COUNSEL	FORTUNE
0	The king goes to his ancestral temple.	Your plea is heard. It is time to see the great one. Good omen for the sacrifice. Now is the time to go on a journey.	Using the great ox will bring good fortune.
1	Capturing does not end. There is chaos, and then, suffering.	If crying "yeow" becomes a laugh, do not fret.	Going on a journey will bring no harm.
2		If there are captives, it is best to use them for the summer sacrifice.	Stretching it out brings good fortune. No harm will come.
3	Suffering and sighing.	No signs are favorable.	Going on a journey will bring no harm. There will be slight regret.
4			There will be great good fortune. No harm will come.
5	Suffering in high position.	No harm will come if no one is captured.	Great good fortune. The long-term omen is that troubles will end.
6	Moaning and groaning, sobbing and sniveling.		No harm will come.

45. Cui, Suffering

The graph of *cui* 萃 combines the "grass" element above a phonetic element (pronounced *zu*), and means "to collect" or "assemble." In the Mawangdui version of this hexagram, the *zu* 卒 graph appears without the "grass" element, in which case it means "to finish" or "to die." However, the same phonetic with the "illness" element means "to suffer," is pronounced *cui* 瘁, and is the meaning that fits the context of the hexagram.

Hexagram statement: The omen shows the king proceeding to his temple, where sacrifices to the ancestral spirits are conducted. Thus, the counsel says it is a good omen for sacrifice. Requiring the services of his Grand Invocator, he is advised to see the great one. The prognostication counsels that good fortune can be obtained if an ox—the greatest of all domestic victims—is used for the ritual.

Line 1: The omen of the hexagram statement shows the king proceeding to the temple to seek advice from his ancestors about the coming conflict. Here we see the battle in progress. The killing and capture of the enemy is interminable. Chaos reigns. The counsel predicts that cries of anguish will turn to smiles when victory is in sight.

Line 2: The stretching out may be of bows, or simply the prolongation of war. Either will bring good fortune in a time of conflict. The omen of the hexagram statement showed the king proceeding to the temple to seek advice from his ancestors in regard to the coming battle. The ox was recommended as the best victim for the sacrifice. But, if prisoners of war are taken, then clearly they would be the victims of choice.

Line 3: This omen depicts the suffering and sighing of battle, all unfavorable signs. However, the prognostication is not one of terrible misfortune, just slight regret.

Line 4: Line 4 has no omen or counsel. The ancient diviners who encountered this line recorded the prognostication of great good fortune. Whatever your question or task, success is predicted.

Line 5: The king is suffering in his position as leader of the rebellion. However, the prognostication is that no harm will come as long as he is not captured. Furthermore, if the king is not captive, there will be great good fortune, and the troubles that led to the original conflict will eventually be resolved.

Line 6: This omen portrays the sobbing and sniveling of those who mourn the suffering and loss of war. In this case, the battle was won. The damage is over and the future is bright.

萃：亨。王假有廟。利見大人，亨利貞。用大牲，吉。利有
攸往。

初六：有孚不終，乃亂乃萃。若號一握為笑，勿恤，往無咎。

六二：引吉，無咎。孚乃利用禴。

六三：萃如，嗟如，無攸利。往無咎，小吝。

九四：大吉，無咎。

九五：萃有位，無咎匪孚。元永貞，悔亡。

上六：齎咨涕洟，無咎。

Sheng, The Climb

	OMEN	COUNSEL	FORTUNE
0		Your primary plea is heard. Use this omen to see the great one. Do not be anxious.	An attack to the south will bring good fortune.
1	They climb earnestly.		Great good fortune.
2		If there are captives, use them for the summer sacrifice.	No harm will come.
3	They climb the hill settlement.		
4		The king used this to offer sacrifice to Mount Qi.	Good fortune. No harm will come.
5	They climb the steps.	Omen of good fortune.	
6	They climb in the gloom.	A good omen for not resting.	

46. Sheng, The Climb

The graph of *sheng* 升 is a pictograph of an ancient measuring utensil similar to a scoop. It resembles the character *dou* 斗, another measuring utensil, but also used to name the constellation Bei Dou 北斗, or the Northern Bushel, better known as the Big Dipper or the Great Bear. Probably based on this resemblance, *sheng* was borrowed to mean "to rise" (as with heavenly bodies), "to ascend" (as sacrifices to Heaven), and "to climb." All of these derived meanings are probably valid here.

Hexagram statement: In general, the topic of the hexagram is "climbing." In particular, the hexagram may refer to The Great Climb, when Danfu led his people across the mountains to the plain of Zhou beneath Mount Qi. There is no omen text here, but the counsel advises seeing the great one, the Grand Invocator, or head diviner of the court. There is no need for the people to be anxious, even though it is a major undertaking. If, after divining, it is determined that military action is necessary, the prognostication predicts good fortune for a campaign to the south. Danfu's exodus was to the south.

Line 1: Danfu's exodus began from the valley of the Jing River 涇水, a tributary of the great Wei River 渭水 that drained the plain of Zhou. Immediately upon leaving the Jing River valley, the refugees had to climb for days in order to cross the Liang Mountains 梁山 and reach the valley in sight of Mount Qi 岐山. According to the *Book of Odes* (#296): "Oh, august are those Zhou! They ascended the high mountains, the long, narrow ridges, the high peaks, they went along the roaring River" 於皇時周陟其高山嶞山喬嶽允猶翕河 (*Maoshi zhengyi* 毛詩正義, 卷28, "Zhousong Minyuxiaozi zhi shi" 周頌閔予小子之什, "Ban" 般, p. 125; Karlgren, p. 253).

Line 2: The migration south and west must have been grueling work because of the mountains and river valleys that hindered their journey. The tribe probably had to fight its way through some districts, in which case captives would have been taken. The counsel advises that the captives be utilized in the summer sacrifice. Danfu arrived at Mount Qi in the summer.

Line 3: After he crossed the Liang Mountains 梁山, Danfu led his tribe west and forded the Qi 漆 and Ju 沮 Rivers. When he arrived in the plain of Zhou, he found the land to be flat and fertile. We know this from the *Book of Odes* (#237), which records the following legend: "The ancient duke Danfu/ Came in the morning, galloping his horses,/Along the banks of the western rivers,/To the foot of Qi;/And there, he and the lady Jiang/Came, and together looked out for a site on which to settle./The plain of Zhou looked beautiful and rich" 古公亶父來朝走馬率西水 滸至于岐下爰及姜女聿來胥宇周原膴膴 堇茶如飴 (*Maoshi zhengyi* 毛詩正義, 卷 23, "Daya Wenwang zhi shi" 大雅文王之什, "Mian" 緜, p. 68; Legge, *Chinese Classics,* vol. 4: p. 438).

Line 4: In addition to their ancestors, the ancient Chinese worshiped the spirits of mountains and rivers. Once he arrived at the foot of Mount Qi, Duke Danfu offered sacrifice to determine if Mount Qi was appropriate for their new home. According to the *Book of Odes* (#237): "There he singed the tortoise-shell,/The responses were—there to stay, and then;/And they proceeded there to build their houses" 爰契我龜曰止曰時築室于茲 ("Mian" 縣, p. 69; Legge, *Chinese Classics,* vol. 4: p. 438).

Line 5: After constructing the ancestral temple and the great walls around the royal compound, Danfu and his warriors erected the altar to the spirits of the Earth. This was a great platform of rammed earth on which excursions of war began. These are probably the steps he climbs. According to the *Book of Odes* (#237): "They reared the great altar [to the Spirits of the land],/From which all great movements should proceed" 迺立冢土戎醜攸行 ("Mian" 縣, p. 78; Legge, *Chinese Classics,* vol. 4: p. 438).

Line 6: Presumably, Danfu's exodus was so intent on escaping the marauding tribes that he marched deep into the night in order to reach the plain of Zhou. Had they stopped to rest, they may have been overtaken by the enemy.

升： 元亨，用見大人，勿恤。南征吉。

初六： 允升，大吉。

九二： 孚乃利用禴，無咎。

九三： 升虛邑。

六四： 王用亨於岐山，吉，無咎。

六五： 貞吉，升階。

上六： 冥升，利於不息之貞。

47

Kun, Distress

	OMEN	COUNSEL	FORTUNE
0		Your plea is heard. Omen of the great one. There is talk but it is not believed.	Good fortune. No harm will come.
1	Thighs distressed by a wooden staff, he enters the dark valley and is not seen for three years.		
2	He is distressed with food and wine, and then come the scarlet knees.	By this omen it is time to offer sacrifice.	An attack will bring misfortune. No harm will come.
3	Distressed by stone, he grasps at thorns. Entering his palace he does not see his wife.		There will be misfortune.
4	He comes slowly, distressed by a bronze carriage.		There will be an end to regret.
5	Distressed with amputation by the burgundy knees, he slowly extricates himself.	By this omen it is time to offer sacrifice.	
6	Distressed by vines and creepers, he is tripped up.	This is called "to act is to regret."	There will be problems. An attack will bring good fortune.

47. Kun, Distress

The graph of *kun* 困 shows a tree enclosed in a wall, which means, "to obstruct," or "distress." In this hexagram, each line text includes the character *kun*. However, in each case, a different shade of meaning is understood by the particular type of "distress"—a beating, overeating, harassment, entanglement, etc.

Hexagram statement: The counsel identifies the hexagram as an omen of the great one. Here the great one may be Chang, the Earl of the West, who encountered many difficulties in his life. The rebellion he instigated caused him great consternation, because he knew that rule was a divine right. At the same time, he was unsure that Heaven had chosen him to be king. Many would condemn him for his actions, but in the end, the Mandate of Heaven was his. His clan ruled for centuries.

Line 1: Here, we see a man punished with a caning and thrown into a dungeon where he is not seen for three years (Gao Heng; Kunst, "Notes," 47.1). This omen may represent Chang, who was thrown into prison by the cruel Zhou Xin, last king of Shang.

Line 2: The scarlet knees—a type of legging, was the insignia of highest office—grand dukes or high ministers. Chang was promoted to the position of Grand Duke before he was thrown into prison. The image of distress while banqueting is reminiscent of lines 11.3, "...his capture at dinner," and 17.5, "captured at the celebration," which both describe the capture of Chang by Zhou Xin.

Line 3: Here we see a nobleman traversing a rocky path surrounded by brambles (see also line 29.6). Even though he seems to extricate himself from this distress, when he returns to his palace his wife is not to be seen. There is no way to escape this distress.

Line 4: Here, we see an image of someone in distress due to a bronze-fitted carriage—the conveyance of the aristocrat. His movement is slowed by the obstruction of the nobleman, but in the end the obstruction is removed.

Line 5: The burgundy knees—a type of legging (not to be confused with the scarlet knees), was the insignia of the feudal lords. In this omen a burgundy knee threatens someone with the penalty of nose and foot amputation. However, he manages to extricate himself from this predicament.

Line 6: Here, we see someone entangled, which may represent the perilous situation faced by Chang as he served in King Zhou Xin's court. Perhaps his rebellion would have ended differently had he acted sooner ("an attack will bring good fortune").

困：　亨，貞大人。吉，無咎。有言不信。

初六：臀困於株木，入于幽谷，三歲不覿。
九二：困于酒食，朱紱方來，利用享祀。征凶，無咎。
六三：困于石，據於蒺藜，入于其宮，不見其妻，凶。
九四：來徐徐，困于金車。吝，有終。
九五：劓刖，困於赤紱，乃徐有說，利用祭祀。
上六：困于葛藟，於臲卼，曰：動悔。有悔，征吉。

48

Jing, **The Well**

	OMEN	COUNSEL	FORTUNE
0	The town is moved, but not the well. They come and go, welling up, but the rope does not reach the depth of the well, and he breaks his jug.		There will be neither loss nor gain. There will be misfortune.
1	The well water is muddy and is not drunk. At an old well there is no game.		
2	He shoots fish in the well bottom. His crock is cracked and leaky.		
3	The well water surges; it is not drunk. My heart is sad since it can be used to draw water.	The king will make a covenant.	All will receive mutual blessings.
4	The well is tiled.		No harm will come.
5	The well water is clear; its cool spring is drunk from.		
6	If the well is retired, do not cover it.	There will be capture.	Great good fortune.

48. Jing, The Well

The earliest depiction of the graph of *jing* 井 shows a nine-cell grid with a dot in the center cell representing the well. It is an illustration of the well-field system used by ancient settlers to open up the wilderness. In particular, Zhou kinsmen, invested by their king with new territories, set out with a party of soldiers, swidden agriculturists, and artisans to colonize the land. Each unit of eight families cleared and farmed a nine-section field. The produce of the ninth section, where the well was dug, went to the maintenance of the non-cultivating leaders in the fortress community.

Hexagram statement: Swidden (slash-and-burn) cultivation required that fields be abandoned after their fertility had declined. Farmers would then move and clear new land. The loss of the depleted land and the old well meant the gain of a fresh well and more fertile land for the millet crops. The prognostication for this hexagram is not good. The omen shows a citizen going on his daily journey to draw water from the well, but it was dry and he broke his water jug before he could use it to fetch water. Perhaps this indicated that the village had waited too long before moving.

Line 1: The omen depicts an old well with water too soiled to drink. Even wildlife will find the stagnant water unfit to drink. You should investigate your resources to see if they are unsound.

Line 2: The Chinese sometimes put minnows in their wells to keep the water fresh. However, a well is for drawing water and is not a source of food. If you shoot at fish in the bottom of the well, you take the chance of damaging the well or the jug that draws the water. This omen is a warning not to misuse resources.

Line 3: The omen depicts a well whose water surges up and seeps down as the water flows underground, yet no one drinks from it. The author of this omen also recorded his emotion regarding the wasted resource. Perhaps this was Chang, the Western Earl, who was sad that loyal subjects like Bi Gan were being ill-treated by King Shou. He then pledged to his ancestors that he would seek blessings for all.

Line 4: Wells will have cleaner water if their walls are lined with tile or stone. This is making the best use of a resource, since solid walls prevent dirt from muddying the water. People will be less likely to be harmed when drinking water from a lined well.

Line 5: This omen depicts a new well whose clear, cool spring is freely utilized. This is a good omen, and symbolizes an ideal situation.

Line 6: When a farming village is forced to move because the land's fertility has been depleted, this counsel recommends that the abandoned well not be covered. Consequently, it would be utilized by wildlife. Hunters could take advantage of this man-made watering hole to stalk their game. Such secondary use of abandoned resources will be a source of great good fortune.

井：改邑不改井，無喪無得。往來井井汔至亦未繘井，羸其
　　瓶，凶。

初六：井泥不食，舊井無禽。

九二：井穀射鮒，甕敝漏。

九三：井渫，不食，為我心惻，可用汲。王明，並受其福。

六四：井甃，無咎。

九五：井洌，寒泉食。

上九：井收，勿幕。有孚，元吉。

49

Ge, Molting

	OMEN	COUNSEL	FORTUNE
0		When the day of sacrifice comes, use captives. Your primary plea is heard. Good omen.	Problems disappear.
1	Bound up with the hide of a yellow ox.		
2		When the day of sacrifice comes, skin them.	An attack will bring good fortune. No harm will come.
3		Omen of danger.	An attack will bring misfortune.
	It is said that change is complete after three.	Captives will be taken.	
4		Captives will be taken.	Regret disappears.
	Change the mandate.		Good fortune.
5	The great one dons the tiger change.	Captives will be taken, even before he has divined.	
6	The nobleman dons the leopard change, while the lowborn change their faces.	Omen of good fortune for settlement.	An attack will bring misfortune.

49. Ge, Molting

The graph of *ge* 革 is a drawing of a cowhide. It means "pelt" or "skin," and, by extension, "to change" or "to molt" ("change the skin"). Both senses of the term are used in the context of this hexagram.

Hexagram statement: All the line texts in this hexagram deal with the subject of change, utilizing three different Chinese characters: *ge* 革, *gai* 改, and *bian* 變. For two-thirds of the lines, it is the donning of a mask or an animal skin that symbolizes the change. Although recent scholarship is convincing in regard to the lack of evidence for shamanistic trance in ancient Chinese texts, nevertheless, the donning of animal hides and the wearing of masks—if that is indeed what this hexagram depicts—does seem to point in that direction. Since this hexagram also pertains to dynastic change, sometimes it is clear that the diviner presides over a sacrifice seeking military success. In this statement, the counsel advises using prisoners for the sacrifice.

Line 1: Here, we see the prisoners bound up using the hide of a yellow ox. Ancestral sacrifices normally called for the bovine victim to be dark-colored, whereas here the ox hide is yellow. Since yellow is the color of the soil of the Yellow River basin, perhaps this sacrifice is to the earth god. It was from the altar to the earth god that military campaigns began.

Line 2: Here, we see that the prisoners bound up with cowhide now have their "hides" removed in sacrifice. When the sacrificial ceremony of the yellow ox has concluded, the army can launch its military campaign. The outcome will be fortunate and no harm will come.

Line 3: The prognostication for line 3 is that misfortune will result if a military campaign is launched. The omen for this line is what must have been a proverb in early Zhou: "Change, it is said, is complete after three." Reminiscent of silkworm metamorphosis—caterpillar, cocoon, and moth, in the political reality of late Shang China, it may mean something like "third time's a charm." That is, the third change of mandate is final. Traditionally speaking, the Zhou was the third change of mandate after the Xia and Shang dynasties, although it is generally understood that the Zhou founders created the concept of Heaven's Mandate passing from Xia to Shang to justify their conquest of Shang. One of the oldest texts to record such a change of mandate is the "Speech of Tang" 湯誓 in the *Book of Documents*, ostensibly the words of the first king of Shang, but probably not recorded until the early Zhou dynasty.

Line 4: Here, we see the final change discussed in the previous line, "a change of mandate" (using the word *gai* 改). Due to the cruelty and perversion of King Zhou Xin, the Shang lost the favor of their god. Heaven then chose Chang of the Ji clan to receive his favor, mandating Zhou rule over all under Heaven.

Line 5: Here, we see "the great one," probably King Wu, donning the skin of a tiger (*bian* 變, as in "changing skins"). The tiger is the most ferocious wild animal in ancient China. Donning a tiger skin would have symbolized gaining the physical powers of the tiger. Upon the threshold of battle in the Wilds of Mu, King Wu addressed his troops, saying: "Display a martial bearing. Be like tigers and panthers!" 尚桓桓如虎如貔 (*Shangshu* 尚書, "Zhoushu" 周書, ch. 4, "Mushi" 牧誓, p. 17; Legge, *Chinese Classics,* vol. 3, p. 304). Sure enough, before the ceremony is complete the army has already captured enemy warriors.

Line 6: Here, we see a vassal of King Wu donning the skin of a leopard. The lowborn commoners, who made up the infantry in Zhou armies, also put on masks to join the ceremony. While this particular omen is not good for military attack, it is appropriate for settling new communities.

革： 巳日乃孚。元亨利貞，悔亡。

初九： 鞏用黃牛之革。

六二： 巳日乃革之。征吉，無咎。

九三： 征凶，貞厲。革言三就，有孚。

九四： 悔亡，有孚。改命，吉。

九五： 大人虎變，未佔有孚。

上六： 君子豹變，小人革面。征凶，居貞吉。

Ding, The Cauldron

	OMEN	COUNSEL	FORTUNE
0		Your plea is heard.	Great good fortune.
1	The caldron's legs are upturned.	Now is the time to expel the bad. Take a consort to get a son.	No harm will come.
2	The caldron is full.	My enemy is ill and cannot get to me.	Good fortune.
3	The caldron sheds its ears. The plump meat of the pheasant is uneaten.	His movement will be blocked. The frontier rains will diminish.	There are problems, but good fortune in the end.
4	The caldron breaks a leg and spills the duke's stew.	His punishment will be execution.	Misfortune.
5	A caldron with yellow ears and a bronze carrying pole.	Good omen.	
6	A caldron with a jade carrying pole.		Great good fortune. All signs are favorable.

50. Ding, The Cauldron

The graph of *ding* 鼎 is a pictograph of a ritual caldron with its three (or four) legs and two handles or "ears." As with Hexagram 27, note the pattern of the hexagram symbol, where the broken lines resemble the legs and handles of the caldron, while the unbroken line at the top represents the carrying pole.

Hexagram statement: Instead of impressing gods by erecting stone monuments, the ruling houses of ancient China lavished all luxury on the ritual of ancestor worship. The bronzes cast for ceremonial reasons are the Parthenons and pyramids of Chinese culture. Among the myriad ritual bronzes—sacrificial swords, concert bells, ceremonial chariots, etc., it was the ornate caldrons, some as big as barrels, which came to represent the glory of the state. In this hexagram the *ding* is the symbol of the state.

Line 1: This omen depicts the caldron turned upside-down. This symbolizes the Shang dynasty being overthrown and its perverse king ("the bad" of the counsel) ousted. The counsel also advises the taking of a concubine in order to insure a male heir. Otherwise, the lineage will come to an end.

Line 2: This omen depicts a full caldron, symbolizing the leadership of King Wen. The ailing enemies are border-states that cannot match the military might of the rising Zhou.

Line 3: This omen depicts a caldron that has lost its handles. This symbolizes the death of King Wen before his rebellion was complete. Until his successor, King Wu, was able to regroup and seek new allies, the political and military movement halted. The rich meat of the pheasant—symbolizing the spoils of war and the glory of victory—is uneaten. The counsel informs the ancient inquirer that frontier rains will diminish. That is, border incursions will decrease.

Line 4: The omen depicts a caldron with broken legs. It symbolizes the rebellion of the three brothers of King Wu who were charged with supervising Wu Geng 武庚, the Shang prince, after the conquest. When King Wu died, his son, Cheng, was still too young to rule, so another brother was appointed regent to assist him. This was Dan 旦, better known as the Duke of Zhou, who penned these lines. It was during his regency, symbolized by the stew, that the rebellion occurred. The leader of the rebellion, Ji Xian 姬鲜, was executed; thus, the prediction of misfortune.

Line 5: This omen depicts newly cast bronze handles and a golden carrying pole for the caldron of state. Dan, better known as the Duke of Zhou, led an expedition east and suppressed a rebellion led by the Shang prince. As regent, the Duke of Zhou ruled in place of his young nephew, Cheng, King Wu's son. The new handles symbolize the duke, under whose rule peace returned to the kingdom.

Line 6: This omen depicts a caldron with a jade carrying pole. It symbolizes King Cheng, who ascended the throne seven years after his father's death. He reigned for some forty years. He is called the Accom-

plished King and his reign was one of the most peaceful in the entire history
of the Zhou dynasty.

鼎： 元吉，亨。
初六：鼎顛趾，利出否。得妾以其子，無咎。
九二：鼎有實。我仇有疾，不我能即，吉。
九三：鼎耳革，其行塞。雉膏不食，方雨虧悔，終吉。
九四：鼎折足，覆公餗。其形渥，凶。
六五：鼎黃耳金鉉，利貞。
上九：鼎玉鉉，大吉，無不利。

51

Zhen, Earthquake

	OMEN	COUNSEL	FORTUNE
0	Tremors come—"shock-shock." Laughter and gossip—"ha-ha."	Your plea is heard. The quake will alarm hundreds of villages, but not a ladle of sacrificial wine is spilled.	
1	Tremors came—"shock-shock," then there was laughter and gossip—"ha-ha."		Good fortune.
2	Tremors come—so alarming, he may lose cowry shells climbing the Nine Hills.	Do not search for them; you will get them in seven days.	
3	Tremors "shake-shake." Tremors shift.		There will be no calamity.
4	Tremors are followed by mudslides.		
5	Tremors come and go—so alarming.	There may be no loss. Perform services.	
6	Tremors "smash-smash." He looks around "blink-blink." The tremor harms his neighbor, not himself.		An attack will bring misfortune. No trouble.
		There is talk about the marriage match.	

51. Zhen, Earthquake

The graph of *zhen* 震 is composed of the element for "rain" on top and, on the bottom, a drawing of the constellation, Scorpio. The character has two meanings: a clap of thunder, and the tremor of an earthquake. Either meaning is appropriate here. However, in the hexagram statement the counsel reports that "hundreds of villages" are alarmed (or hundreds of "leagues"—the character is the same). Since the sound of thunder travels less than ten miles, it would appear a quake is described, since it can be so much more widespread.

Hexagram statement: The omen describes the fearful sound of an earthquake striking a village--*xiak-xiak* in the original dialect. But, in the aftermath, the people's terror turns to laughter and conversation. The counsel warns that hundreds of villages will be terrified, but not a ladle of sacrificial wine will be spilled at the ceremonies of propitiation conducted to ward off the evil. Clearly, the rituals succeed. The people are saved.

Line 1: The omen describes the fearful sound of an earthquake striking a village—*xiak-xiak* in the original pronunciation. But, in the aftermath, the people's terror turns to laughter and conversation. The prognostication is good fortune. If you obtain this line, what appears to be a coming disaster will pass without harm. Someone else's disaster will be your good fortune.

Line 2: The omen describes the arrival of an earthquake, which is very threatening to the inhabitants of the village. When the first tremor is felt, villagers grab their valuables and head for the burial mounds to get away from the collapsing houses and walls. On the way, someone loses strings of cowry shells (a form of money). The counsel advises against conducting a search for the lost cash. You will get it back in a matter of days.

Line 3: The omen describes the fearful sound of a tremor shaking a village—*sag-sag* in the original pronunciation. Things shift as the tremor passes. But, the prediction is that calamity will be avoided.

Line 4: The omen describes mudslides triggered by the earthquakes. There are no counsel or prognostication texts in this line. However, the prognosis is certainly threatening.

Line 5: The omen describes an earthquake followed by tremors, a threatening situation. There will be no loss incurred, but the counsel advises that sacrificial services be conducted.

Line 6: The omen describes the fearful sound of a tremor shaking a village—*sak-sak* in the original pronunciation. We see a villager glancing about anxiously. But the damage is to his neighbor's house, while his property remains unscathed. The omen portends no trouble, unless the line is used to initiate a military attack. In that case, misfortune will result. If there are those contemplating marriage, the suitability of the match will be the topic of gossip.

震：　　亨。震來虩虩，笑言啞啞。震驚百里，不喪匕鬯。

初九：震來虩虩，後笑言啞啞，吉。

六二：震來厲，億喪貝，躋於九陵，勿逐，七日得。

六三：震蘇蘇，震行，無眚。

九四：震遂泥。

六五：震往來厲，億無喪，有事。

上六：震索索，視矍矍，征凶。震不于其躬，於其鄰，無咎。
　　　婚媾有言。

52

Gen, Obstruction

	OMEN	COUNSEL	FORTUNE
0	Obstruction in the back.	It will not strike the belly. If you travel to the court, you will not see the man.	No harm will come.
1	Obstruction in the feet.	 Good omen for the long term.	No harm will come.
2	Obstruction in the legs.	It will not save the marrow. The heart is unwell.	
3	Obstruction in the waist.	Sear the loin. There will be the danger of fuming of the heart.	
4	Obstruction in the belly.		No harm will come.
5	Obstruction in the jaw.	Speech will continue.	Problems disappear.
6	Staunch the obstruction.		Good fortune.

52. Gen, Obstruction

The graph of *gen* 艮 is composed of an "eye" and the pictograph of a person turned backwards. It means "to turn the back on" or "to resist." By extension, it can mean, "to obstruct" or "obstacle." The earliest commentary on this hexagram, the *Tuan* 彖, or "Commentary on the Hexagrams," of the "Ten Wings," says that *gen* means, *zhi* 止, "to stop." The subject of this hexagram concerns illness, in particular, the malady of stoppage, blockage, or obturation. From the point of view of traditional Chinese medicine (TCM), obturation is a disorder that arises when wind, cold, and dampness penetrate the skin and block conduits of blood and *qi*, resulting in joint and bone pain or numbness. Although the concept of "conduits" may be anachronistic here, there is some likelihood that primitive precursors to such therapies as moxibustion did exist in the Zhou period since the *jianshi* 箴石, "needle stone" (the ancestor of the acupuncture needle) is attested in the *Classic of Mountains and Seas* (*Shanhaijing* 山海經, 卷 4, p. 110; Birrell, p. 56). Furthermore, the Gen hexagram opened the lost book of divination titled, *Lianshan* 連山, which is attributed to Shen Nong 神農, the Divine Husbandman. In his role as the god of agriculture, to him is ascribed the invention of the plow and swidden farming. But he is also the patron deity of Chinese medicine for his classification of the medicinal herbs and for the invention of both moxibustion and acupuncture.

Hexagram statement: In each line of this hexagram a different portion of the anatomy is blocked—the foot, the calf, the waist, the mouth, etc. In the hexagram statement, the first omen depicts an obstruction in the back, that is, the posterior portion of the body. The counsel advises that the obstruction will not extend to the front of the body, that is, the belly or the womb. A search of the court for help (perhaps a doctor) will be unsuccessful.

Line 1: This omen diagnoses obstruction in the feet. The prognosis is good, and the person with a foot obstruction has a good chance for long-term recovery.

Line 2: This omen diagnoses obstruction in the legs. Whatever treatment is attempted unfortunately will not save the marrow, causing the heart to falter. This appears to be the affliction that affected Yu the Great. See Hexagram 39, where excerpts from the *Lüshi chunqiu* accredit the lameness of Yu to bodily vital ethers that would "not flow," and the five organs of the body that were "clogged."

Line 3: This omen diagnoses obstruction in the small of the back. The treatment is searing (reading *lie* 列 with the "fire" radical: 烈), most likely something like cauterization (moxa therapy). With searing of the loin or reins (kidney) area of the back, there is the risk of *xun* 薰, or "fuming, steaming," of the superior organs—the heart in this case. *Xun* is a TCM term indicating internal "heat-evil" such as "spleen damp-heat fuming up into the lungs" (Wiseman, p. 233).

Line 4: This omen diagnoses obstruction in the belly. It is not a serious malady. The prognostication is that no harm will come.

Line 5: This omen diagnoses obstruction in the jaw. The obstruction is not serious enough to affect speaking, and the prognosis is that the malady will go away.

Line 6: This omen shows the obstruction being *dun* 敦 "staunched," that is, compressed. This is most likely some type of massage, or primitive acupressure, assuming primitive knowledge of "conduits." This treatment is the most therapeutic of the six diagnoses, since the prognosis is excellent.

艮其背，不獲其身。行其庭，不見其人，無咎。

初六：艮其趾，無咎，利永貞。

六二：艮其腓，不拯其隨，其心不快。

九三：艮其限，列其夤，厲薰心。

六四：艮其身，無咎。

六五：艮其輔，言有序，悔亡。

上九：敦艮，吉。

Jian, Progression

	OMEN	COUNSEL	FORTUNE
0		Send a girl off as a bride. Good omen.	Good fortune.
1	The wild goose advances to the bank of the river.	Dangerous for a child. There will be talk.	No harm will come.
2	The wild goose reaches an outcropping.	They eat and drink, "cronk-cronk."	Good fortune.
3	The wild goose progresses to high land.	The husband goes to war and will not return. The wife is pregnant but will not give birth. Now is the time to defend against bandits.	There will be misfortune.
4	The wild goose advances to the tree.	Perhaps you'll get your roof beams.	No harm will come.
5	The wild goose reaches the hills.	The wife will not conceive for three years. In the end no one can overcome it.	Good fortune.
6	The wild goose progresses to high land.	Its feathers can be used in the dance.	Good fortune.

53. Jian, Progression

The graph of *jian* 漸 is composed of the "water" element on the left, and a phonetic on the right. The original meaning is "to moisten, seep into." By extension, it means "gradually" (as in drop by drop), or "to advance, progress."

Hexagram statement: The subject of this hexagram is a wild goose that gradually migrates from the shore to the hilltop. Since geese mate for life, it may be a lone goose indicated here, which is a symbol of separation. The hexagram statement and various line texts make predictions regarding marriage and the married couple. Although this hexagram statement has no omen, the counsel is clear: it is a good omen for giving away the bride. Since the topic of Hexagram 54, "The Young Bride," is the marriage of Shang King Di Yi's daughter to King Wen, the omen of this hexagram statement likely refers obliquely to that event (Shaughnessy, *Before Confucius*, 21).

Line 1: This omen shows a wild goose swimming to the shore of a great river. For children, this is an omen of danger. The "talk" may be a reprimand from parents, which serves to warn the child so that danger is averted (Gao Heng; Kunst, "Notes," 53.1).

Line 2: This omen shows a wild goose hopping atop a rocky outcrop in the middle of the river. Here, a flock of migrating geese are eating and drinking contentedly. Good fortune is predicted.

Line 3: This omen shows a wild goose reaching dry land. Here, the omen is a metaphor for two ominous situations in the human realm. In the first scenario a wife is separated from her husband when he goes to war and does not return. This is a stock image in ancient Chinese poetry. The *Book of Odes* (#181) records the following poem: "The wild geese are flying;/ Suk, suk go their wings./ The soldiers are on the march;/...Sad are their wives, left all alone" 鴻雁于飛肅肅其羽之子于征...哀此鰥寡 (*Maoshi zhengyi* 毛詩正義, 卷18, "Xiaoya Tonggong zhi shi" 小雅彤弓之什, "Hong Yan" 鴻雁, p. 98; Waley, 1937: p. 118). In the second scenario the wife is separated from her unborn child. Both scenes have unhappy endings. The counsel warns those who obtain this line to bolster their defenses against those who would separate them from their possessions. The image of marauding bandits also appears in Hexagrams 3 and 4, where the "thieves" are "abducting" the wedding bride.

Line 4: This omen shows a wild goose flying over a treetop. The image of the waterfowl reaching the tree line prompts the recording of an early inquirer who probably sought trees large enough to cut down for roof beams. This may be an example of a later accretion.

Line 5: This omen shows a wild goose flying even higher to the hill. Another ominous scenario similar to those in line 3 is presented in the counsel text here. A wife is deprived of her future child when she is unable to conceive for three years. However, in this line the woman is unable to overcome her barrenness—perhaps a reference to the daughter of King Di Yi (Shaughnessy, *Before Confucius*, 21). Otherwise, the counsel refers to the hunters who are unable to bag the goose. Whichever is the case, the prognosis is good fortune.

Line 6: This omen shows a wild goose flying back to high land. When it returns, the hunter who wants its feathers to use in a sacrificial dance shoots it. This is good fortune for the hunter, and for the object of sacrifice—perhaps the married couple.

漸：　　女歸吉，利貞。

初六：鴻漸于幹，小子厲。有言，無咎。

六二：鴻漸於磐，飲食衎衎，吉。

九三：鴻漸于陸，夫征不復，婦孕不育，凶。利禦寇。

六四：鴻漸於木，或得其桷，無咎。

九五：鴻漸於陵，婦三歲不孕，終莫之勝，吉。

上九：鴻漸于陸，其羽可用為儀，吉。

54

Gui Mei, **The Young Bride**

	OMEN	COUNSEL	FORTUNE
0		No signs are favorable.	An attack will bring misfortune.
1	A maiden is given in marriage along with a younger sister. The lame can walk.		An attack will bring good fortune.
2	The weak-sighted can see.	Good omen for the man in the dark.	
3	A maiden is given in marriage along with a lady in waiting.	She will go back and return with a younger sister.	
4	The maiden given in marriage exceeds her period.	She is overdue and will return to wait.	
5	King Di Yi gave his daughter in marriage.	The sleeves of her gown will not be as fine as those of her younger sister. The moon is almost full.	Good fortune.
6	The young girl offers a basket, but it has no fruit. The young man stabs the lamb, but it does not bleed.		No signs are favorable.

54. Gui Mei, The Young Bride

The first graph, *gui* 歸, is composed of "burial mounds" on the left and a "broom" on the right. The broom is an abbreviation of the graph for "wife." The burial mounds represent the ceremony of ancestral worship. In Chinese culture the wife takes responsibility for conducting the sacrifices for her husband's ancestors. The character *gui* means the ceremony of giving a maiden in marriage. Three days after the ceremony the woman returns to her own family for a visit. Thus, the character can also mean, "to return." The second graph, *mei* 妹, means "younger sister."

Hexagram statement: The hexagram describes the marriage of a Shang princess, a daughter of King Di Yi, to Chang, Earl of the West, otherwise known as King Wen. This was the standard procedure for subduing a recalcitrant neighbor short of going to war with him. However, the hexagram texts also draw attention to an unusual aspect of the marriage. High officials were customarily married to two sisters plus one of their nieces. We know from other sources that King Wen's second wife was a Lady of Shen 有莘氏女, who was probably the mother of King Wu and the Duke of Zhou. The "younger sister" of lines 1 and 5 is the Lady of Shen.

Line 1: The omen shows Di Yi's daughter given in marriage to King Wen, along with a "younger sister" from Shen 有莘. In this context, younger sister means "younger secondary wife." The omen that "the lame will be able to walk" refers to the reversal of fortunes for the Lady of Shen, the secondary wife who became the mother of King Wu.

Line 2: The counsel of the blind gaining their eyesight refers to the reversal of fortunes for the people of Zhou. The counsel identifies this as a good omen for the man in the dark, who represents King Wen. He is called the man in the dark because he was imprisoned by Shang King Zhou Xin. After he was released, he began his rebellion against the Shang. See Hexagram 10 for a similar counsel statement.

Line 3: Di Yi's daughter is shown here being given in marriage accompanied by a *xu* 須, "lady in waiting." In the Mawangdui manuscript this character is replaced by *ru* 嬬 "concubine," which clearly indicates the secondary wife—the Lady of Shen. The counsel depicts the maiden being sent back to her home (the palace of Di Yi) before returning again with her "younger sister."

Line 4: Here, we see an image of King Wen's new bride remaining barren after an allotted amount of time. The counsel notes that the expected pregnancy is overdue and then indicates that there will be another "return," at which time all will await the secondary wife, the Lady of Shen.

Line 5: In this omen King Di Yi appears in person giving his daughter in marriage to King Wen. However, the princess is depicted as inferior to her "younger sister," the Lady of Shen. The counsel warns that "the moon is almost full," which means her period is almost up. If the Shang princess does not produce an heir, the secondary wife will become the primary wife.

Line 6: The images of this omen symbolize the barren couple. The young girl with an empty basket is the Shang princess unable to conceive. The young man sacrificing a lamb is King Wen, whose prayers for a son are unanswered. No signs are favorable for such a scenario.

歸妹：征凶，無攸利。

初九：歸妹以娣，跛能履，征吉。

九二：眇能視，利幽人之貞。

六三：歸妹以須，反歸以娣。

九四：歸妹愆期，遲歸有時。

六五：帝乙歸妹，其君之袂，不如其娣之袂良，月幾望，吉。

上六：女承筐，無實，士刲羊，無血，無攸利。

55

Feng, The Royal Capital

	OMEN	COUNSEL	FORTUNE
0	The king approaches. It is in the middle of the sun.	Your plea is heard. Do not grieve. It is appropriate.	
1		He will meet his noble counterpart. To go on a journey will be rewarded.	For a cycle of ten days at least, no harm will come.
2	The Capital in shadow, the ladle appears in the middle of the sun.	One who takes a journey will get the doubting disease. There will be captives, as if commencing.	Good fortune.
3	The Capital under a veil, stars appear in the middle of the sun.	He will break his right bow.	No harm will come.
4	The Capital in shadow, the ladle appears in the middle of the sun.	He will meet a lord of Yi.	Good fortune.
5	He comes to Shang.	There will be celebration and joy.	Good fortune.
6	His house in the Capital, in the shadow of his home. Peer through the door; it is vacant and no one is there.	For three years no one is seen.	Misfortune.

55. Feng, The Royal Capital

The graph of *feng* 豐 is a pictograph of a ritual vessel filled with grain and generally means "full" or "abundant." *Feng* was also the name of the Zhou capital founded by King Wen, which is the meaning in this hexagram (Marshall, p. 48). Minford's translation as "Citadel" is an excellent alternate (p. 736), in light of the omen of the hexagram statement. In conjunction with the location of the Zhou capital city is the ominous sighting of what are probably sunspots when the sky is sufficiently "veiled." According to Needham, haze due to dust storms would have permitted the observation of sunspots (Needham, vol. 3: pp. 411, 436). Here they are referred to as "stars" in the middle of the sun.

Hexagram statement: The omen of this hexagram statement shows King Wu approaching the *lingtai* 靈臺, his Numinous Tower, where he may properly observe celestial phenomena. Something has appeared in the middle of the sun. The counsel advises that it is appropriate not to grieve.

Line 1: The counsel predicts that King Wu will meet a noble ally. For the next week (the Shang week was ten days in length) he will be free from harm. A journey (perhaps the campaign against Shang) will be rewarded.

Line 2: The omen describes a shadow spreading over the capital city (perhaps a dust cloud from the Gobi Desert). When the brightness of the sun is obscured enough, the ladle appears in the middle of the sun. "Ladle" is the translation of *dou*, the name of the circumpolar constellation known in the West as the Bear or the Plough. Here it describes the configuration of spots on the sun. According to David Pankenier, a Chinese sunspot record for November 19, 904, uses similar language (Pankenier, 2003: p. 277). This is an appropriate time for prisoners of war to be taken, as it initiates the beginning of rebellion, for which good fortune is predicted.

Line 3: The omen describes darkness spreading over the capital city (perhaps a dust cloud from the Gobi Desert). When the brightness of the sun is obscured enough, *mei* 沫 "stars" appear in the middle of the sun. The counsel predicts that someone will break his weapon (*yougong* 右弓, borrowing the Mawangdui variant reading), rather than his *yougong* 右肱 "right arm," in this darkness. However, no further harm will occur.

Line 4: The omen describes a shadow spreading over the capital city (perhaps a dust cloud from the Gobi Desert). When the brightness of the sun is obscured enough, the ladle appears in the middle of the sun. Good fortune is predicted when King Wu meets a lord of the Eastern Yi barbarians.

Line 5: This omen shows King Wu arriving in Shang (reading *zhang* 章 as *shang* 商, according to Gao Heng; Kunst, "Notes," 55.5). Now that the king is here to vanquish the evil Zhou Xin, there is celebration and joy among the oppressed Shang people.

Line 6: The omen depicts the mourning hut of King Wu in the shadow of the palace. But the king has abandoned his hut and departed on his campaign to overthrow the king of Shang. The mourning hut by tradition is occupied for three years.

豐：　　亨，王假之。勿憂，宜。日中。
初九：遇其配主，雖旬無咎，往有尚。
六二：豐其蔀，日中見斗。往得疑疾，有孚發若，吉。
九三：豐其沛，日中見沬。折其右肱，無咎。
九四：豐其蔀，日中見斗。遇其夷主，吉。
六五：來章，有慶譽，吉。
上六：豐其屋，蔀其家，闚其戶，闃其無人。三歲不覿，凶。

56

Lü, The Traveler

	OMEN	COUNSEL	FORTUNE
0		Your minor plea is heard. Omen of good fortune for the traveler.	
1	The traveler is miserly. This is the disaster he takes on.		
2	The traveler approaches a lodge with his cherished provisions. He gains a servant boy.	Omen of good fortune.	
3	The traveler burns down his lodge and loses his servant boy.	Omen of danger.	
4	The traveler goes to settle and gets his goods and weapons.	My heart is not glad.	
5	He shoots a pheasant with one arrow, and it dies. In the end he wins honor and the mandate.		
6	A bird burns up its nest. At first the traveler laughs, but afterward he weeps.	He loses his cattle in Yi.	Misfortune.

56. Lü, The Traveler

The graph of *lü* 旅 shows men marching under a banner, and originally meant a troop of soldiers. By extension, the character means "traveler" (as in, "to troop"), or "to lodge." Based on the appearance of the Shang ancestor Wang

Hai, domesticator of livestock, in line 6, some scholars believe *lü* here means "nomad," which might have described the lifestyle of Hai's tribe (Ping Xin; Kunst, "Notes," 56.2). Wang Hai (*circa* 2000 BCE) was an early ancestor of the Shang ruling house when the Zi clan was pastoral (see line 34.5). He and his brother were pasturing their sheep and cattle in the neighboring state of Yi. In their unfortunate involvement with the Yi people, Hai lost his life and his livestock. Hai's son Wei eventually traveled to Yi and massacred the citizenry. His line endured, and the kings of Shang are descended from him.

Hexagram statement: Travel in ancient China was a difficult proposition for commoners because banditry was widespread. In far west China there would also have existed seasonal travel of nomads moving their flocks and herds.

Line 1: This omen shows the traveler courting disaster due to his penurious lifestyle. This scenario is likely a depiction of Wang Hai and his brother, Heng, who were sojourning near the land of Yi, pasturing their herds and flocks. The disaster that was soon to befall them was due to their tendency to take handouts from their neighbors.

Line 2: This omen shows the traveler arriving at a lodge clutching his possessions. At the lodge he gets a servant, probably a shepherd boy to help him take care of his flocks. Arriving safe and sound on the first leg of his journey, this is an omen of good fortune. This scenario describes Wang Hai's arrival in the land of Yi, where the king has invited him into his realm.

Line 3: This omen depicts the traveler burning down his lodge; that is, by his own negligence, his comfortable situation in the land of Yi comes to a tragic end. If it is Wang Hai depicted here, he loses his shepherd boy and his herds when he dallies with the queen and is murdered by his jealous brother (see Hexagram 23).

Line 4: This omen indicates that the traveler will no longer be a sojourner; he goes there to settle. There he has means of support as well as an axe to defend himself. This probably depicts Heng, the younger brother of Wang Hai, who conspired to murder his brother and was banished from the land of Yi. However, when he returned later to recover the tribe's lost sheep, he learned that the king and queen had forgiven him, so he stayed and continued his intemperate lifestyle. The ancient diviner who recorded this omen expressed his unhappiness with the immoral behavior of Heng.

Line 5: This omen depicts the traveler hunting. He shoots a pheasant with one arrow, and kills it, which results in honor and the throne. The hunter of this omen represents Jia Wei, the son of Wang Hai. When Hai did not return home with the cattle, his people installed Jia Wei as king. Wei crossed the river and destroyed the kingdom. His line endured, and the kings of Shang are descended from him.

Line 6: Here, the bird symbolizes the traveler of line 3 who burnt down his lodge. As we speculated in line 3, here the traveler is indeed Wang Hai, who first laughs because of his life of ease in the land of Yi, but afterward weeps because he loses his cattle. Since Hai eventually loses his life in addition to his livestock, the prognostication is misfortune.

旅：　　小亨，旅貞吉。

初六：旅瑣瑣，斯其所取災。

六二：旅即次，懷其資，得童僕，貞。

九三：旅焚其次，喪其童僕，貞厲。

九四：旅於處，得其資斧，我心不快。

六五：射雉一矢，亡。終以譽命。

上九：鳥焚其巢，旅人先笑後號咷。喪牛于易，凶。

Xun, Crouching

	OMEN	COUNSEL	FORTUNE
0		Your minor plea is heard. Now is the time to go on a journey. It is time to see the great one.	
1	He advances and then retreats.	Good omen for a warrior.	
2	He crouches at the foot of the bed.	Use a combination of scribes and diviners.	Good fortune. No harm will come.
3	He crouches, frowning.		There will be cause for regret.
4		On the hunt he will bag three kinds of game.	Problems disappear.
5		Omen of good fortune. What has a poor beginning will end well.	Problems disappear. All signs are favorable. Three days before and three days after the seventh day of the week there will be good fortune.
6	He crouches at the foot of the bed.	He will lose his goods and weapons. Omen of misfortune.	

57. Xun, Crouching

The graph of *xun* 巽 depicts two people crouching before an altar. By extension it means, "to be humble" (Gao Heng; Kunst, "Notes," 57.2).

Hexagram statement: In this hexagram text a healing ritual is being conducted. We see three pictures of the subject crouching next to the convalescent bed of the invalid. It is probably the Duke of Zhou at the deathbed of his brother, King Wu. In the hexagram statement the charge by the counsel to "see the great one" probably refers to the Grand Invocator, the imperial diviner.

Line 1: This omen shows King Wu advancing against the enemies of Zhou, and then retreating when his health deteriorates. Since the army withdraws from the battlefield, the lives of the soldiers are no longer at risk. Thus, the counsel identifies this as a good omen for the warrior.

Line 2: Here, we see the Duke of Zhou, brother of King Wu, crouching at his brother's bed. According to the *Book of Documents*, King Wu contracted an epidemic illness and was close to death. His brother placed a jade *bi* 璧 on the altar, held up his jade *gui* 圭 mace, and prayed to King Wen, Wang Ji, and Tai Wang, his three immediate ancestors, and offered his own life for that of the dying king. Then, he had his scribe record the prayer on tablets. Next, he divined using three turtles, all of which were favorable. Lastly, he consulted the oracular texts, which also indicated that the king would suffer no harm. He reported the results to King Wu. When he returned to his palace he placed the prayer tablets in a golden coffer. Only then did his elder brother's health improve. See *Shangshu* 尚書, "Zhoushu" 周書, ch. 8, "Jinteng" 金縢, p. 17; tr., Legge, vol. 3, pp. 351-61.

Line 3: After the Duke of Zhou had offered his own life in place of that of his dying brother, King Wu, the king's health improved (see line 2). However, the king suffered a relapse. This omen shows the Duke of Zhou kneeling at his brother's bed again, his brow wrinkled in anxiety.

Line 4: Here we see the nobleman successful in his hunt, and bagging three kinds of game—fish, fang, and fowl. Such prowess in the chase predicts an end to problems for the inquirer.

Line 5: King Wu died only two years after the conquest of Shang, unleashing a three-year rebellion by the Shang prince. However, with the help of his upright brother, the Duke of Zhou, the rebellion was suppressed and the young King Cheng was placed on the throne. Thus, the counsel advises that, "What has a poor beginning will end well." The prognostication text foretells good fortune "three days before and three days after the seventh day of the week" (that is, day 4 and day 10). In the Shang dynasty, on the last day of every ten-day week, the fortune of the following week would be divined. In such fashion, the king would know what days were proper for taking action. This is a remnant of that divination practice. See line 18.0.

Line 6: King Wu lay dying on his bed, when his younger brother offered a prayer to his ancestors, offering his life in place of the king's. King Wu's health improved, but later he suffered a relapse and died. This omen shows the Duke of Zhou at his brother's bed again. In the previous hexagram, at the end of his journey the traveler settles down and, as a result, gets provisions and weapons (see 56.4). The counsel of this line shows the provisions and weapons being lost by King Wu upon his death. When Wu died, his son, Cheng, was too young to ascend the throne, so the Duke of Zhou assumed regency of the kingdom. His other brothers feared that he would usurp the throne, beginning a dangerous chapter in the history of the Zhou dynasty. Thus, the line predicts misfortune.

巽：　　小亨，利有攸往，利見大人。

初六：進退，利武人之貞。

九二：巽在床下，用史巫紛若，吉，無咎。

九三：頻巽，吝。

六四：悔亡，田獲三品。

九五：貞吉，悔亡，無不利。無初有終，先庚三日，後庚三日，吉。

上九：巽在床下，喪其資斧，貞凶。

58

Dui, Discussions

	OMEN	COUNSEL	FORTUNE
0		Your plea is heard. Good omen.	
1	Reconciliation talks.		Good fortune.
2	Prisoner-of-war talks.		Good fortune. Problems disappear.
3	Pending negotiations.		Misfortune.
4	There is negotiation with Shang, but no reconciliation as yet.		With a great illness, there will be joy.
5	Prisoners at a skinning.		There will be danger.
6	Talks are extended.		

58. Dui, Discussions

The graph of *dui* 兌 has an "eight" 八 (meaning "to differentiate") over a kneeling man with a big "mouth" 兄 (meaning "to supplicate"). With the "heart" radical 悅, the character means, "pleasure," which is the standard gloss for *dui*. However, with the "word" radical 說, the character means, "to talk, explain" which is the likely context in this hexagram.

Hexagram statement: From the context of this hexagram *dui* means diplomatic "talks" or "discussions."

Line 1: Good fortune is predicted for reconciliation talks, that is, diplomatic discussions with peace as the objective.

Line 2: Good fortune is predicted for talks regarding captives, or prisoners-of-war. With an exchange or release of captives, enmity disappears.

Line 3: Those awaiting the coming negotiations will be disappointed. The prognosis for a pleasant outcome is poor.

Line 4: This omen identifies the Shang state as one party in the negotiations, but there is still no peace or reconciliation. In the meantime, the leader of one side contracts a serious illness. This would normally be an omen of misfortune. However, since this particular negotiation is that between the Shang and Zhou states, even the death of a king is merely a setback and the prognostication is excellent.

Line 5: This omen shows prisoners present at a sacrifice, where the victims are being flayed or skinned alive. Understandably, the prognostication is danger.

Line 6: This omen reports that reconciliation talks have been extended. Although no counsel or prognostication texts are available, indications are that this is a promising situation.

兑： 　亨，利貞。

初九：和兑，吉。

九二：孚兑，吉，悔亡。

六三：來兑，凶。

九四：商兑未寧，介疾有喜。

九五：孚于剝，有厲。

上六：引兑。

59

Huan, Overflow

	OMEN	COUNSEL	FORTUNE
0	The king goes to his ancestral temple.	Your plea is heard. Now is the time to cross the great river. Good omen.	
1		If this omen is used to geld a horse, it will grow strong.	There will be good fortune.
2	Spraying, it gushes over the table.		Problems disappear.
3	Pouring over their bodies.		No harm will come.
4	Swelling is the herd. Swelling, it has reached the hills.	Not what one would ordinarily expect.	Great good fortune.
5	Spurting is the liver; it squeals loudly. Flooding the king's palace.		No harm will come.
6	Overflowing is the blood.	He will depart and go far away.	No harm will come.

59. Huan, Overflow

The graph of *huan* 渙 combines the "water" element on the left with the *huan* phonetic element on the right. It means the swell of floodwaters after the spring rains and, by extension, "to disperse."

Hexagram statement: The image of overflow in this hexagram is manifested in various ways (either swelling, spraying, pouring, spurting, or flowing), depending on what is overflowing in each case. For the most part, it is the blood of sacrifice, the sustenance of choice for ancestral spirits. But some lines depict swelling floodwaters, while others picture milling herds. In this hexagram statement, the king proceeds to his ancestral temple to offer sacrifice. This is a good omen and a good time to take a journey.

Line 1: The ancient diviner who obtained this omen determined that it was an appropriate sign for gelding a horse. Any action taken by the inquirer will bring good fortune.

Line 2: This omen depicts the sacrificial victim on the altar. The spray of blood as it is cut open gushes over the table. The original sacrifice would have been conducted in order to placate the gods or seek guidance from the ancestral spirits. According to the prognostication, the problem that prompted the sacrifice will disappear.

Line 3: The spray of blood from the sacrifice in line 2 gushes over the altar and pours onto the bodies of the spectators. Since the blood is the food of the spirits, it is a consecrated liquid and, thus, will bring no harm.

Line 4: Here, we see a herd of horses milling about in the valley and swelling up the hillside like floodwaters. The ancient diviner who encountered this omen considered it an unexpected image, but one that predicted a flood of good fortune.

Line 5: In this line, the original graph *han* 汗, "sweat," is replaced with the borrowing, *gan* 肝, "liver," which occurs in the Mawangdui manuscript. The liver and heart were considered to be the seat of the soul, and were thus the organs of choice for live sacrifices. Here, we see the sacrificial knife stabbing the victim in the liver, causing the blood to spurt. The animal squeals in pain. The second omen shows floodwaters reaching the king's palace. If it is a flood of the Yellow River that is recorded here, then this is a Shang king (perhaps King Wuyi, see Hexagram 42), whose capitals were in the middle reaches of the Huang He, rather than in the Wei River valley of Mount Qi. If it is the swelling waters of the spring rains, which is an image of abundance and fertility, not of devastation, then it may be King Wu in Feng.

Line 6: The omen depicts the blood of sacrifice overflowing the altar. In this line it is an image of warning. The ancient diviner who encountered this line advised the inquirer to depart, and go far away. If you take this advice no harm will come.

渙：　　亨。王假有廟，利涉大川，利貞。

初六：用拯馬壯，吉。

九二：渙奔其機，悔亡。

六三：渙其躬，無悔。

六四：渙其群，元吉。渙有丘，匪夷所思。

九五：渙汗其大號。渙王居，無咎。

上九：渙其血，去逖出，無咎。

60

Jie, Stem Nodes

	OMEN	COUNSEL	FORTUNE
0	Bitter nodes.	Your plea is heard. Omen of disapproval.	
1	He will not go out the door into the courtyard.		No harm will come.
2	He will not go out the gate from the courtyard.		Misfortune.
3	If he is not node-like, then he will be knell-like.		No harm will come.
4	Calming nodes.	Your plea is heard.	
5	Sweet nodes.	Going on a journey will bring rewards.	Good fortune.
6	Bitter nodes.	Omen of misfortune.	Problems disappear.

60. Jie, Stem Nodes

The graph of *jie* 節 combines the "bamboo" element on top and a phonetic element on bottom. The original meaning of *jie* was a section or "joint" of bamboo or a stem "node" in other plants. By extension it meant a "regular division" or "measured, moderated." Just like Hexagram 27 Jawbones, which depicts a bone-cracking ritual, this hexagram depicts a ritual employing the jointed stalks of the yarrow, or milfoil, plant. However, in addition to counting the yarrow stem nodes, in the ritual depicted here they were apparently tasted with the prognosis based on their palatability. In particular, it was the herb's bitter or sweet quality that indicated one's fortune, in addition perhaps to its medicinal properties. Shen Nong, the Divine Husbandman, mentioned previously in relation to traditional Chinese medicine (see Hexagram 52), is said to have "savored the taste and flavor of the hundred plants and sweetness and bitterness of the streams and springs so that the people would know which to take and which to leave" (嘗百草之滋味，水泉之甘苦，令民知所辟就: *Huainan hongliejie* 淮南鴻烈解, 卷19, "Yangwuxun" 脩務訓, p. 74).

Hexagram statement: The omen of the hexagram is a yarrow node with a bitter flavor. While the bitter flavor is probably the plant's best quality (see line 6), overall, it is an omen of disapproval.

Line 1: The omen pictures a space called the *hu ting* 戶庭, or the courtyard outside the temple door. In this case, someone is not exiting the temple door to enter the courtyard. This is not perceived to be unlucky, because the temple is a safe haven.

Line 2: The omen pictures a space called the *men ting* 門庭, or the courtyard within the outer gate. In this case, someone is not exiting the outer gate of the temple compound. This is perceived to be unlucky, because the temple courtyard is a safe haven while the street outside is not.

Line 3: To be *jieruo* 節若 "node-like" is to be moderate. If someone is not node-like, then the situation will be *jieruo* 嗟若 "knell-like," or sorrowful, and the person will therefore suffer the consequences. However, in the end no harm will come.

Line 4: The yarrow plant, in addition to its use as a counting wand, is also known for its medicinal qualities, including its function as a sleep aid.

Line 5: The yarrow plant, in addition to its use as a counting wand, is also known for its medicinal qualities. The herb, when fresh, has a sweet taste.

Line 6: The yarrow plant, in addition to its use as a counting wand, is also known for its medicinal qualities. The herb, when dried, has a bitter flavor. However, the bitter flavor is probably what gives the plant its useful medicinal qualities.

節： 　亨。苦節，不可貞。

初九：不出戶庭，無咎。

九二：不出門庭，凶。

六三：不節若，則嗟若，無咎。

六四：安節，亨。
九五：甘節，吉。往有尚。
上六：苦節，貞凶，悔亡。

61

Zhong Fu, Score the Capture

	OMEN	COUNSEL	FORTUNE
0	Piglets and fishes.	Now is the time to cross the great river. Good omen.	Good fortune.
1		There will be unexpected injury and no rest.	Good fortune for the gamekeeper.
2	A crane calls. In the shade its chicks respond.	"Here is a beaker of wine. I will drink it with you."	
3	They get the enemy. Some are drumming; some are resting. Some are weeping, some singing.		
4	The moon is almost full.	One of the teamed horses bolts.	No harm will come.
5	There are captives tied up together.		No harm will come.
6	Wings flapping, it rises up to heaven.	Omen of misfortune.	

61. Zhong Fu, Score the Capture

The graph of *zhong* 中 is a circle pierced by a vertical pole. It can mean, "center," and, by extension, "to pierce the center," as in "hitting the target." The graph of *fu* 孚 depicts a "claw" or "hand" above a "child," and literally means "to hatch," or "hatchling," and by extension, the "trust" of the hatchling for its mother. If the "man" element is joined to this graph, the new word means "captives" or "the catch" (of game in a hunt). In the *Yijing* all thirty instances of the graph *fu* are missing the "man" element, yet all but one of them mean "captive" or "capture" (see line 14.5). Thus, the two graphs *zhong* and *fu* together mean, "to score the capture."

Hexagram statement: The omen here is the image of piglets and fishes, two common objects of the "catch." Coming in this hexagram, they are not domestic but wild. Bagging them is an omen of good fortune.

Line 1: The hexagram of "Score the Capture" is the ideal image for the hunt. The prognostication for this line is good fortune for the gamekeeper, the manager of the royal hunting park. Still, a plentiful catch does not mean a problem-free hunt. There will be unexpected injury and no rest for the gamekeeper.

Line 2: The image of this omen text is an appropriate representation of the original meaning of *fu*, "hatchling," noted under the hexagram name above. A derived meaning of "hatchling" is "confidence"—the fragile chicks have total trust and dependence on the hen that hatches them. Here, it is a symbol of allegiance. The counsel text continues the same image. The beaker is a bronze goblet used by the nobility for ceremonial toasts. A negotiation or alliance is being consecrated.

Line 3: This omen shows the captured enemy. Some of the captives are celebrating and singing, while others are tired and weeping. It would appear that their defeat is not a total disappointment. This may describe the warriors of Zhou Xin, who abandoned their king when the Zhou armies entered the Shang capital.

Line 4: The waxing moon represents cyclical change. One horse from a double team runs off, but it will return.

Line 5: The omen shows captives on a tether. When the raid is successful, no harm will come.

Line 6: The *hanyin* 翰音 (literally "sound of wings spread") is a sacrificial cock. The pheasant (or chicken) is not known for its flying skills. When it does fly, it is in a straight line away from trouble (see line 36.1). The image of a cock flying up to heaven is a bad omen (Rutt, p. 354). This recalls the story of Shang King Wu Ding 武丁 (r. 1324-1265 BCE), who was sacrificing to his ancestors during the first year of his reign. Unexpectedly, the pheasant victim flew up and lighted on the "ear" of the caldron (see line 50.3). This omen was taken by the shaman-priest to mean that the king's conduct was incorrect. If he did not rectify his behavior, his reign would come to an end.

中孚：豚魚吉。利涉大川，利貞。

初九：虞吉，有它不燕。

九二：鶴鳴在陰，其子和之。我有好爵，吾與爾靡之。

六三：得敵，或鼓或罷，或泣或歌。

六四：月幾望，馬匹亡，無咎。

九五：有孚攣如，無咎。

上九：翰音登於天，貞凶。

八過 62 ䷽

Xiao Guo, **The Young Surpass**

	OMEN	COUNSEL	FORTUNE
0		Your plea is heard. Good omen. Small things are possible; big things are not.	
	A flying bird leaves behind its cry.	It is not proper to go up, but proper to go down.	Great good fortune.
1	A flying bird.		With it will come misfortune.
2	He passes over his ancestor and faces his ancestress.	He will not reach his lord, but will meet his minister.	No harm will come.
3	He does not pass over but stands up to him.	So someone may injure him.	Misfortune.
4	He does not pass over, but faces him.	Going on a journey is dangerous. You must be cautious. Do not use this omen for a long-term query.	No harm will come.
5	Dark clouds are building in the west, but there is no rain.	The duke shot and bagged it in its hole.	
6	He does not meet him, but passes him by.	The flying bird, he leaves it.	Misfortune. This means disaster.

62. Xiao Guo, The Young Surpass

The graph of *xiao* 小 originally consisted of three small dots, representing "little" in number and in size. *Guo* 過 combines a phonetic element with the "walking" element to mean, "pass through, pass by," or "fault, mistake." In this hexagram *xiao* and *guo* combine to mean the young pass by or surpass the old.

Hexagram statement: Unlike Hexagram 28, "The Old Surpass," in which the old manages to survive or endure by making use of the young, in this hexagram it is the young who surpass the old. One way the young get by is in small increments. Thus, the counsel advises "Small things are possible; big things are not." Another means is by movement downward rather than upward. This is the message of the omen text: a bird flies up, but it "bequeaths" or "passes down" its sound. Thus, the counsel advises, "It is not proper to go up, but proper to go down." As long as these are the means used by the young to get by, there will be great good fortune.

Line 1: The flying bird here represents the spirit of the ancestor, which flies up to Heaven. In the hexagram statement above, the young inherited the cry of the flying bird. Since there is no cry here, there is no inheritance. This spells misfortune.

Line 2: This line depicts the actions of the son at a funeral. When a grandfather or grandmother dies, the spirit of the departed is given a permanent resting-place in a wooden tablet placed in the ancestral shrine. At the funeral a sacrifice of repose conducts the spirit from the tomb—where the bones and flesh are buried—to the shrine. During the time between the burial and the sacrifice of repose, the spirit is invited to reside temporarily in an impersonator—usually a grandchild. In this omen text the mother has just died, and the sacrifice of repose is being performed. The son quickly passes by the tablet of his father in order to face the impersonator of his mother. As he encounters her spirit, he is facing her grandchild. In other words, as he looks up to his ancestress, he is simultaneously looking down at his descendant. This was represented in line 1 as the flying bird bequeathing its cry. The counsel advises that the inquirer will not reach his lord, but will meet his minister. In other words, he will not communicate with those above, but will connect with those below.

Line 3: Here we see the son unable to ignore his deceased father—he can no longer "pass him by" as he did in line 2. His disrespect in the past has brought retaliation. The son must defend against the wrath of the father's spirit. However, it is not too late to show contrition. If he does not submit, he could be injured. Although there is no record of the death of King Wu's mother, this hexagram may describe such a funeral. The transgression implied in such a scenario would have been King Wu's failure to properly mourn his father's death when he took up arms against the Shang.

Line 4: The line begins with the prognostication that no harm will come. That is because the son is depicted in the omen as properly respecting ("facing") his ancestor. Still, encountering the ghost of the father is a frightening prospect, even if the behavior is appropriate. The ancient diviner who encountered this omen determined it would be dangerous to take a trip. Caution is called for in all actions. If your question has long-term implications, then this omen is not appropriate.

Line 5: The vassal state of Zhou was located in the west of the Shang kingdom. The storm brewing in the west represents the rebellion that originated there, eventually leading to the downfall of Shang. That the rain has yet to fall means the revolt is still in its infancy. The counsel depicts a nobleman hunting with a tethered arrow. These were used mainly for fowl to keep them from flying away with the arrow. Here we see the duke tracing his arrow to the bird's hole. The bagging of the game represents the successful conclusion of the rebellion alluded to in the omen. King Wu will eventually "bag" his quarry—Zhou Xin—in the Shang king's pleasure dome.

Line 6: Here, we see the son avoiding the father, refusing to meet him. Moreover, after capturing the flying bird, he abandons it. Not only is this the sign of misfortune, it will spell disaster.

小過： 亨，利貞，可小事，不可大事。飛鳥遺之音，不宜上，
　　　 宜　下，大吉。

初六： 飛鳥，以凶。

六二： 過其祖，遇其妣，不及其君，遇其臣，無咎。

九三： 弗過防之，從或戕之，凶。

九四： 無咎，弗過遇之，往厲，必戒，勿用永貞。

六五： 密雲不雨，自我西郊，公弋取彼在穴。

上六： 弗遇過之，飛鳥離之，凶，是謂災眚。

63

Ji Ji, Across the Stream

	OMEN	COUNSEL	FORTUNE
0		Your plea is heard. Good omen for small matters.	Good fortune in the beginning, disorder in the end.
1	His wheels are dragging. It drenches its tail.		No harm will come.
2	His wife loses her hairpiece.	Don't look for it. In seven days she will find it.	
3	The High Ancestor attacked the Land of Ghosts, and conquered it in three years.	The lowborn should not use this omen.	
4	He drenches his wadded jacket.	Be vigilant all day long.	
5	The eastern neighbor slaughtered an ox.	It will not receive as full a blessing as the western neighbor's sacrifice.	
6	It drenches its head.		Danger.

63. Ji Ji, Across the Stream

The graph of the initial *ji* 既 combines a food vessel on the left and on the right a man kneeling with his mouth open. It means, "to finish a meal" or, simply, "to complete." The graph of the second *ji* 濟 combines the "water" element on the left with a phonetic component. It means, "to ford a stream." Together, the two characters mean "already across the stream." Edward Shaughnessy believes that this hexagram symbolizes the Shang state, whose king, Wu Ding, is referenced in line 3. In other words, the country is past its prime and is in decline ("Composition," pp. 263-4).

Hexagram statement: This hexagram describes the fording of a stream. In ancient China bridges were rare. When streams had to be crossed, it was necessary to find a shallow location, usually a sandbar, to enable the traveler to wade across. Here, the stream has already been crossed, although not without mishap. The counsel advises you to focus only on minor questions, not major life decisions. The crossing of the stream, while only a minor step in the journey, is a fortunate one. It is likely that confusion will increase as the journey progresses.

Line 1: Here, we see the nobleman's carriage wheels leaving a trail in the mud as its team of horses drags it out of a sandbar. Similarly, we see a fox wetting its tail as it loses its footing or falls into a hole when it misjudges the depth of water. Neither scenario is deadly. The prediction is that no harm will come.

Line 2: When the carriage was trapped in the sandbar, its passengers were soaked. In the process the nobleman's wife lost her hairpiece when the water carried it down the stream. The counsel advises not to go looking for it. Seven days later the ornament will turn up of its own accord. If you obtain this line, don't worry if there is a slight setback in your journey. You will recover the lost ground in a week's time.

Line 3: *Gao Zong* 高宗 "High Ancestor" was the posthumous title of Shang King Wu Ding, who reigned 1324-1266 BCE. This omen text records his three-year long campaign against Guifang 鬼方, or Ghost-land, a barbarian state in the arid plateau above the Fen River 汾水 (in present day northern Shanxi). Records of conflict between this state and both Shang and Zhou armies abound. In such battles the infantry did most of the fighting, while the nobles directed the combat from their chariots. This is not a good omen for the lowborn.

Line 4: When the carriage was trapped in the sandbar trying to cross the stream, its passengers were soaked. In the process the nobleman's wadded silk jacket was drenched (reading *ru* 濡 with the "water" radical for the same character with the "silk" radical, 繻, according to Gao Heng). The counsel warns the inquirer to be cautious the remainder of the day.

Line 5: This omen shows two neighbors conducting sacrifices. The eastern neighbor slaughters an ox, the ultimate sacrificial victim. We assume the western neighbor's sacrifice is not as lavish. However, the western neighbor receives more blessings than the eastern neighbors. This symbolizes the favor from Heaven accorded to the Zhou people, whose homeland was in the west, as opposed to the Shang people who resided in the east.

Line 6: This omen depicts a fox (or a man) that is completely submerged as it attempts to ford the stream. In ancient societies people in general could not swim, so an accident like this was very dangerous.

既濟：亨，小利貞，初吉終亂。

初九：曳其輪，濡其尾，無咎。

六二：婦喪其茀，勿逐，七日得。

九三：高宗伐鬼方，三年克之，小人勿用。

六四：繻有衣袽，終日戒。

九五：東鄰殺牛，不如西鄰之禴祭，實受其福。

上六：濡其首，厲。

64

Wei Ji, Not Yet Across the Stream

	OMEN	COUNSEL	FORTUNE
0	Just when crossing the stream the kit fox drenches its tail.	Your plea is heard. No signs are favorable.	
1	It drenches its tail.		There will be regret.
2	His wheels are dragging.	Omen of good fortune.	
3	He is not yet across the stream.	Now is the time to cross the great river.	An attack will bring misfortune.
4	Zhen used this omen to attack the Land of Ghosts. In three years he was rewarded in the great state.	Omen of good fortune.	Problems disappear.
5	It is glory for the nobleman.	Omen of good fortune. There will be captives.	There will be no problems. Good fortune.
6	There is a capture of those who go drinking wine. It drenches its head.	The captives will lose this.	No harm will come.

64. Wei Ji, Not Yet Across the Stream

The graph of *wei* 未 is a pictograph of a plant, and was originally a number, the eighth of the cycle of twelve numbers called the Earth Branches. It was borrowed early on to mean "not yet." *Ji* combines the "water" element with a phonetic component, and means, "to ford a stream." Together, the two characters mean "not yet across the stream." Edward Shaughnessy believes that this hexagram symbolizes the Zhou realm, whose leader, Ji Li, is referenced in line 4. In other words, their people are on the rise and their fortunes will eventually supersede those of their neighbors to the east ("Composition," pp. 263-4).

Hexagram statement: This hexagram describes the fording of a stream. In ancient China bridges were rare, so when streams had to be crossed it was necessary to find a shallow location, usually a sandbar, to enable the traveler to wade across. The fox has a long, bushy tail that trails as it scurries along. When it wades across water, however, the fox raises its tail because a wet tail will drag it down. In this picture, the inexperience of the fox causes it to fail in its attempt to stay dry. No signs are favorable for such a failed crossing. When the fox wets its tail in the middle of the stream, the chance is great that it will drown.

Line 1: The omen describes a young fox drenching its tail just in the process of crossing the stream. Since the fox's tail is long and bushy, wetting it in the middle of the stream will make crossing dangerous. Such an accident might be cause for regret.

Line 2: Here, we see the nobleman's carriage wheels leaving a trail in the mud as its team of horses drags it across a sandbar. This is the human version of the animal tale of line 1.

Line 3: This omen shows the nobleman crossing the stream, but not yet across. In such a precarious position it would be unwise to initiate new actions, especially something as dangerous as a military attack. However, the experience gained from crossing a stream will be advantageous in the crossing of the great river.

Line 4: This omen text records the three-year long campaign conducted against Guifang 鬼方, or Ghost-land, some 150 years before the founding of the Zhou dynasty (see line 63.3). According to the omen, a warrior named Zhen 震 used this omen to launch the attack. At the completion of the campaign he was rewarded in the great state of Shang. Although history has no record of this warrior, the fact that he appears in this text is a good indication that Zhen (the Thunderbolt) was a Zhou ancestor. Shaughnessy ("Composition," 263) believes Zhen is Zhou duke Ji Li who is known to have fought the Gui Rong 鬼戎 (*rong* is a name for non-Chinese tribes) during the last year of the reign of Shang King Wu Yi 武乙 (died 1123 BCE). According to the *Bamboo Annals*, this king was frightened to death by a *zhen* thunderbolt in the same year that Ji Li conquered the Ghost people (*Zhushu jinian* 竹書紀年, 卷上, "Di Yi" 帝乙, p. 65).

Line 5: The line text begins with the counsel declaring this to be an omen of good fortune. Then the omen praises the glory of the nobleman. It is the warrior of line 4 who is depicted. The *Bamboo Annals* recorded that Ji Li received "30 *li* of ground, ten pairs of gems, and ten horses [from Shang King Wu Yi]" 賜地三十里玉十穀馬十匹 (*Zhushu jinian* 竹書紀年, "Di Yi" 帝乙, 卷上, p. 65; Legge, *Chinese Classics,* vol. 3: "Prolegomena," p. 138). The counsel declares there will be captives. Indeed, although it is not recorded how many prisoners were taken in this particular campaign, in one early Zhou battle over 13,000 enemy soldiers were captured.

Line 6: The Shang nobility were known to be fond of drinking. The founders of the Zhou dynasty considered drunkenness to be one of the reasons for the Shang loss of mandate, so they prohibited it. Those caught drinking were to be put to death, according to *Jiu Gao* 酒誥 "The Announcement About Drunkenness" in the *Book of Documents*. The omen of this line reports the capture of those who *yin jiu* 飲酒 "drink the wine." The second omen repeats the omen of line 63.6, "It drenches its head." It literally describes a fox (or a man) that is completely submerged as it attempts to ford the stream. But the expression eventually gained the meaning "very drunk," probably because of its association with *yin jiu* in this line text. The counsel warns that "the captives will lose this," which probably pertains to Shang captives, who were to be treated more leniently, according to the "Announcement." In other words, they would lose their wine and keep their heads.

未濟：亨，小狐汔濟，濡其尾，無攸利。

初六：濡其尾，吝。

九二：曳其輪，貞吉。

六三：未濟，征凶。利涉大川。

九四：貞吉，悔亡。震用伐鬼方，三年有賞於大國。

六五：貞吉，無悔。君子之光，有孚，吉。

上九：有孚於飲酒，無咎。濡其首，有孚失是。

Part 3. Practical Applications

3.1 Casting the *Yijing*

3.1.1 Preparing for the Ritual

In chapter 2 we saw a re-enactment of an oracle bone ritual. Doubtlessly, a ceremony just as rich with religious symbolism was conducted when the milfoil oracle was consulted in ancient times. But no records survive of such rituals. Some of the religious significance of the *Zhouyi* was certainly lost over the Zhou dynasty, especially the terminology of worship and sacrifice borrowed from the older form of divination. But that does not mean what eventually became the *Classic of Changes* was any less respected or revered. That is the point one should keep in mind when preparing to consult this ancient text.

The reader is encouraged to ponder the role of sacred texts in contemporary society. Those raised in Judeo-Christian, Muslim, or Buddhist households probably learned at an early age that their parents paid great respect to the book that recorded the sacred words of God or the Buddha. The *Yijing* is no less a record. At the very least, it records the words of the venerable ancestors of one of the greatest dynasties in the history of China. For this reason, it is natural that the same honor should be accorded to the sacred words of other cultures as is given to the Bible and Koran and Buddhist Sutras.

One way to pay respect is for the contemporary diviner to create a ritual space in which to cast the *Yijing*. Some diviners prefer to carry a portion of that space wherever they carry their book by wrapping it in a cloth that represents sanctuary and reverence. A good choice would be a silk scarf large enough to spread out like a prayer mat, but small enough to wrap the book in when it's not in use. The Chinese believe a person's fate is not carved in stone—it can be changed by a person's actions in the present. So every family owns a *lishu* 曆書, or almanac, which is consulted for the more commonplace questions faced in one's life. The *Yijing* is reserved for more important questions—those that will impact life for years.

If faced with a quandary—a situation where doubt about the proper path to take renders a person unable to act—then the *Yijing* is the proper consultant. Take out the *Yijing* from its place of respect. Choose a surrounding conducive to meditation, where nothing in view will be a distraction. Unwrap the *Yijing* from its silk bundle, and take the scarf or cloth and spread it out on a flat surface. Then place the book in the center of the cloth and put the casting paraphernalia to either side. Close the eyes and clear the mind. This is the most important aspect of the ritual for those who believe the *Yijing* has numinous powers. In many religions such mental clarity is called prayer or meditation. Such an attitude is an ideal one to bring to a consulting session. On the other hand, those who choose not to see the *Yijing* as a sacred oracle (which is also a valid viewpoint), rely on the power of the human mind. To realize the full potential of the mind we must reduce the clutter of thoughts that normally occupy conscious thinking and thereby open up the resources of the subconscious.

3.1.2 Formulating the Question

In the re-enactment of an oracle bone ritual we learned the charge given to the gods or spirits was a statement of what the diviner thought may or may not happen. It was something like a true or false question. When the diviner read the bone, he determined whether the answer was yes or no. Such a system of questioning was required for an oracle that could not answer in words and sentences. The *Yijing*, on the other hand, is not so constrained. Containing over 8000 words in some 1500 sentences (in English translation), the book is capable of answering questions in surprising detail. It is therefore appropriate to ask questions that demand specific answers. The yes/no question should be avoided, because the statements of the hexagram and line texts are difficult to narrow down to such either/or simplicity. Instead, ask questions which demand specific answers. Ask what, why, and how questions, and it will be easier to interpret the hexagram or line statement.

While it is not possible to create a template or formula of the perfect question, it is possible to generalize somewhat. Limit the subject of the question to proposed actions, if at all possible. Questions about specific actions tend to be focused. A vague question will get a vague answer. The structure of the question is also essential.

1. Instead of asking if such and such will happen (which is a yes/no question), ask "what" or "what if" questions, or "how" or "why" questions.

2. Avoid specific "when" or "where" questions. Instead, put a time or space limit into a "what" or "why" question.

3.1.3 How to Cast the Milfoil

When the question has been properly formulated, record it in a journal kept just for this purpose. Write down the current date and then the question, before beginning the cast. There are two different ways to cast the *Yijing*—the counting of milfoil lots, which is the traditional method, and the coin tossing method, which is more popular. The traditional stalk casting ritual will be outlined first.

Milfoil, or yarrow, is an ornamental flowering herb available as a dried cutting. The stalks of the milfoil are long and straight with fern-like leaves and a cluster of white or yellow flowers at the top. Obtain a count of 50 and cut them all to an equal length of ten inches and locate a container in which to store them.

With the formulated question in mind, unwrap your *Yijing*, spread out the ritual cloth, and place the book in the center. Then, remove the 50 stalks from the stalk container. Put one stalk back into the container and set it aside. Although the ritual must begin with 50 stalks, only 49 are used for counting. The following 14 steps are required for Lot 1 of the six-lot procedure:

Step 1. Separate the 49 stalks into two similar bunches, and place one on either side of your *Yijing*.

Step 2. Beginning with the right bunch, take one stalk and place it between the little finger and ring finger of the left hand.

Step 3. Count off the remainder of the right bunch by fours until there are only 1, 2, 3, or 4 stalks left. Place this remainder between the ring finger and the middle finger of the left hand.

Step 4. Move to the left bunch and count off by fours until only 1, 2, 3, or 4 remain. Place this remainder between the middle finger and the index finger of the left hand. In the left hand now will be a total of either 5 or 9 stalks. Place these on top of the book.

Step 5. Now pick up the stalks that were counted off by fours and bunch them together again (there will be a total of either 40 or 44 stalks). Separate them into two similar piles and place one on either side of the *Yijing*.

Step 6. Beginning with the right bunch, take one stalk and place it between the little finger and ring finger of the left hand.

Step 7. Count off the remainder of the right bunch by fours until there are only 1, 2, 3, or 4 stalks left. Place this remainder between the ring finger and the middle finger of the left hand.

Step 8. Move to the left bunch and count off by fours until only 1, 2, 3, or 4 remain. Place this remainder between the middle finger and the index finger of the left hand. In the left hand will now be a total of either 4 or 8 stalks. Place these on top of the book.

Step 9. Now pick up the stalks counted off by fours and bunch them together again (there will be a total of either 32, 36, or 40 stalks). Separate them into two similar piles and place one on either side of the *Yijing*.

Step 10. Beginning with the right bunch, take one stalk and place it between the little finger and ring finger of the left hand.

Step 11. Count off the remainder of the right bunch by fours until there are only 1, 2, 3, or 4 stalks left. Place this remainder between the ring finger and the middle finger of the left hand.

Step 12. Move to the left bunch and count off by fours until only 1, 2, 3, or 4 remain. Place this remainder between the middle finger and the index finger of the left hand. In the left hand will now be a total of either 4 or 8 stalks. Place these on top of the book.

Step 13. Now pick up the stalks counted off by fours, bunch them together again, and count them (there will be a total of either 24, 28, 32, or 36 stalks). Divide this number by 4. The answer will be 6, 7, 8, or 9.

Step 14. The possible outcomes and their corresponding lines are as follows:

28 / 4 = 7, the number of **young** *yang*
32 / 4 = 8, the number of **young** *yin*
36 / 4 = 9, the number of **old** *yang*
24 / 4 = 6, the number of **old** *yin*

Record the line as indicated. This is the conclusion of Lot 1. Begin from the lowest line of the hexagram and move upward as lots are cast.

Repeat steps 1 through 14 five more times, in each case recording the line obtained in the journal. When finished with all six lots, a hexagram will be the outcome, which will then correspond to a chapter of the *Yijing*.

3.1.4 How to Cast the Coin Oracle

The stalk oracle is a complex and time-consuming procedure. When manipulating the stalks of the milfoil the person will come closest to reproducing the ritual as it was conducted thousands of years ago. However, in the fast-paced modern world many people will not have an hour or two to dedicate to a casting ceremony. The Chinese themselves developed their own simpler techniques that utilize coins instead of stalks, which are outlined below—one in use since the Song dynasty (960-1126), and another in use among contemporary fortune-tellers in Hong Kong.

3.1.4.1 The Coin Tossing Method

To utilize this system all that is needed is three coins of the same denomination. For this casting technique cup the hands around the three coins and shake, then throw them onto the ritual cloth. Record the throws in heads and tails obtained. As the coins are cast, record each line in the journal using the symbols shown in table 7. Line 1 is at the bottom of the hexagram, and with each succeeding throw move upward until six lines are obtained. There are only four possible outcomes for each individual throw, as indicated below:

Table 7. How to record the coin toss.

3 heads	**old** *yang*	—o—
2 heads, 1 tail	**young** *yang*	——
2 tails, 1 head	**young** *yin*	▬ ▬
3 tails	**old** *yin*	—x—

The term **young** is used to describe the hexagram line that does not change. The term **old** describes the line that will change into its opposite and form the second hexagram of a casting session. Thus, **old** *yang* will change into an *yin* line, and **old** *yin* will change into a *yang* line. Throw the three coins a total of six times, and each throw will produce one line of the hexagram. When finished, proceed to the text of the *Yijing*.

All methods for casting the *Yijing* are based on random number generation. The ancient diviners realized the only way to insure the king was not skewing the answer to his question was to seek complete randomness in the oracular response. The more complex the casting technique, the more likely there was no cheating involved. However, the various techniques commonly employed today result in different probabilities for particular lines. For example, the stalk-casting method returns a *young yin* (non-changing broken line) 7 times out of 16, and a *young yang* (non-changing solid line) 5 times out of 16. It returns an *old yang* (changing solid line) 3 times out of 16, and an *old yin* (changing broken line) 1 time out of 16. With the coin tossing method just discussed, the chances of getting either of the non-changing lines is 6 out of 16, whereas the chances of getting either of the changing lines is 2 out of 16. For those who believe the oracle taps into the realm of spirits, probabilities should not be of any great concern. Those with a more philosophical approach to the classic may prefer the yarrow stalk method, because of its purported antiquity. For those with neither of these concerns, the following system may be the most appropriate.

3.1.4.2 The Baqian System

Baqian 八錢 means "eight coins." To utilize this system a small container to store the coins is required, which can also double as a shaker. Choose eight coins of the same denomination, one of which must be marked to distinguish it easily from the others. To cast with *Baqian*, the Pre-Heaven sequence of the *bagua*, or eight trigrams, will be used, as seen in figure 16:

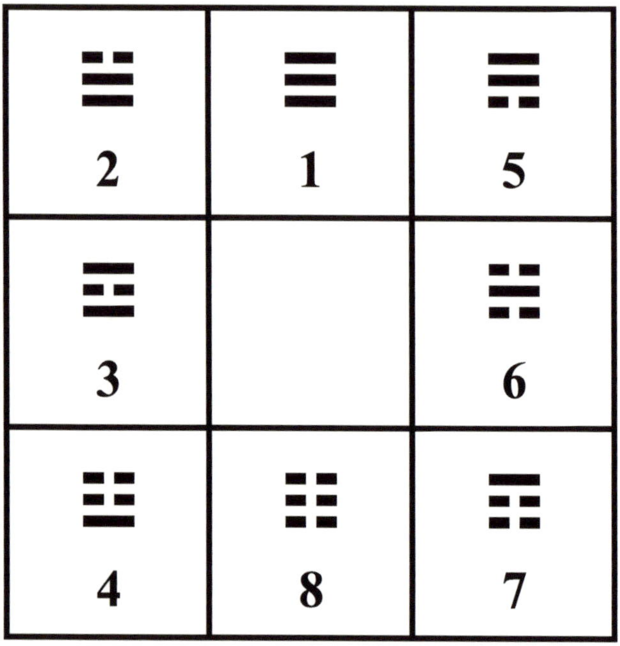

Illustration 16. The Pre-Heaven Sequence of *Bagua* with Numbers

The following steps are required for Lot 1 of the three lot procedure:

> **Step 1.** With all eight coins in the container, shake to mix thoroughly. Then remove one coin and place in on the Heaven trigram, numbered 1 in the figure.
>
> **Step 2.** Shake again, then remove another coin and place it on the Lake trigram, numbered 2.
>
> **Step 3.** Shake again, then remove another coin and place it on the Fire trigram, numbered 3.

Step 4. Shake again, then remove another coin and place it on the Thunder trigram, numbered 4.

Step 5. Shake again, then remove another coin and place it on the Wood trigram, numbered 5.

Step 6. Shake again, then remove another coin and place it on the Water trigram, numbered 6.

Step 7. Shake again, then remove another coin and place it on the Mountain trigram, numbered 7.

Step 8. Shake again, then remove another coin and place it on the Earth trigram, numbered 8.

Stop whenever the marked coin has been removed. The trigram chosen by the marked coin of Lot 1 will be the lower trigram in the hexagram. Draw this trigram in the journal.

Return the coins to the container and repeat the procedure for Lot 2. The trigram chosen by the marked coin of Lot 2 will be the upper trigram in the hexagram. Draw this trigram in the journal above the one derived in Lot 1.

For Lot 3, begin with the hexagram obtained from Lots 1 and 2 above. Return only six coins to the shaking container, including the marked coin.

Step 1. Shake to mix thoroughly. Then Remove one coin and place it on the bottom line of the hexagram.

Step 2. Shake again. Then remove one coin and place it on the second line from the bottom of the hexagram.

Step 3. Shake again. Then remove one coin and place it on the third line from the bottom of the hexagram.

Step 4. Shake again. Then remove one coin and place it on the fourth line from the bottom of the hexagram.

Step 5. Shake again. Then remove one coin and place it on the fifth line from the bottom of the hexagram.

Step 6. Shake again. Then remove one coin and place it on the top line of the hexagram.

Stop whenever the marked coin has been removed. The line chosen by the marked coin of Lot 3 will be the "changing line" of the hexagram. Record this line in the journal by drawing a small circle in the center of the line if it is a solid, *yang* line, or by drawing an X between the broken pieces of an *yin* line.

3.2 How to Interpret a Reading

In this chapter we will discuss how to proceed from the hexagram cast to the omen, counsel, and prognostication texts of the *Yijing*. In the last chapter we learned three different methods of casting. Regardless of which method chosen, in all cases a six-line hexagram will be obtained which is made up of two trigrams, one on top of the other. To find out which hexagram has been cast, look for the two trigrams on the Hexagram Location Chart on the last page of this book. Upper trigrams are located in the top row, and lower trigrams are located in the first column. Once the trigrams have been found, move down the column from the upper trigram and across the row from the lower trigram. Where they meet is a number from 1 to 64. This is the hexagram number.

We have learned that the *yi* of the *Zhouyi* probably came from the "changing" line of the hexagram. In the record of milfoil divination, each cast produced one hexagram changing into another. In the terminology of the "Ten Wings," it is the age of the line that determines its potential. Young lines maintain their original nature, while the old lines change into their opposites.

King Wen combined the eight trigrams to create the 64 hexagrams, and then attached to each one a statement called a *guaci* to explain its meaning. The Duke of Zhou attached an additional statement called a *yaoci* to each of the six lines of the hexagram. Thus, there are seven lines of text attached to each hexagram—one general *hexagram statement*, and six specific *line statements*.

Possibility 1. No lines change. It is possible that none of the six lines will be old. If no lines are old—that is, if none of them are changing—then the guaci, or original hexagram statement, is the proper oracle. The line texts should not be read.

Possibility 2. One line changes. If one line is old—that is, if only one of them is changing, then that single yaoci, or line text, of the original hexagram is the oracle. Do not read the guaci hexagram statement or any other line statements.

Possibility 3. Two to five lines change. If two, three, four, or five lines out of the six are old, then these lines change into their opposite, and a new hexagram is formed. The guaci hexagram statement of both hexagrams is the oracle. Usually the situation of the first hexagram is seen to change into that of the second. None of the yaoci line texts of either hexagram is taken into account.

Possibility 4. All lines change. It is conceivable, although rare, that all six lines obtained will be old yang or old yin. That means all six lines of the hexagram will change. Except for the two cases mentioned below, when all lines change the oracle is the guaci hexagram statement of the second, or changed, hexagram. The two exceptions are Hexagram 1 (all yang lines) and Hexagram 2 (all yin lines). Each of these hexagrams includes a special "Line 7." Therefore, if the cast is all old yang lines or old yin lines, then line 7 is the oracle.

These four possibilities are more or less likely to be obtained, depending on which casting method is used. The *Baqian* method always returns one and only one changing line. So if that system is used, Possibility 2 will always be encountered. If the stalk-casting method is used, it is common to obtain no changing lines at all. So if that system is used, Possibility 1 will often be encountered. Finally, when using the three-coin toss, it is uncommon that no changing lines are obtained. More than one changing line is common. So users of this method will often encounter Possibility 3.

The choice of casting method may depend on which of the four possibilities is preferred. If one is content with receiving only one *hexagram statement*, use the stalk method. If one prefers to base the consultation on a single *line text*, then use the *Baqian* system. If two *hexagram statements* are preferred, one from the original hexagram and one from the changed hexagram forming a "before and after" scenario, then the three-coin toss is the best choice.

Glossary

Attack 征 (*zheng*). To send the military on an punitive expedition against an enemy or recalcitrant tribe.

Counsel. Signs from nature are rarely intelligible to the untrained individual, so they must be interpreted by sages. Such interpretation is called a counsel. In the *Yijing*, the counsel originated as a diviner's clarification of the omen text he encountered. Normally a connection can be seen between the two. For example, line 2.1a (the omen) says, "Frost is underfoot," while line 2.1b (the counsel) says, "A hard freeze is coming." It is the duty of the inquirer to intuit a connection if one is not apparent, and to interpret both the omen and the counsel from the inquirer's own particular standpoint.

Crossing the great river 涉大川. In ancient China bridges were rare. When rivers had to be crossed primitive barges were used, which were easily swamped in the swift and deep waters. So fording was a perilous activity. In the *Yijing* crossing a great river symbolizes undertaking hazardous enterprises, for which one may encounter great difficulties.

Di Yi 帝乙. Second to the last ruler of the Shang dynasty and father of Zhou Xin, Di Yi is mentioned in the *Yijing* because he married his sister to Chang, the ruler of the vassal state of Zhou. Chang eventually overthrew Zhou Xin and became King Wen of Zhou.

Duke of Zhou 周公. Born Ji Dan, in 1085 BCE, the fourth son of King Wen, he was given the title, Zhou Gong, or the Duke of Zhou, when he founded the eastern capital, Cheng Zhou (modern Luoyang). When his elder brother, King Wu, died only two years after founding the Zhou dynasty, Zhou Gong ruled as regent until his nephew, King Cheng, was old enough to take the throne.

Explaining the *Gua* (Trigrams) 說卦傳. The *Shuogua*, or "Explaining the Trigrams" commentary of the "Ten Wings," discusses the eight trigrams, and expands each of the general trigram categories into as many as twenty distinct terms. A Table of Trigram Attributes that organizes the data from the *Shuogua* commentary is provided in chapter 1.4.

Good fortune. See *Ji*.

Good omen 利貞. Literally "favorable divination," but in the context of the hexagram or line statement, the phrase normally means that the omen prompts a determination of good fortune.

Grand Invocator 太祝. The royal diviner, whose duties were to lead the crack-making and stalk-casting ceremonies. The Grand Invocator interpreted the omens in conjunction with the king. The counsel texts often appear to originate from him.

Great one 大人. Usually a sage, or man of wisdom, from whom to seek advice. In several instances the great one is the Grand Invocator, or royal diviner. On other occasions he is the king.

Great river. See *Crossing the great river*.

Guaci 卦辭. The statement attached to each hexagram by King Wen, according to legend. It is usually composed of three parts—the omen, a counsel that interprets the omen, and a prognostication of good or bad fortune. When referring to the *guaci* by number in this book, they are given the number "0" to distinguish them from the *yaoci* line texts, which are numbered 1-6. For example, 12.0 is the *guaci* of Hexagram 12, whereas 12.4 is line 4 of the same hexagram. If necessary, omen, counsel, and prognostication portions of individual lines are designated by a, b, and c.

Harm 咎 (*jiu*). A prognosticatory formula indicating minor misfortune—usually appearing in the negative, such as line 9.4c: "No harm will come."

Heng 亨. A counsel statement indicationg that "Your plea is heard." In the *Yijing* it records the establishment of a link between the diviner and the ancestral spirit through an initial sacrifice or between the inquirer and the oracle through the casting of yarrow stalks.

Hexagram statement. Also called "judgment"; see *Guaci*.

Hui 悔. A prognosticatory formula indicating a problem—usually a minor misfortune that is beyond someone's control. In the context of the line text, this formula often appears in negative form: "There will be no problems."

Jiu 咎. A prognosticatory formula indicating minor misfortune, usually appearing in negative form, i.e., "There will be no harm." See *Wu jiu*.

Journey 往. Travel was perilous in ancient China because of bandits and wild animals (especially tigers), and because river-crossing was so difficult. So, embarking on a journey was a major undertaking. In the *Yijing*, going on a journey symbolizes making difficult decisions and the willingness to change directions in one's life.

Ji 吉. A prognosticatory formula indicating that an action undertaken according to the counsel would be auspicious and result in good fortune.

Junzi 君子. See *Nobleman*.

King Wen 文王. Born Chang 昌, of the House of Ji, he became the ruler of the vassal state of Zhou in 1099 BCE, during Di Yi's reign. Eventually, he was named Chief of the West—ruler of the western states—by Zhou Xin, the last king of Shang. Chang initiated the rebellion against the Shang, but died in 1050. His son overthrew Zhou Xin in 1046 and named his father, King Wen, posthumous founder of the Zhou dynasty.

King Wu 武王. Born Fa 發, of the House of Ji, in 1095 BCE, he inherited the position of Chief of the West upon his father's death. He continued the rebellion begun by King Wen, succeeding in 1046, when he was named King Wu. He died unexpectedly in 1043, and was succeeded by his son, Cheng.

Li 利. A counsel formula indicating "advantageous" or "favorable," but in the context of the hexagram or line statement, this term is usually translated "good for (something)," or "now is the time to (do something)."

Li 厲. A counsel formula indicating danger. See, for example, line 1.3b.

Li zhen 利貞. A counsel formula meaning "favorable divination." In context the phrase normally indicates that the omen of a given line text indicates a determination of good fortune. See, for example, line 1.0b.

Lin 吝. A prognosticatory formula indicating minor humiliation or regret. See, for example, line 4.4c.

Line text. See *Yaoci*.

Lowborn 小人. Literally "little men" or "lesser men," the lowborn consisted of all those not considered noble or aristocratic—farmers, artisans, foot soldiers, and merchants.

Mawangdui 馬王堆. The oldest manuscript of the *Yijing* was discovered in a tomb dating from the 2nd century BCE. It is called the Mawangdui version, after the village where the tomb was located.

Misfortune. See *xiong*.

Nobleman 君子. Literally "sons of rulers," the term *junzi* was first used to designate the hereditary noblemen, consisting of the king and the landed gentry. By the time of Confucius the *junzi* was the "gentleman," a man who pursued the moral path. There is no indication the latter use is ever indicated in the lines of the original *Zhouyi*.

Omen 貞 (*zhen*). In divination by augury, an omen is a sign from nature that is interpreted by the diviner to be ominous. In divination by oracle bones the omen is the image intuited by the diviner from the shape of the crack. In the *Yijing* the omen is a record of some natural phenomenon or human action that prompted a determination of good or bad fortune in the life of the oracle's author. When a hexagram is cast, the omen obtained mirrors the situation of the inquirer.

Problems 悔 (*hui*). A prognosticatory formula indicating a minor misfortune that is usually beyond someone's control. See, for example, line 1.6c.

Prognostication. The prognostication is the prediction—like a prognosis, of good or bad fortune in the future. Action based on the advice of the counsel texts will result in the fortune expressed in the prognostication.

Regret 吝 (*lin*). A prognosticatory formula indicating minor humiliation. If one recognizes that the path is in error and subsequently changes directions, good fortune can still be achieved.

Shang Di 上帝. Shang Di was the principle deity of the Shang Chinese, who ruled over all other gods, including the spirits of the ancestors.

Sheng 眚. A prognosticatory formula indicating calamity or disaster. See, for example, 6.2c.

Shuowen jiezi 說文解字, or *Explaining the Characters.* China's oldest dictionary, compiled in 100 CE.

Use/Do not use this omen 用/勿用. Advice from the ancient diviners who had determined specific uses for particular omens. Equivalent to "act" or "do not act."

Wujiu 無咎. A prognosticatory formula indicating that no harm will come. Actions that would normally result in harm do not do so here. Often it is because mistakes one has made were corrected, or improper directions one has taken were changed due to the advice of the counsel.

Xiong 凶. A prognosticatory formula indicating misfortune.

Yaoci 爻辭. The text attached to each line by the Duke of Zhou, according to legend. It is usually composed of three parts—the omen, a counsel that interprets the omen, and a prognostication of good or bad fortune. In the commentaries that follow the hexagram tables, the *yaoci* are given the numbers 1 through 6. For example, 12.4 is line 4 of Hexagram 12, whereas 12.0 is the *guaci* of the same hexagram.

Your plea is heard. See *Heng.*

Zheng 征. To field troops against. See, for example, line 15.6b. See *Attack.*

Zhou Xin 紂辛. Also known as Shou 受, Zhou Xin, son of Di Yi, became king of Shang in 1078 BCE. An intelligent, strong and talented prince, when he ascended the throne, he became ostentatious, greedy, and cruel. He was overthrown by Wu, second king of Zhou.

Bibliography

1. Primary Sources

Baihu tong 白虎通. Ban Gu 班固 (Eastern Han dynasty), ed. *Baihu tong delun* 白虎通德論: 10卷. In *Sibu congkan chupian* 四部叢刊初編, vols. 431-432. Reprint. Shanghai: Shangwu yinshuguan, 1922.

Chuci 楚辭. Wang Yi 王逸 (Eastern Han dynasty), ed. *Chuci zhangju* 楚辭章句. Hong Xingzu 洪興祖 (Song dynasty), ed. *Chuci buzhu* 楚辭補注. In *Sibu congkan chupian* 四部叢刊初編, vols. 577-581. Reprint. Shanghai: Shangwu yinshuguan, 1922.

Chunqiu Zuozhuan zhengyi 春秋左傳正義. Du Yu 杜預 (Jin dynasty), ed. 孔穎達 Kong Yingda (Tang dynasty), ed. In *Wuyingdian shisanjing zhushu* 武英殿十三經注疏. Reprint. Taipei: Taiwan guji, 2001.

Erya 爾雅. Guo Pu 郭璞 (Jin dynasty), ed. In *Sibu congkan chupian jingbu* 四部叢刊初編經部, vol. 42. Reprint. Taipei: Taiwan shangwu yinshuguan, 1975.

Huainan hongliejie 淮南鴻烈解. In *Sibu congkan chupian zibu* 四部叢刊初編子部, vols. 425-428. Reprint. Shanghai: Shangwu yinshuguan, 1922.

Liezi 列子. In *Qinding siku quanshu zi bu* 欽定四庫全書子部, vol. 276. Reprint. Changchun: Jinlin chuban jituan youxian gongsi, 2005.

Liji 禮記. *Zuantu huzhu Liji* 纂圖互註禮記. Kong Yingda 孔穎達 (Tang dynasty), ed. In *Sibu congkan sanpian jing bu* 四部叢刊三編經部, vols. 20-24. Reprint. Taipei: Taiwan shangwu yinshuguan, 1967.

Lunheng 論衡. Wang Chong 王充 (Han dynasty). In *Sibu congkan chupian* 四部叢刊初編, vols. 433-440. Reprint. Shanghai: Shanghai shangwu yinshuguan, 1967

Lunyu jishuo 論語集說. Cai Jie 蔡節 (Song dynasty), ed. In *Qinding siku quanshu jingbu sishu lei* 欽定四庫全書經部四書類. Reprint. Shanghai: Shanghai guji chubanshe, 1987.

Lüshi chunqiu 呂氏春秋. Gao You 高誘 (Eastern Han dynasty), ed. In *Sibu congkan chupian zibu* 四部叢刊初編子部, vols. 420-24. Reprint. Taipei: Taiwan shangwu yinshuguan, 1965.

Maoshi zhengyi 毛詩正義. Zheng Xuan 鄭玄 (Eastern Han dynasty), ed. Kong Yingda 孔穎達 (Tang dynasty), ed. In *Wuyingdian shisanjing zhushu* 武英殿十三經注疏. Reprint. Taipei: Guangwen shuju, 1972.

Shangshu 尚書. Kong Anguo 孔安國 (Han dynasty), ed. Lu Deming 陸德明 (Tang dynasty), ed. In *Sibu congkan chupian jingbu* 四部叢刊初編經部, vols. 3-4. Reprint. Shanghai: Shangwu yinshuguan, 1919.

Shanhaijing 山海經. Guo Pu 郭璞 (Jin dynasty), ed. In *Sibu congkan chupian zibu* 四部叢刊初編子部, vols. 465-66. Reprint. Taipei: Taiwan shangwu, 1965.

Shiji jijie 史記集解. Pei Yin 裴駰 (Song dynasty), ed. In *Qinding siku quanshu, shibu yi, zhengshilei* 欽定四庫全書史部一正史類. Reprint. Taipei: Taiwan shangwu yinshuguan, 1984.

Shuowen jiezi zhu 說文解字注. Duan Yucai 段玉裁 (Qing Dynasty), ed. In *Xuxiu siku quanshu* 續修四庫全書. Reprint. Shanghai: Shanghai guji chubanshe, 2002.

Taiping yulan 太平御覽. In *Sibu congkan sanpian zibu* 四部叢刊三編子部, vols. 234-369. Reprint. Taipei: Taiwan shangwu yinshuguan, 1968.

Yixue qimeng 易學啓蒙. Zhu Xi 朱熹 (Song dynasty). Reprint. Taipei: Huangji chubanshe, 1980.

Zhouli shuzhu 周禮述註. Li Guangpo 李光坡 (Qing dynasty), ed. In *Qinding siku quanshu jingbu* 欽定四庫全書經部. Reprint. Taipei: Taiwan shangwu yinshuguan, 1971.

Zhouyi *benyi* 周易本義. Zhu Xi 朱熹 (Song dynasty), ed. In *Siku quanshu zhenben liu ji* 四庫全書珍本六集. Reprint. Taipei: Taiwan shangwu yinshuguan, 1976.

Zhouyi zhengyi 周易正義. Wang Bi 王弼 (Three Kingdoms), ed. *Zhouyi zhu* 周易注. Kong Yingda 孔穎達 (Tang dynasty), ed. In *Wuyingdian shisanjing zhushu* 武英殿十三經注疏. Reprint. Taipei: Taiwan guji, 2001.

Zhushu jinian 竹書紀年. In *Sibu congkan chupian shibu* 四部叢刊初編史部, vol. 86. Reprint. Shanghai: Shanghai shudian, 1989.

2. Secondary Sources

Ames, Roger T. and Henry Rosemont, Jr., trs. *The Analects of Confucius: A Philosophical Translation.* New York: Ballantine, 1998.

Bamboo Annals [*Zhushu jinian* 竹書紀年] (ca. 281 CE). Translated by James Legge, vol. 3, *The Shoo King*, "Prolegomena," ch. iv, "The Annals of the Bamboo Books."

Birrell, Anne, tr. *The Classic of Mountains and Seas.* London: Penguin, 1999.

Bodde, Derk. *Festivals in Classical China*. Princeton, NJ: Princeton University Press, 1975.

Chang, K.C. *Early Chinese Civilization: Anthropological Perspec-tives*. Cambridge, MA: Harvard University Press, 1976.

Chang, Kwang-chih. *The Archaeology of Ancient China*. New Haven, CT: Yale University Press, 1977.

—. *Art, Myth, and Ritual: The Path to Political Authority in Ancient China*. Cambridge, MA: Harvard University Press, 1983.

Chikudō (Takatsuka 高塚) 竹堂, et al., ed. *Hanzi shuti zidian: teji Hanzi mingji* 汉字书体字典：特集汉字名迹. Nanning: Guangxi minzu chubanshe, 1993.

Ching, Jeffrey R., et al., tr. "Interpretation of the Divinatory Inscriptions on Early Chou Bronzes," *Early China 6* (1980–81): 80-96.

Chou, Hung-hsiang. "Chinese Oracle Bones," *Scientific American* 240.4 (April 1979): 135-149.

Chow, Tse-tsung. "The childbirth myth and ancient Chinese medicine: a study of aspects of the *wu* tradition," in David Roy and Tsuen-hsuen Tsien, eds., *Ancient China: Studies in Early Civilization*, 43-89. Hong Kong: Chinese University Press, 1978.

Cline, Eric H. *1177 B.C.: The Year Civilization Collapsed*. Princeton, NJ: Princeton University Press, 2014.

Creel, Herrlee G. *The Origins of Statecraft in China*. Chicago: University of Chicago Press, 1970.

Davis, Scott. *The* Classic of Changes *in Cultural Context: A Textual Archaeology of the* Yi jing. Amherst, New York: Cambria Press, 2012.

Eberhard, Wolfram. *The Local Cultures of East and South China*. Leiden: E.J. Brill, 1968.

Eliade, Mircea. *Shamanism: Archaic Techniques of Ecstasy*, tr. Willard R. Trask. Princeton University Press, 1964.

Elvin, Mark. *The Retreat of the Elephants: An Environmental History of China*. New Haven, CT: Yale University Press, 2004.

Eno, Robert. "Inscriptional Records of the Western Zhou," Indiana University, History G380—class text readings—Spring 2010. 13-8-10, http://www.indiana.edu/~g380/3.10-WZhou_Bronzes-2010.pdf.

Field, Stephen, tr. *Tian Wen: A Chinese Book of Origins*. New York: New Directions, 1986.

Field, Stephen. "Recovering the Lost Meaning of the *Yijing* Bagua: a Literary Archaeology," *The Oracle* 2.9 (1999): 20-27.

—. "Who Told the Fortunes: The Speaker in Early Chinese Divination Records," *Asia Major* 13.2 (2000):1-14.

—. *Ancient Chinese Divination*. Honolulu. University of Hawai'i Press, 2008.

Forke, Alfred, tr. *Lun-Heng, Part I. Philosophical Essays of Wang Ch'ung.* New York: Paragon Book Gallery, 1962.

Gao, Heng 高亨. Zhouyi *gujing jinzhu* 周易古經今注. Hong Kong: Zhonghua shuju, 1963, 1980.

Gao, Wence 高文策. "Shilun *Yi* de chengshu niandai yu fayuan diyu" 試論易的成書年代與發源地域, *Guangming ribao* 光明日報, June 2, 1961.

Graham, A.C., tr. *Chuang Tzu: The Inner Chapters.* London: George Allen & Unwin, 1981.

Gu, Jiegang 顧頡剛, ed. *Gushi bian* 古史辨 vol. 3. Shanghai: Shanghai guji chubanshe, 1926-1941, 1982.

Ho, Ping-Ti. *The Cradle of the East.* Hong Kong: Chinese University of Hong Kong, 1975.

Hsu, Cho-Yun and Katheryn M. Linduff. *Western Chou Civilization.* New Haven: Yale University Press, 1988.

Huang, Kerson, tr. *I Ching, The Oracle.* Singapore: World Scientific Publishing Co., 1984.

Keightley, David. *Sources of Shang History.* Berkeley: University of California Press, 1978.

—, ed. *The Origins of Chinese Civilization.* Berkeley: University of California Press, 1983.

Knoblock, John, and Jeffrey Riegel, trs. *The Annals of Lü Buwei,* Stanford, CA: Stanford University Press, 2000.

Kunst, Richard A. "The Original *Yijing*: A Text, Phonetic Transcription, Translation, and Indexes, with Sample Glosses." Ph.D. dissertation, University of California, Berkeley, 1985.

—. "Rick Kunst's unpublished *Yijing* Notes" (1979-85). 13-8-10, http://www.humancomp.org/ftp/yijing/yi_hex.htm.

Legge, James. *The Chinese Classics: with a Translation, Critical and Exegetical Notes, Prolegomena, and Copious Indexes,* vol. 3, *The Shoo King*; vol. 4, *The She King*; vol. 5, *The Ch'un Ts'ew, with the Tso Chuen.* London: Oxford University Press, 1861–72.

—. *Sacred Books of the East,* vol. 27, *The Li Ki,* Part I; vol. 28, *The Li Ki,* Part II. London: Oxford University Press,1885.

Li, Feng 李峰. "'Feudalism' and Western Zhou China: A Criticism." *Harvard Journal of Asiatic Studies* 63.1 (Jun., 2003): 115-144.

—. *Early China, A Social and Cultural History.* New York: Cambridge University Press, 2013. Kindle edition.

Li, Jingchi 李鏡池. "*Zhouyi* shici kao" 周易釋辭考 (1930), in Gu, ed. *Gushi bian,* vol. 3, 187-251.

—. "*Zhouyi* jiaoshi" 周易校釋, in *Lingnan xuebao* 嶺南學報, 9.2 (1949): 52-148.

—. "Guanyu *Zhouyi* jitiao yaoci de zaijieshi—da Liu Huisun Tongzhi" 關於周易幾條爻辭的再解釋——答劉蕙孫同志 (1961), in *Zhouyi tanyuan* 周易探源, 178-190.

—. *Zhouyi tanyuan* 周易探源. Beijing: Zhonghua shuju, 1978, 1982.

—. *Zhouyi tongyi* 周易通義. Beijing: Zhonghua shuju, 1981.

Lynn, Richard John. *The Classic of Changes: A New Translation of the* I Ching *as interpreted by Wang Bi*. New York: Columbia University Press, 1994.

Marshall, S. J. *The Mandate of Heaven: Hidden History in the* Book of Changes. London: Curzon, 2001.

Mesker, Harmen. 易學 "Yijing Research." 15-2-8, http://www.yjcn.nl/wp/.

Minford, John, tr. *I Ching (Yijing): The Book of Change*. New York: Viking, 2014.

Moore, Steve. *The Trigrams of Han: Inner Structures of the* I Ching.

Needham, Joseph, et al. *Science and Civilisation in China,* vols. 2-4. London: Cambridge University Press, 1956.

Nivison, David. "Royal 'Virtue' in Shang Oracle Inscriptions," in *Early China 4* (1978-79): 52-55.

Pankenier, David. "Astronomical Dates in Shang and Western Zhou," in *Early China 7* (1981-82): 2-37.

—. "S.J. Marshall, *The Mandate of Heaven: Hidden History in the* Book of Changes," book review in *Journal of Chinese Religions 31* (2003): 277-78.

—. "A Brief History of Beiji 北極 (Northern Culmen), With an Excursus on the Origin of the Character *di* 帝." *Journal of the American Oriental Society* 124.1 (2004): 211-236.

—. *Astrology and Cosmology in Early China: Comforming Earth to Heaven*. New York: Cambridge University Press, 2013.

Pankenier, David, Ciyuan Y. Liu, and Salvo De Meis. "The Xiangfen, Taosi Site: A Chinese Neolithic 'Observatory'?" in *Archaeologia Baltica: Astronomy and Cosmology in Folk Traditions and Cultural Heritage*, vol. 10: 141-148. Klaipeda, University of Klaipeda, 2008.

Ping Xin 平心 (Zhao Yiping 趙一萍). "*Zhouyi* shishi suoyin" 《周易》史事索隱, in *Lishi yanjiu* 歷史研究 1963.1: 141-160.

Porter, Deborah Lynn. *From Deluge to Discourse: Myth, History, and the Generation of Chinese Fiction*. Albany: SUNY Press, 1996.

Puett, Michael J. *To Become a God: Cosmology, Sacrifice, and Self-Divination in Early China*. Cambridge, MA: Harvard University Press, 2002.

Qu, Wanli 屈萬里. "*Zhouyi* yaoci zhong zhi xisu" 周易爻辭中之習俗 in *Wenshizhe jikan* 文史哲季刊 1.2 (1943): 43-48.

Raphals, Lisa. *Divination and Prediction in Early China and Ancient Greece.* New York: Cambridge University Press, 2013.

Rickett, W. Allyn, tr. *Guanzi: Political, Economic, and Philosophical Essays from Early China.* Princeton: Princeton University Press, 1985.

Rong, Zhaozu 容肇祖. "Zhanbu de yuanliu" 占卜的源流 (1928), in Gu, ed. *Gushi bian,* vol. 3, 252-308.

Rutt, Richard. *The Book of Changes (Zhouyi): A Bronze Age Document Translated with Introduction and Notes.* Richmond, UK: Curzon Press, 1996.

Schuessler, Axel. *A Dictionary of Early Zhou Chinese.* Honolulu: University of Hawaii Press, 1987.

Shaughnessy, Edward L. "The Composition of the *Zhouyi.*" Ph.D. dissertation, Stanford University, 1983.

—. *Sources of Western Zhou History: Inscribed Bronze Vessels.* Berkeley: University of California Press, 1991.

—. I Ching*: The Classic of Changes.* New York, Ballantine, 1996.

—. *Before Confucius: Studies in the Creation of the Chinese Classics.* Albany: State University of New York Press, 1997.

—. "The Origin of an *Yijing* Line Statement." *Early China 20* (1995): 223-240.

—. *Unearthing the* Changes: *Recently Discovered Manuscripts of the* Yi Jing (I Ching) *and Related Texts.* New York: Columbia University Press, 2014.

Shelach-Lavi, Gideon. *The Archaeology of Early China: From Prehistory to the Han Dynasty.* New York: Cambridge University Press, 2015.

Schmitt, Gerhard. *Sprüche der Wandlungen auf ihrem geistesgeschichtlichen Hintergrund.* Berlin: Akedemie-Verlag, 1970.

Smith, Richard J. *Fortune-tellers and Philosophers: Divination in Traditional Chinese Society.* Boulder, CO and Oxford, England: Westview Press, 1991.

—. *Fathoming the Cosmos and Ordering the World: The* Yijing *(I Ching or Classic of Changes) and Its Evolution in China.* Charlottesville: University of Virginia Press, 2008.

Stover, Leon E. *China: An Anthropological Perspective.* Pacific Palisades, CA: Goodyear Publishing Co., 1976.

Sturgeon, Donald. "Chinese Text Project." 13-8-10, http://ctext.org.

Tang, Yi 唐頤, ed. *Tujie hetuluoshu: heluozhenshu* 图解河图洛书：河洛真数. Xi'an: Shaanxi shifan daxue chubanshe, 2009.

Waley, Arthur. "The *Book of Changes*," in *Bulletin of the Museum of Far Eastern Antiquities* 5 (1934): 121-140.

—, tr. *The Book of Songs*. New York: Grove Press, 1937, 1960.

Wen, Yiduo 聞一多. "Putang zashi" 璞堂雜事, in *Gudian xinyi* 古典新義, vol. 2 of *Wen Yiduo quanji* 聞一多全集. Beijing: Sanlian shudian, 1948, 1956, 1982: 581-602.

—. "*Zhouyi* yizheng leizuan" 周易義證類纂, in *Gudian xinyi*, vol. 2 of *Wen Yiduo quanji*. Beijing: Sanlian shudian, 1948, 1956, 1982: 3-65.

Wheatley, Paul. *The Pivot of the Four Quarters: A Preliminary Enquiry into the Origins and Character of the Ancient Chinese City*. Chicago: Aldine Publishing Company, 1971.

Wilhelm, Richard. *The I Ching; or, Book of Changes*, rendered into English by Cary F. Baynes. Princeton, N.J.: Princeton University Press, 1967.

Wiseman, Nigel and Ye Feng. *A Practical Dictionary of Chinese Medicine*. Brookline, MA: Paradigm Publications, 1998.

Wu, Shu-hui. "The Great Migration: Inception of the Zhou Identity," in *Studia Orientalia* 3 (2011): 407-446.

Zhang, Qicheng 張其成. *Yifu yu Yitu* 易符與易圖. Beijing: Zhongguo shudian, 1999.

Zhang, Yachu 張亞初 and Liu Yu 劉雨. "Cong Shang Zhou bagua shuzi fuhao tan shifa de jige wenti" 從商周八卦數字符號談筮法的幾個問題, *Kaogu* 考古(1981.2): 155-164.

Zhang, Zhenglang 張政烺. "Shishi Zhou chu qingtongqi mingwen zhong de *Yi* gua" 試釋周初青銅器銘文中的易卦, in *Kaogu xuebao* 考古學報 (1980.4): 403-415. See Jeffrey Ching for translation.

Index

Hexagram Location Chart

Upper → / Lower ↓	☰	☵	☶	☳	☷	☴	☱	☲
☰	01	34	05	26	11	09	14	43
☷	25	51	03	27	24	42	21	17
☵	06	40	29	04	07	59	64	47
☶	33	62	39	52	15	53	56	31
☷	12	16	08	23	02	20	35	45
☴	44	32	48	18	46	57	50	28
☱	13	55	63	22	36	37	30	49
☲	10	54	60	41	19	61	38	58